CAMBRIDGE LIBRARY COLLECTION

Books of enduring scholarly value

History

The books reissued in this series include accounts of historical events and movements by eye-witnesses and contemporaries, as well as landmark studies that assembled significant source materials or developed new historiographical methods. The series includes work in social, political and military history on a wide range of periods and regions, giving modern scholars ready access to influential publications of the past.

The Story of the 'Domus Dei' of Portsmouth

The 'Domus Dei', otherwise known as the Garrison Church, in Portsmouth is a familiar landmark to ships sailing into and out of Portsmouth Harbour. It was originally founded about 1210 as a 'hospital' for travellers – especially pilgrims – arriving at the port. After the Reformation its main building became a church, and was frequently used by naval and army personnel before embarkation. In 1814 the sovereigns and leaders of the Allies against Napoleon gathered there during the peace celebrations following his abdication, but by the middle of the century it had become dilapidated. A restoration project was begun in 1865, and this history of the building was published in 1873 by Henry P. Wright, 'chaplain to the Forces', with the intention of raising further donations towards the refurbishment, which he describes in detail. The church was severely damaged by bombing in 1941, but remains consecrated and is occasionally used for services.

T0381851

Cambridge University Press has long been a pioneer in the reissuing of out-of-print titles from its own backlist, producing digital reprints of books that are still sought after by scholars and students but could not be reprinted economically using traditional technology. The Cambridge Library Collection extends this activity to a wider range of books which are still of importance to researchers and professionals, either for the source material they contain, or as landmarks in the history of their academic discipline.

Drawing from the world-renowned collections in the Cambridge University Library and other partner libraries, and guided by the advice of experts in each subject area, Cambridge University Press is using state-of-the-art scanning machines in its own Printing House to capture the content of each book selected for inclusion. The files are processed to give a consistently clear, crisp image, and the books finished to the high quality standard for which the Press is recognised around the world. The latest print-on-demand technology ensures that the books will remain available indefinitely, and that orders for single or multiple copies can quickly be supplied.

The Cambridge Library Collection brings back to life books of enduring scholarly value (including out-of-copyright works originally issued by other publishers) across a wide range of disciplines in the humanities and social sciences and in science and technology.

The Story of the 'Domus Dei' of Portsmouth

*Commonly called
the Royal Garrison Church*

HENRY PRESS WRIGHT

CAMBRIDGE
UNIVERSITY PRESS

CAMBRIDGE UNIVERSITY PRESS

Cambridge, New York, Melbourne, Madrid, Cape Town,
Singapore, São Paolo, Delhi, Mexico City

Published in the United States of America by Cambridge University Press, New York

www.cambridge.org
Information on this title: www.cambridge.org/9781108044622

© in this compilation Cambridge University Press 2012

This edition first published 1873
This digitally printed version 2012

ISBN 978-1-108-04462-2 Paperback

THE STORY OF THE

'DOMUS DEI' OF PORTSMOUTH,

Commonly called

THE ROYAL GARRISON CHURCH.

By H. P. WRIGHT, M.A.

CHAPLAIN TO THE FORCES, AND CHAPLAIN TO H.R.H. THE DUKE
OF CAMBRIDGE, K.G.

Nihil scriptum miraculi causâ.

Tacitus.

London:

JAMES PARKER & Co., 377, STRAND.

1873.

THE STORY OF THE

'DOMUS DEI' OF PORTSMOUTH,

Commonly called

THE ROYAL GARRISON CHURCH.

By H. P. WRIGHT, M.A.

CHAPLAIN TO THE FORCES, AND CHAPLAIN TO H.R.H. THE DUKE
OF CAMBRIDGE, K.G.

Nihil scriptum miraculi causâ.

Tacitus.

London:

JAMES PARKER & Co., 377, STRAND.

1873.

PREFACE.

As early as the time when Lord Frederick Fitz-Clarence was Governor of Portsmouth, the restoration of the Garrison Church was talked of; but nothing was then done, as that highly esteemed officer soon after left Portsmouth (1851) for India. In due time Lt.-Gen. Lord William Paulet, G.C.B., became Governor, and then, through the active exertions of the Reverend J. E. Sabin, Senior Chaplain of the Garrison, Sir J. Wm. Gordon, K.C.B., Commanding Royal Engineer, Colonel Shadwell, C.B. Quarter-Master-General, and Captain Molesworth, R.E., Executive Officer, supported by the generous nobleman at the head of the Garrison, that restoration was determined on, which has now I am happy to think, after a labour of eight years, drawn so near completion. But if Lord Wm. Paulet gave so liberally, and for nearly six years laboured so strenuously as Chairman of the first Committee, in Lt.-Gen. Viscount Templetown, K.C.B., the present Governor of Portsmouth, and Chairman of the Military Committee appointed by the Secretary of State for War to arrange the interior of the Church, the work has found a very able and large-hearted supporter. Indeed, from the General down to the private soldier, the Garrison has from the first taken the liveliest interest in the preservation of our ancient and highly valuable ecclesiastical relic.

Nor has the Navy been forgetful of a Church so long used by the Royal Marines, in and around which lie the remains of so many distinguished naval officers. Admirals Sir Henry Chads, G.C.B., Sir Michael Seymour, G.C.B., Sir Thomas Pasley, Bart., G.C.B., G. G. Wellesley, C.B., and Major Generals Alexander, R.M.A., C.B., and Schomberg, R.M.A., C.B., were active members of the Committee, and, with other leading officers of the sister service, furthered the restoration in every possible way.

And so also did the citizens of Portsmouth, among whom must be especially named, R. W. Ford, Esq., Mayor of the Borough, when the great Restoration gathering took place on the 8th of August, 1865, in the Guildhall, W. G. Chambers, Esq., J.P., Captain McCoy, J.P., and C. B. Hellard, Esq., who, as members of the Executive Committee, rendered valuable assistance by their ready enterprise and sound practical advice.

It, however, signifies little who did the work, let the glory be entirely and solely to God, who moved the faithful to do it.

As to the " Story of the ' Domus Dei ' " for that I must hold myself alone responsible ; and I do so with confidence, because, I feel certain, all who know the difficulty of avoiding errors when writing the history of an ancient building will deal kindly with me, if I assure them that, while not professing myself an antiquarian, I have taken all possible pains to be accurate. I am thankful to say that I have found some very kind friends who have greatly lightened my labors.   To Sir Frederick Madden, K.H., the leading archæologist of the day, I owe very much, so I do to the Rev. Mackenzie E. C. Walcot, B.D., F.S.A., the Rev. C. Collier, M.A., and F. I. Baigent, Esq., of Winchester.   They have rendered me services for which I can never sufficiently thank them.   Nor must I forget my respected friend B. J. Jeffery, Esq., of the British Museum, whose able and continuous exertions to help me have been only the more acceptable, because they were always so heartily rendered.   I also owe a debt, I may say a great debt, to Mr. Ubsdell, of Portsmouth, who provided me with many rare and interesting sketches and not a little valuable information.

It now only remains for me to add that, throughout the restoration of the "Domus Dei," the Committees have received the kindest consideration and support from the Secretaries of State for War, the Earl de Grey and Ripon K.G., and the Right Honorable E. Cardwell, from H. R. Highness The Duke of Cambridge, K.G., Commanding in Chief, and from the Rev. G. R. Gleig, M.A., Chaplain General of the Army. The present state of the Royal Garrison Church will, I feel sure, be ample proof to them that their confidence has been in no way misplaced.

The sum of £700 is still wanted to complete the long and arduous undertaking. I trust that my unpretending Story will so inform and interest the friends of the Army, and all who value an ancient and beautiful* House of Prayer, that the money will be speedily supplied, and the alms of the public be directed to some other equally holy object.

HENRY PRESS WRIGHT.

Portsmouth, Jan. 1st, 1873.

---

* It is due to subscribers and to the Committees to state, that all ornament in the Church has been supplied by special gifts for memorials.

It is also due to the builder, Mr. Alfred Smith, of Lion Terrace, Portsea, to say that, during the seven years he has superintended the restoration of the Garrison Church, his attention has been unremitting. His tenders have always been the lowest, but the work done has given general satisfaction. The Porch and Vestry lately built by Mr. Smith are considered remarkably fine examples of stone work.

CONTENTS.

ILLUSTRATIONS.

DOMUS DEI.

THE Royal Garrison Church of Portsmouth is all that remains of the ancient Hospital, Maison Dieu or Domus Dei, which once occupied a part of the now Governor's Green and the ground lying between the south side of the church and the ramparts. These Hospitals in England were generally founded at seaport towns or near the sea, so that they might receive pilgrims and strangers, both men and women, on their way to any renowned shrine; and they were usually within the walls of the town with the principal population in their immediate vicinity, in order that the inhabitants might have assistance in case of sickness; the Brethren, in those days, being for the most part the only persons who at all understood the art of medicine. In its original constitution the God's House was not purely ecclesiastical, the Master being sometimes a layman, sometimes a priest; but, as a rule, when the revenue permitted, the office of Master was filled by a priest. We find these Hospitals at Southampton, Portsmouth, Dover, Arundel, &c., because they were there conveniently placed for pilgrims making for the great

shrines of Winchester, Canterbury, Chichester, &c. They
are generally of the 12th, 13th and 14th centuries
and had a common plan; a long hall with vaulting and
divided into bays by pillars. At one end was usually a
porch, and at the other invariably a chapel. The central
part of the hall was kept free, the occupants being housed
in the aisles. Beside being Hospitals for the sick and aged
like St. Mary's Hospital,* Chichester, which preserves its
ancient arrangement with dwellings or cells in the aisles,
they were true Houses of God; the poor, the houseless, and
the wanderer found a home there; not with advantage I
fear to the community at large, since the gathering together
of distressed strangers must have tended greatly to spread
the various contagious diseases, which proved such terrible
scourges during the middle ages. The government was
vested in a Master; Brethren aided by Sisters carried on
the duties of nursing, prescribing, cooking, &c., while the
spiritual care of the Hospital was entrusted to Priest
Chaplains.

The Portsmouth "Domus Dei" was founded by Peter
de Rupibus, Bishop of Winchester.† The exact time is
not known, although the year 1205 is commonly given
by antiquarians. As the founder was consecrated Bishop
of Winchester, A.D. 1204, it is clear that the above date is
too early. There is a charter‡ of John, dated 2nd November,
16th year of his reign (1214) in which the king confirms to the
Hospital built at Portesmuthe five messuages in St. Mary's
street, and five others in Ingeles Street, given by charter to
the Hospital by William (de Wrotham), Archdeacon of
Taunton; also a certain land called "Westwode," given by
charter by the burgesses of Portesmuthe, and 15s. rent from
Richard Britone, given by Simon Forestarius. Witnessed by
Peter, Bishop of Winchester, W. Earl of Arundel, Saer Earl
of Winchester and others. We may therefore fairly conclude
that the "Domus Dei" was built not long before this confirmation by King John, or about 1212. Dugdale observes under

* The plan may also be seen in Brown's at Stamford, and in Hospitals at
Wells and Sherborne.
† "Domos plurimas religiosorum construxit. Hæc sunt nomina domorum
quas fundavit....Hospitale de Portsmue" Matt. Par. Hist. Angl. III. 277.
‡ Calendarium Rot. Cart. Joh. p. 202.

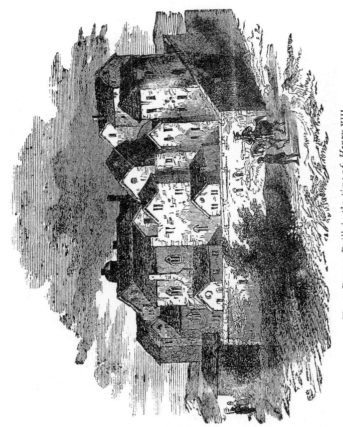

The "Domus Dei" in the time of Henry VIII.

the head 'Portsmouth,' "Peter de Rupibus founded here
temp. Johannis a Hospital called God's House, dedicated
to St. John the Baptist and St. Nicholas."*

It is worthy of notice that, although the "Domus Dei"
has by tradition been dedicated to St. John the Baptist and
St. Nicholas, there is no ancient document, that I am aware of,
in which both these Saints are mentioned together. It is
sometimes designated as of St. John Baptist (in 1283, 1284,
1305 and 1308), but more frequently as of St. Nicholas (in
1235, 1298, 1314, 1349, 1361, 1356, 1376, 1393, 1462,
1492, &c.) In early times it was simply styled "Domus
Dei de Portesmuthe," but, what is very strange, in the
earliest document now known relative to the Hospital (the
Charter above noticed) the King confirms land to the Hospital built at Portsmouth in honour of the Holy Trinity, the
Blessed Virgin Mary, the Holy Cross, and St. Michael and
All Angels. We can only suppose that the dedication had
not then been actually made, and was afterwards altered.
This also supports 1212 as about the year when "Domus
Dei" was founded.

Of the history of the Hospital from its foundation to
its surrender little is known. The following are a few facts
gathered chiefly from registers and papers in the Library
of Winchester Cathedral, in the British Museum and the
Tower, and from the records of the Borough of Portsmouth.

It is supposed by many that the now Garrison Church
is an older building than St. Thomas's, the parish church,
and they base their opinion upon the fact that in the year
1229, the parish church is mentioned as the new† church
of Portsmouth ; and further, they hold that in all probability it was consecrated in that year, for in 1229, special
provision was made that the privileges of God's House
should not encroach on the rights of the parish church.‡
This is altogether a mistake, as St. Thomas's Church was

* Dugdale (last Edition.)
† Allen's History of Portsmouth, p. 121. The word is *nonæ* not *novæ*.
‡ See Deed of Amicable Settlement, A.D. 1229.

not built during the episcopate of Peter de Rupibus, nor
during that of his predecessor Godfrey de Lucy, but was,
we have every reason to believe, entirely the work of Bishop
Richard Toclive between 1173 and 1188. The exact year
of its consecration I cannot discover, but the following
notices of the church will bring us near the date. A
grant we know was made by John de Gisors to the church
and canons of St. Mary, Southwick, of a place on his
land named Sudewede "apud insulam de Portesia" (then
in the occupation of a certain Lucas) 13 perches in length
by 12 perches in width, for the purpose of building a
chapel in honour of St. Thomas the Martyr, (" ad erigen-
dam in eo Capellam in honore gloriosi Martyris Thomæ
Cantuariensis quondam archipresulis.") Now this John
de Gisors was contemporary with Richard Toclive, Bishop
of Winchester, 1173—1188 and Godfrey de Lucy 1188—
1204. He also granted a messuage "in villâ meâ de
Portesmuthe" (in my town of Portsmouth) "ad reparacionem capellæ Sancti Thomæ" (for the repair of the
chapel of St. Thomas). In addition to this we find in a
charter of William, Prior of St. Swithun, mention made
of a charter of Richard (Toclive) Bishop of Winchester,
in which he (the Bishop) confirms to the Priory of
Southwick the chapel of St. Thomas the Martyr, which
with his consent they had *begun* to build in their Parish
of Portsea. This is dated 1185.* The church, therefore,
in 1185 could not have been completed ; and did we want
further proof of this, we possess it in the fact that St.
Thomas's Church is not mentioned in a Bull of Pope Urban
III. of that year, confirming to the Priory of Southwick all
their churches by name. It is then just possible, but not
very probable, that St. Thomas's Church was not quite
completed, and therefore not consecrated, until shortly after
the death of Bishop Toclive. The Churchyard was consecrated by Godfrey de Lucy, A.D. 1196.

---

* See Cartulary of Southwick Priory in possession of T. Thistlethwayte
Esq. for all the above quotations.

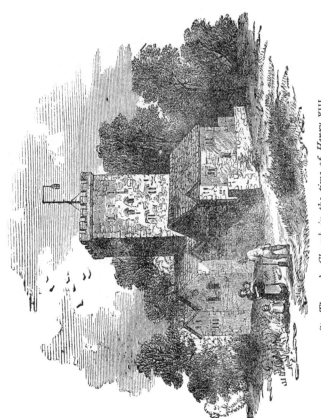

St. Thomas's Church in the time of Henry VIII.

The time thus fixed as about that when St. Thomas's was consecrated, well explains the jealousy which soon sprang up between the parish church and the "Domus Dei;" for if the Hospital of God's House was built say—nearly a quarter of a century after the mother church, we can easily understand that the Master and Brothers of an interesting and influential Hospital would soon invite to them the fees and legacies of the faithful, and so seriously interfere with the monetary prosperity of the parish church. This at once caused complaints, and when matters became serious the dispute was referred to the Bishop, and was settled by the following ancient and curious deed :—

"To all the Sons of Holy Mother Church, Master ALANUS DE STOKES, Official of Peter, Bishop of Winchester, Greeting in the Lord. Be it known to all, that every controversy argued before any Judges, between the Prior and Convent of Southwick on one part, and the Master and Brothers of the Hospital of God's House of Portsmouth on the other, concerning the parochial right of their Church of Portsmouth, is amicably settled after this form before us :—The said Prior and Convent concede that in the aforesaid Hospital, Divine Service may be celebrated, according to the parochial right of their Church of Portsmouth, by two priests, only the Rector of the Hospital is to be employed if he be a priest; and if any stranger priest, visiting the same for the purpose of going abroad, or travelling, shall wish to celebrate, it shall be lawful for him to do so ; and they may have two bells, not exceeding the weight of the bells of the Mother Church, which shall only ring at Matins, and Masses, and Vespers, and for the Dead, and a short None after the ringing of the None of the Mother Church. The said Brothers shall not receive the Parishioners of Portsmouth to confession, nor to Communion of the Body of Christ, unless any shall be sick and specially ask confession of any priest of the Hospital, the requisite consent of the parish priest being first obtained. They shall not receive any stranger to confession publicly in Lent, except the brothers, sisters, own family, sick persons lying there, and inmates. Nevertheless if any stranger shall seek advice from any priest of the Hospital, it shall be lawful to receive him privately. Moreover on Sundays, and on the eight chief festivals, namely, the Birth-day of our Lord, the Epiphany, the Purification, the Annunciation of the Blessed Mary, the Ascension of our Lord, the Assumption and Nativity of the Blessed Mary, and the Feast of All Saints, the aforesaid Brothers of the Hospital shall not receive the Parishioners of Portsmouth. If however, it shall happen, that any of the aforesaid Parishioners shall come to

hear Divine Service on the aforesaid festivals, or on Sundays, at the aforesaid
Hospital, they shall be admitted, and their offering, if any be brought, shall be
restored whole and in good faith to the Mother Church, under the penalty here-
under expressed, unless the said Parishioners shall have made satisfaction
on the aforesaid days to the aforesaid Mother Church.

" Moreover it shall not be lawful for any one of the said Hospital to enter
ships, in order to give Benediction, or preach, or read the Gospel, but he
may lawfully beg alms, the Gospel being read and rites performed by
the Chaplain of the Mother Church. Moreover the aforesaid Canons concede,
that the Hospital shall have a Cemetery only for the Brothers and the Sisters of
the said Hospital, and for the servants and poor persons dying in the said
Hospital : but we mean Brothers and Sisters in this sense :—those who have
received and wear the habit there or have bequeathed their estates to the said
Hospital. Besides, if any stranger shall chuse to be interred in the said
Hospital, it shall be lawful for them to receive them, but the body shall be first
carried to the Mother Church and mass celebrated there. And be it known
that it becomes the Parishioners of Portsmouth to leave their first legacy to the
Mother Church, and the Parish Priest shall be bound to be present at the
making of the Will of the Parishioners; for the damage however, that
the Mother Church will suffer by this concession, the said Brothers of the
Hospital shall pay to the Mother Church every year twenty shillings sterling,
viz. :— five shillings at the Feast of St. Michael, five shillings at the Circum-
cision of our Lord, at Easter five shillings, and at the Feast of St. John the
Baptist five shillings. And for the greater security the said Brothers, by
their corporal oaths, the Evangelists being touched, have bound themselves
under a stipulated penalty, to wit, forty shillings to be paid to the aforesaid
Prior and Convent, if any penalty be incurred, so that if after the offence,
being canonically warned, they shall not give satisfaction within eight days,
the penalty incurred shall be paid without contradiction to the said Prior and
Convent; which is to be understood alike on the part of the Prior and Convent.
This Composition is executed in the first year after the decease of Stephen de
Langton, Archbishop of Canterbury, and in testimony thereof the parties have
strengthened the present deed with their seal; and the Lord Bishop of Winchester being absent, we by his authority confirm it, and append our seal, toge-
ther with the seal of Master B., Archdeacon of the same place. These being
witnesses, Master A. de Ellesburne, Master R. Canon, Master J. de Wallingford,
R. Dean of Winchester, W. and S. Chaplains of the Official, Oliver, clerk,
John, clerk, Adam de Portesie, knight, Andrew, Richard, and John his sons,
G. de Basevile, H. de Burgh, knights, and many others.''

During the life of the noble founder, the Hospital attracted much the generous attention of the faithful, and after his death, throughout the 13th and 14th centuries, received a variety of valuable endowments and privileges. The first gift, that of William de Wrotham, I have already noted. On the 22nd of September, 3 Hen. III., (1219) the king ordered the Sheriff to give seisin to the Knights Templars in England of the land in Seleburne, which Emeric de Sacy left to them " agens in extremis " at the siege of Damietta ; reserving to the Brethren of the Hospital of Portesmuthe a rent of 10s., which the said Emeric had given to them before he took journey to Jerusalem ; as also the outgoings for one year, which the said Emeric had farmed to them in his lifetime. This charter was witnessed by Peter, Bishop of Winchester.*

At the close of the same year the Sheriff is ordered to give seisin to Hugh de Vivonia of the land which belonged to Aemeric de Sascy in Bertone (Bartone Stacy) ; reserving to the said Aemeric or assignee the outgoings for one year, and reserving also to the Prior and Brethren of the Hospital of Portesmuthe, the land which the said Aemeric had granted to them in the same manor, in alms. Tested at Winchester by the Justice and the Bishop of Winchester, 14th of December, 4 Hen. III. (1219.)† In the years 1236, 1253, and 1268, proceedings were instituted before the itinerant justices relative to certain property in Winchester and Portsmouth, and for the settlement of some points at issue between the Master of the Hospital, the Vicar of Portesmuthe and the convent of Southwick. " In 1252 the Prior of Portesmuthe and others had right of common in Kington Wood Co. Dors.‡ In 1268 a fine was levied between Robert Walerand and Robert, Custos of the Hospital of Portesmuthe, concerning some messuages and 200 acres of land in Kington Magna and Parva. The

---

* Calend. Rot. Claus. p. 401.

† Calend. Rot. Claus. p. 409.

‡ MS. Harl. 4120. f. 3.

said Robert Walerand granted to the said Custos and Brethren a moiety of the Manor of Laseham in Dorsetshire.* We also find that during the reign of Edward I. the Prior of God's House held half a knight's fee in Froditon (Fratton) under Hugh de Plains, of ancient foeffment.† He also in conjunction with Jordan de Kyngestone held under William Russell, a quarter of a fee in Wippingham, Isle of Wight.‡ By a deed dated in 1272, Richard le Coveror gave to the Brethren of God's House, yearly for ever, three silver pennies, out of a piece of land granted by him to the convent of Southwick; and by a similar deed dated 1276, Robert of St. Denis gave to the Brethren four shillings for ever, yearly charged upon a house and premises in the High Street of Portsmouth, and payable on the Feasts of St. Michael and St. John the Baptist.

In 1283 a writ was addressed by the King to the Sheriff dated 8th May, directing him to order John, Bishop of Winchester, to surrender to the King the advowson of St. John Baptist of Portsmouth.‖ A suit was commenced in the King's court in consequence, and the Bishop presented a petition to the King's council offering to give up the manor of Swenstone, (Swainstou, Isle of Wight) and 3000 marks, *causá pacis*, on consideration of being confirmed by the King in the manors and advowsons of which he was patron.§ The result was a charter dated 5th June, 1284, granted by the King to the Bishop, giving to him the manor of Menes and the advowsons of Menestoke and of the Hospital at Portesmuthe. For this concession a fine of £2000 was paid and the manor of Swainstone.¶ An entry was afterwards made on the Claus Roll of the 2 Richard II., (1387) stating that the Bishops of Winchester were always seized of the advowson of the

* Pedes Fin. temp. Hen. III. f. 76.
† Testa de Neville, p. 234.
‡ Testa de Neville, p. 240.
‖ Regist. Pontissaia, f. 101.
§ Regist. Pontissara, f. 179.
¶ Regist: Pontissara, f. 195.

Hospital, as granted by Edward I. in the 12th year of his reign. In 1298 a further struggle began. A plea took place in the King's bench of the Prior of God's House against John Walerand for the moiety of the manor of Lasham, with the church which the said Prior held by charter of Robert Walerand, uncle of the said John. This was again contested in 1315 and 1319, and the Custos of the Hospital received the value of the said moiety in the manor of Burghton (Broughton near Stockbridge) which belonged to Adam Plukenet.*

In the thirty fifth year of Edward I. (1307) Robert de Harwedone, the then Master of the Hospital, obtained a grant from the Crown of free warren over land situate in Portsmouth, Froddington (Fratton) and Feldershe.† In the reign of Edward II. the chantry at the east end of the south aisle was founded (1325.) The following story of its foundation is highly interesting The Bishop of Winchester (John de Stratforde) confirmed at Waltham, 8 Kal Feb. (25 January) 1325, letters of William de Harwedone, Custos of St. Nicholas of Portesmuthe and his Brethren, in which they state that by the pious liberality of Joan, sister and heir of Alan Plokenot, deceased, lady of Kilpeke and widow of Henry de Bohun, they had received many benefits; and in consideration that the said lady had relinquished to the said Custos, and Brothers and Sisters, her right in the manor of Berughton (Broughton), they agree to admit to their fellowship and maintain a chaplain, to be presented by the said lady, who was to assist at the offices in the said house, like the other chaplains, and daily recite the offices for the souls of the said lady Joan, of Robert de Harwedone, formerly Custos, and of the said William de Harwedone. This deed is headed 'Confirmacio Cantarie de Portesmuthe', and dated Portesmuthe, 20th January, 1325.‡ The piscina of the chantry is still remaining.

---

* Abbrev. Placit. Pasch. 12 Edward II.

† Calend. Rot. Cart. 35, Edward I. p. 38.

‡ Stratford Reg. 1323—1333 fo. 14.

It would appear from an entry in the rent roll of the
Priory of Southwick 7th Edward III. (1333) that for the
privilege of having this Chantry, "Domus Dei" paid
to the Priory annually twenty shillings—surely a large
sum ! In 1341 Edward III. confirmed to William de
Overton in fee, one messuage 151 acres of land, 25 acres
of meadow, 64 acres of pasture, 18 acres of wood and £5
11s. 6½d. rent, in the villes of Estdene, Lokerley, and Hole-
berg, county Southampton, quit from a feefarm rent of £8
a year; to be held of the Custos of Domus Dei of Portesmuthe as of his manor of Brighton (Broughton) by the
service of 59s. 10d. a year.*

And in the year 1349, the King further confirmed
to William de Overton in fee divers lands in La
Frenschmore near the manor of Burghton (Broughton)
granted in feefarm to him by Edmund Arundell, Custos
of St. Nicholas of Portesmuthe, for the annual payment of
100s.†

The Master of "Domus Dei" also petitioned the King
relative to the thirtieths and fifteenths due from the Hospital to the Exchequer, and received a favourable answer
to his prayer. In the year 1380, we find that " the Master
of God's House of the Town of Portsmouth held freely of
the Lord of Portsea the manor of Froddington," " rendering yearly at the Feast of St. Michael, one pound of
pepper and one pound of cummin, doing suit of court
from three weeks to three weeks, paying a heriot, and
giving a relief after the death of each tenant."‡ In right
of this manor the Master claimed, as the mesne lord,
a fine on wreck within the ambit of his manor, and the
following entry is extracted from the Portsea Records of
Title to show the way in which the case was established
and the fine apportioned between the chief and the mesne
lord :—

---

* Pat. 15 Edw. III. m. 25.

† Pat. 22 Edward III. pars. 2, m. 41.

‡ Rental of Portsea Manor (3rd Richard II.) under the head Froddington.

" Concerning the wreck happening at Portesey on the first day of February, in the year of our Lord, 1384, and in the seventh year of the reign of King Richard II. divers ships, were endangered in the sea, and the wine in the same ships, being 300 pipes of wine, came upon the land of the Lordship of Portesey, and of the Keeper of "Domus Dei" of Portsmouth. All which Richard Foghill, the Bailiff of Sir John Thornie, the Abbot of Tychfeld, the Lord of the manor of Portesey, did arrest. Whereupon came the citizens of London, and the merchants of the wine aforesaid, and prayed livery of the said wine, for that two seamen of the aforesaid ships were saved and got up alive upon the soil aforesaid. And the aforesaid citizens of London and merchants faithfully proved that all the aforesaid goods were and are their own, and paid a fine to the aforesaid Lord the Abbot, and to the Keeper of "Domus Dei" of Portesmuthe, to have again and possess the aforesaid goods, because they were saved upon the soil of the two lords aforesaid, seven pounds six shillings and eight-pence, whereof the aforesaid Abbot received for his part seventy-three shillings and four-pence."[*]

The last bequest of which we have any record is that of William of Wykeham, the noble founder of Winchester College, who in his will, dated 1404, left to St. Nicholas Hospital, Portsmouth, one suit of vestments and a chalice.

While, as we have seen, the interests of the Hospital were duly cared for by Henry III. the following extract from the Patent Rolls shows that in those early days the property of the Crown was as fully protected:—"At Portesmouth on the 3rd August, 1253, Henry III. granted to the Master and Brethren of the Hospital of Portesmouth, that by view of his Bailliffs and men of the town, they might enclose five feet of land by the side of the royal road near the said Hospital towards the south, also eight feet similarly situated near the Hospital towards the west, provided that from their enclosure they enlarge the King's

---

[*] Court Roll of Portsea, 1384.

common way on the other side towards the east, to the same
extent as they enclose from the same towards the west."*

The Superior of the Hospital was called from time to
time by various titles. He is designated as Prior in 1215,
1250, 1251, 1298, and twice so in the Festa de Neville
(temp. Edward I.). As Custos or Warden in 1307, and preserved that title until towards the close of the fourteenth
century. In 1376 we find Magister or Custos and also in
1462. In 1482 and 1492 Magister is applied, and that is
the designation in the deed of surrender.

The ancient seal of the Hospital attached to the
surrender in the Record Office is of the usual monastic shape
surrounded by the words "Sigillum comune Domus† Dei
de Portesmowth." At the upper part is a hand projecting
from a cloud emblematic of the first Person of the Blessed
Trinity and still used as a masonic emblem. Below this
on either side the Sun and Moon, the latter represented as
a horned crescent enclosing the profile of the human
countenance; between these and in the centre of the seal
a double cross with angels worshipping. This represents
the Second Person of the Trinity. At the lower part immediately below the cross is either an altar, or (as some
think it) a roll of vellum; if the latter, it indicates the
Holy Scripture produced by the inspiration of the Third
Person of the Trinity, the Holy Ghost. The common seal
of the Borough of Portsmouth is not unmindful of the Old
Hospital. It bears the following inscription carried round
a suit of three tabernacles, the centre and more elevated containing a figure of the Virgin and child, the others figures of
St. Nicholas & St. Thomas of Canterbury: "Portum : Virgo :
Iuva: Nichola: Fove: Roge: Thoma:"—"The Port O
Virgin assist! O St. Nicholas cherish it! O St. Thomas
pray for it!" These prayers were addressed to the Virgin
in whose honour a chapel was dedicated in the Town, to
St. Nicholas the special protector of sailors and the Patron

* Patent Rolls, 37, Henry III.
† The word 'Domus' is on the Surrender seal almost destroyed. I could
only see clearly ' om.' The other words are very distinct.

Saint of the "Domus Dei," and to St. Thomas of Canterbury, the Patron Saint of Portsmouth parish church.

From the death of William of Wykeham in 1404, to the surrender of the Hospital by John Incent, on the 2nd of June, 1540, there is only one occurrence recorded of any special interest; indeed, as far as I have been able to discover, with that solitary exception, the old "Domus Dei" for nearly 150 years remained almost unnoticed. I need scarcely say that I allude to the murder of Adam Moleyns, Bishop of Chichester, "through the procurement of the Duke of York by shipmen slaine" on the 9th of January, 1449. The exact spot where the murder took place is unknown, but the current story that the Bishop fell close to the high altar is untrue. The Process,* in Bishop Fox's Register, distinctly states that he was *inhumanly and with sacrilegious hands dragged by the inhabitants 'out of' the said Church called the 'Domus Dei;'* while the same record tells us, that he was subjected to a cruel death "committed *at* the aforesaid church called the 'Domus Dei.'" The word '*extra*' cannot be misunderstood, it clearly signifies that the murderers were not *inside* the building when the crime was perpetrated; while the words "*at* the aforesaid church" as clearly declare that they were not far from it. It is quite possible that the "shipmen" sought the Bishop in the Church, while he was ministering by night† at the altar, and that, on his passing out by the south door, they dragged him through the Churchyard towards the beach, and there murdered him. But a little care will, I think, enable us to fix within a few yards the very spot where the murder took place. The Process informs us that the Vicar and inhabitants of Portsmouth were required to erect, first a cross and afterwards a chapel "in the same place of the

---

* See Process, pp. 142-153.

† 1446 5 id. Jan. interfectus fuit *in nocte* Magr. Adam Moleyns, Episc. Cicestr. apud Portesmouth."

Hist. Eccl. Chr. Cant. per John Stone, MS. in Corp. Coll. Cant.

crime." On the map of Portsmouth, drawn in the reign
of Henry VIII. before 1540, also on that of the reign of
Elizabeth, (Cott. MS.) there is a little building between the
Church and the present Memorial Cross. In the Elizabeth
plan will be found over the little building the word
'Chappel.' We may therefore fairly conclude that there
the foul deed was done. The statement that the murder
occurred in a boat is altogether unsupported. That Adam
Moleyns was preparing to embark for the continent is true,
and that he was by "shipmen slaine" is very probable, but
the tale that he was struck down while embarking seems
scarcely worthy of our attention.

The last notice we have of the "Domus Dei" as a
House of Mercy is by Leland in the reign of Henry VIII.
"There is also (he writes) in the west southwest part of the
town a fair hospital some time erected by Peter de Rupibus,
Bishop of Winchester, wherein were twelve poor men and
yet six be in it." This statement about six poor men only
being yet in the Hospital is, I think, explained by the
following passage found in a MS. at the Record office :—

"The alms at Portsmouth included four score pounds
from the temporal lands, out of which were maintained
a chaplain priest, and further six men and six women
received every week sixpence a piece, and every fortnight
seven loaves of bread and five gallons of ale a piece."*

We can easily believe, that, when the Hospital was
founded, there were twelve brethren, but that afterwards it
was deemed better for the sick that half the establishment
should be sisters, and so a change was made accordingly
by the Visitor's authority. Leland was evidently only par-
tially informed, as nothing is said by him of the sisters,
who were certainly half of the working staff† of the
"Domus Dei" at the time of its surrender.

---

* See Page 126.—Letter to Mr. Forest.
† See Page 106 "Payments to the Poor with their diets."

Soon after came the terrible visit of the Commissioners. The deed of surrender is dated June 2nd 1540.* The dread of an onslaught upon ecclesiastical property had been felt, we may be sure, for many years, still to the last purchases were made by the Master of the " Domus Dei." As late as October, 1835, John Raynolds of Portsmouth, shipwright, sells to John Incent, Clerk, Magister or Custos of the Hospital, two acres in Kingstone, paying 4d. a year to the king for all service ; this is dated April 11th, 1530. Again, Thomas Carpenter of Kingestone, husbandman, sells to the same Master or Custos of the Hospital of St Nicholas called Goddys House de Portesmouthe, one acre in Frodington, to be held of the lord of the fee, at the rent of ½d. Dated 2nd October, 27, Henry VIII (1535.)

The valuation of the Hospital in the Valor Ecclesiasticus in 1534 is thus stated. The total value £79 13 7½, reprisals in alms, fees, &c., £45 14 2, leaving the net amount £33 19 5½. In a Roll of Accounts of Richard Poulet, one of the receivers of the Court of Augmentations during the year, from Michaelmas, 22 Henry VIII (1530) to Michaelmas 1531, we find the " Hospital of St. Nicholas of Portesmouth vulgarly called Goddeshous " among those voluntarily surrendered; the receipts then amounted to £39 18 5 (exclusive of certain allowances) from lands in Broughtone, Frodingtone, and Burgwelle (parish of Hameldone) and in Kingestone and Portesmouthe as also in Broke, Freshwater and Wippingham in the Isle of Wight. (Rotul. Harl. I. 14.)

Full particulars of all the estates and rights belonging to the Hospital have been preserved. A strict and accurate account of all the property was taken by Roger Tychebourne,† and duly forwarded to the Chancellor of the Court of Augmentations. From it we learn as already stated

---

* See pp. 157-160.

† See No. viii. Page 163.

that for charitable gifts, fees, and other repayments, £45 14 2 were expended, leaving £33 19 5½ as the amount of the Warden's income, subject to tithe ; equal at least to £400 of the present day.* We can therefore well understand that the Wardenship of Portsmouth "Domus Dei" was always considered good preferment, and especially so in lax days, when non-residence was deemed the great divine's privilege but never his shame.

Much of the landed property of the Hospital passed away into the possession of the Powerscourt family.

During the rule of the House of York, the church and buildings about it received, we may suppose, the usual care and were kept in decent condition ; but after the surrender, when the endowments had been alienated, there must have been at least 20 years of sad neglect. Indeed judging by the two estimates for repairs made during the reign of Elizabeth, the once highly favoured Hospital had been allowed to fall into a sadly dilapidated state.

Changes however took place which happily tended to save the "Domus Dei" from utter ruin. As soon as Elizabeth came to the throne it was determined to protect Portsmouth by powerful defences. To "good Queen Bess" Portsmouth is greatly indebted for increased importance, for she helped, in a very marked way, to make it the first arsenal of the world. Among other means of providing money to meet the heavy expenses these defences entailed, a great lottery was put forth in 1569, the proceeds to be applied for fortifying Portsmouth. The works were commenced in 1559, and were vigorously carried on for nearly thirty years ; so much so that we find in 1586 the new fortifications were thoroughly supplied with

---

* Mr. Hallam considers " any given sum under Henry III. and Edward I., as equivalent on general command over commodities, to be about twenty four or twenty five times their nominal value at present." We may therefore say with safety twelve times in the days of Henry VIII.

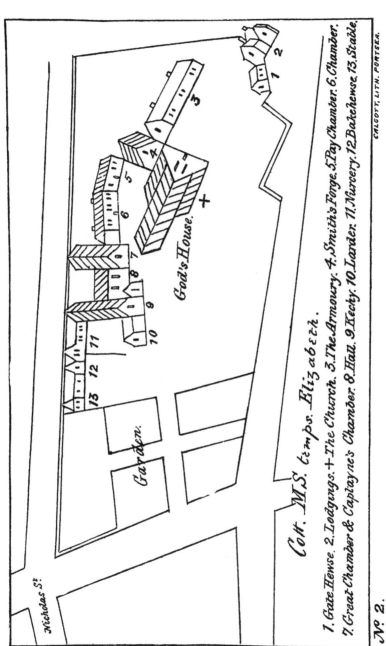

Cott. MS. temps. Elizabeth.

God's House.

Garden.

Nicholas St.

No. 2.

1. Gate House. 2. Lodgings. + The Church. 3. The Armoury. 4. Smith's Forge. 5. Pay Chamber. 6. Chamber.
7. Great Chamber & Captayne's Chamber. 8. Hall. 9. Kechy. 10. Larder. 11. Nursery. 12. Bakehouse. 13. Stable.

CALGOTT, LITH. PORTSEA.

Ordnance. All this necessarily tended to increase the importance of the Governor's position, and rendered it requisite to provide him with quarters in every way becoming his high office. As early as June, 1564, charges were made for "felling and preparing timber for the flooring of God's House,*" but very soon after we find the authorities actively engaged in thoroughly repairing all.the buildings of the " Domus Dei." In the Lansdowne MSS., Nos. 69 and 72, we are expressly told that the outlay set forth in the two estimates dated 1581, and July 24th, 1582 was " for converting God's House and other buildings into a residence for a Governor."

The estimate dated 1581 is of great interest, inasmuch as we are able by it and the plan of God's House in the Cottonian MS. to give the name and position of every building then existing. It is thus worded :—

The gate hous with the lodginges† withoute the north ile of the Church iii score and xv foote long ; the rafter x foote and a halfe ; the church xxv foot wide ; the Armory sixe and fifty foot longe ; the Smithe's forge xxxii foot longe ; the Pay-Chamber at the end of the forge ; the Chamber from the Pay-chamber to the Captayne's chamber sixe score foot long ; the roofe over the Captayne's chamber and the Great Chamber‡ fifty and sixe foot long ; the roofe over the Dyning Chamber xxx fote longe ; the Pigeon hous ; the Hall roofe fifty foot longe ; the Kechin and the Larder‖ one hundred foote longe ; the roofe over the Back

---

* State Papers, 'Domestic Elizabeth,' Vol. 34, No. 31.

† " The Gate hous with the lodginges." These consisted of a small building for the Porter and a larger for the use of guests. They may be seen on the plan, " Cott. MS., temp. Elizabeth," occupying very nearly the spot where the entrance gate now stands.

‡ The Great Chamber was the Guest House in the reception chamber, called also the Hoostrye, sometimes the Ostre. This often comprised several chambers under one name. The Captayne's Chamber was the Master's Chamber but called the Captayne's Chamber when the Hospital became occupied by the Governors of Portsmouth.

‖ The Kechin and Larder were very large because great numbers of poor persons were fed from the Hospital.

gate xviii foot longe ; Bakehous and the Stable iii score
and eight foot longe ; the roofe over the Nurcery* sixe and
fifty foot longe. Repairs estimated at £99.

The accompanying plan (No. 2) shows each of the
buildings above specified.

The other estimate, by Richard Popynjay, is dated
July 24th, 1582, and is principally confined to the cost of
repairing the church. The sum here required is £500 6s. 8d.
This estimate has also especial value attached to it, explaining as it does discoveries recently made at the west
end of the church. It runs thus :—

The churche ther wher the store of· pouther doth lye,
pykes, bowes, bylles, and other provysion and munition ;
the roofe ys covered with leade, which must be taken up
and newe cast, and three tonnes of newe leade for to
supply the wantes of those roofes ; and the gutters in the
howse about the Captayne's lodging and others, th' offices
and rooms to the same apperteyning ; the walles of the
church to be cooped with asheler and crest for keeping the
walles from receveing of rayne and other moysture ; and the
repaiering of the same roofes, which are mooche decayed
allredy by want of good and tyght covering ; vidz : two
of the arches in ruyne, and one pyller of stone standing
betwen the two arches, which hath and doth take sooch
rayne and moysture, that, onles present remydy be had and
provyded, the same churche, or howse for store will utterly
decaye and come to ruyne ; the charge whereof will
amount to £240.   The roofe of the Hall in Gode's howse
without the kytchen roofe, larders, stabelles, armory, forge,
the Dynning Chamber, and all the lodgings in the same
howse are to be striped and newe healed, for that the
nayles, lathe, pynes, and mooche of the stone ys rotten, and
so farre spent and gone that patching, byeting or mending
will not serve, for every meane blast of wynde and wether
teres, breakes, rypes up, and caryeth awaye th' old with

---

* Nurcery—sometimes called the Fermery. It was used for the sick and
infirm.

the newe, as Mr. Captayne himself hath syene, and therein
is best wytnes; the charge for stone, slat, lathe, nayles,
pynnes and workmanshp will amount to £258. The
breach in the wall at Gode's Howse over against the ar-
moyry ys fyfty footes in length and XII footes in height.
The making thereof up againe with cariage of stuffe will
cost 46s. 8d. Sum total £500 6s. 8d.

The church must have been converted into a store for
arms before the days of Edward VI. for, in the first year of
his reign (1547), we find in a MS. in the library of the
Society of Antiquaries, No. 129, a curious list of the
"Munycions within the Churche at Goddeshouse sent by
the L. Grete Mr. from the Towre, 27 Sept. 3. Edw. Sexti."

In the *Churche* were placed: "Sacre and Fawcone
shott of yrone (and other shot), coilles of wollen roopes
for bumbardes," shovels and spades, "skoopes, bloke billes,
morispickes, chestes of bowes and arrowes, serpentyn powder, leade sowes, dryfattes with flaskes and toucheboxes,
cassementes with hand gonnes and bowstrings." In the
Chancelle we have more blocke billes and chestes of bowes
and arrowes, also "collers and traces for horses," and lan-
terns; while in the *Vestrie* were stored "serpentyne and
corne powder" and "lodells of latten for culveryns." Besides all these there were deposited in the *Church* some
"munychions for fireworke," consisting of linseed oil,
turpentine, rosin, saltpetre, pitch, tar, canvas "marlynlyne,"
packthread, twine, "okeham," flax and "packenedells."
Other munitions were in *the Lofte in the Armory,* and in
the *Armory* itself were "Almayne ryvettes" (suits of
armour made in Germany) with splentes and salletts (head
pieces) xxvi paire."

It is evident, from the particulars set forth in the
estimate, that the church was then in a dangerous state;
we may therefore fairly conclude that steps were taken
to prevent the building becoming a mere ruin; and further,
we have every reason to believe that, to avoid expense,
the whole of the west end bay was pulled down and the

church made so much shorter. If it be asked on what ground such belief is based, I answer that when, in 1866, the west wall was taken down to add a bay, according to the plan of the eminent architect, G. E. Street, Esq., R A., complete pillars were found embedded in the wall, and one or two of the stones of an arch remained above the capital of the south pillar. Some have supposed that it was originally intended to make the church one bay longer, but the plan was not carried out for want of funds. Few who know anything of Peter de Rupibus will accept such an explanation of the matter. That great bishop and the men of his day were not architects who failed in a work when so near its completion, as the church must have been if the supposition that funds were wanted be maintained. It is in every way far more probable that one bay was removed, and so the danger and difficulty set forth in the repair document were avoided.

Indeed we may say that such was certainly the case. But there is a riddle connected with the story. When the workmen, in 1866, were preparing the foundation of the new bay they came upon old foundations and found, at the north west corner, a bottle deposited in a bed of rubble work, four feet under ground; the very spot now occupied by the corner stone of the restored building. This bottle, strange to say, is not older than the time of Charles I. and possibly was manufactured as late as the early part of the reign of George I. How is this to be accounted for? What object could there have been in placing the bottle where it was found? I can only suppose that, after the marriage of Charles II. or at a somewhat later period, it was intended to restore the church to its original length, that the foundations were commenced and the bottle deposited, but the work was then abandoned for want of funds or for some other cause. There is a curious plan drawn by Talbot Edwards in 1716, which evidently implies a great change in the Church; that change we know was never carried out, but if we suppose that the foundations were laid and

THE MANER OF THE QUEENES MA.^{tie} LANDING AT PORTSMOUTH. DIS EMBARCANT DE RAINHA DA GRAN BRETAN EM PORTSMVIT *by* 1662

then the undertaking or part of it was abandoned as too expensive, the discovery of the bottle and the date of its manufacture will be fully accounted for. (See Plate No. 4.)

As the Church and buildings about it were, at the close of Elizabeth's reign, at least, in decent repair, it is only reasonable to suppose that they continued so during the next sixty years. The Governor would take due care that his own residence and all about it were kept in good order; and that they were so kept, we may infer from the fact that Catherine of Braganza was received in Government House on her arrival from Portugal, and in it was celebrated her marriage with Charles II. on the 21st May, 1662. His Majesty, writing to Lord Clarendon early on that day, speaks very hopefully of his matrimonial prospects.

" Portsmouth, 21st May, 8 in the morning.

" I arrived here yesterday about two in the afternoon, and as soon as I had shifted myself I went to my wife's chamber. Her face is not so exact as to be called a beauty, though her eyes are excellent good, and not anything in her face that in the least degree can shoque one ; on the contrary, she hath much agreeableness in her looks altogether as ever I saw ; and if I have any skill in physiognomy, which I think I have, she must be as good a woman as ever was born. Her conversation, as much as I can perceive, is very good ; for she has wit enough and a most agreeable voice. You would wonder to see how well we are acquainted already ; in a word, I think myself very happy, for I am confident our two humours will agree very well together. I have not time to say any more. My Lord Lieutenant will give an account of the rest.*   C.

The gathering on the wedding day must have made Portsmouth very gay, and old " Domus Dei " must have presented a striking sight on the great and extraordinary occasion. Samuel Pepys tells us " I followed in the crowd

* MS. Lansdowne, 1236 fol. 117.

of gallants through the Queen's lodging to Chapel, the
rooms being all rarely furnished, and escaped hardly being
set on fire yesterday.   The Mayor, Mr. Timbrell, our
anchorsmith showed me the present they have for the
Queen—a salt-cellar of silver, the walls of chrystal with
four eagles and four greyhounds standing up at the top to
bear up a dish.   I lay at Ward's the chirurgeon's in
Portsmouth."*

In the Register Book of St. Thomas's Church the
marriage is entered as follows :—

" Our Most Gracious Sovereign Lord, Charles the II. by
the grace of God,King of Great Britain, France, and Ireland,
Defender of the Faith, &c., and the most illustrious
Princess Donna Catarina, Infanta of Portugal, daughter of
the deceased Don Juan IV. and sister to the present Don
Alphonso, King of Portugal, were married at Portsmouth,
on the two and twentieth day of May, in the year of our
Lord God, 1662, being in the 14th year of His Majesty's
reign ; by the Reverend Father in God Gilbert, Lord
Bishop of London, Dean of the Chapel Royal, in the
presence of several of the Nobility of his Majesty's
dominions and of Portugal."   Anno 1662."

It is a remarkable fact that the date of the marriage,
as entered in this Register is wrong !   The date there given
is *Thursday, the 22nd of May*, whereas all contemporary
authority concurs in stating it to have taken place on
Wednesday, the 21st of May.   In the Journal of Edward,
Earl of Sandwich, (the Admiral who brought the Queen
over) printed by Kennett in his *Historical Register*, 1728,
he says that she landed on the 14th of May, and went in
her own coach attended by the Lords, the Portugal Ambassador and himself walking on foot before the coach,
" to the *King's House* in Portsmouth."   On Wednesday,
21st May, the Earl tells us that the King and Queen came
into the Presence Chamber, upon the throne, and the

---

* Memoirs of Samuel Pepys.

The Domus Dei, time of Charles 11

CALCOTT, LITH. PORTSEA.

contract made with Portugal was read, after which the King
took the Queen by the hand and said the words of matrimony appointed in the Common Prayer, the Queen also
declaring her consent. Then the Bishop of London
(Gilbert Sheldon) stood forth and made the declaration of
matrimony and pronounced them man and wife.*

It is with regret that I give up the once cherished
belief that Charles II. was married in the Garrison Church,
but, from the record of Lord Sandwich, it is quite evident
that the marriage did not take place in the Church, but in
the Presence Chamber of the King's House. This is confirmed in the Memoirs of Lady Fanshawe (wife of Sir
Richard Fanshawe, the ambassador who had negotiated the
marriage) who no doubt was present on the occasion. She
says " upon the 21st of May, the King married the Queen
at Portsmouth, in the Presence Chamber of His Majesty's
House. There was a rail across the upper part of the
room, in which entered only the King and Queen, the
Bishop of London, the Marquis Desande, the Portuguese
Ambassador, and my husband ; in the other part of the
room there were many of the nobility and servants to
their Majesties. The Bishop of London declared them
married in the name of the Father, and of the Son, and of
the Holy Ghost, and then they caused the ribbons Her
Majesty wore to be cut in little pieces, and as far they
would go every one had some."†

It is supposed that the old altar cloth, on which was
emblazoned a view of Lisbon and the Royal Arms of
Portugal, was an offering made by the King to the Royal
Chapel on his marriage.

This was not the only royal marriage which took
place in the County of Hants, for in the year 1445,
Margaret of Anjou, attended by a large assemblage of
nobility, landed at Portsmouth, and proceeded to the

* Hist. Reg. p. 965.
† 8vo. 1829 p. 143.

Priory of Southwick, (to which the "Portsmouth Domus
Dei" was attached) and was there married to Henry VI.
on the first of April.*

Ten years after the marriage of Charles II. another
royal visit was paid to the old "Domus Dei." "In
September, 1672, the Mayor and Aldermen, with their
mace, and in their peculiar robes, standing at the entrance
of the Fort, the mayor made a speech to welcome James II.
to Portsmouth. The guns were fired and 3000 troops lined
the streets and platform as His Majesty proceeded to God's
House, the Governor's residence."†

The next important gathering in the Chapel, if not
royal, was, we may be certain, thoroughly real. The inhabitants met in 1693 in God's House to settle a quarrel,
which had arisen about the expenditure of money in the
destruction of the beautiful tower and nave of the Parish
Church, and placing in their stead deformities which will,
I fear, long contrast with the brilliant architecture of its
chancel; a church only wanting fitting restoration to render it equal to any in England. The particulars of this
calamity and the use made of the "Domus Dei" are thus
recorded in an old vestry book:—

"In the year 1693, a new rate was agreed upon, and
towards the re-building and repairing the Parish Church,
every inhabitant shall be assessed to the said rate, at six
tymes the sum that he, she, or they were rated to the last
poor-book; and Mr. Ambrose Stanyford shall goe forward
in the finishing the Church, and the parish shall be obliged
to pay him what shall be due, and the money shall be
raised by rate. After some time, dissatisfaction arose, and
Mr. Henry Maydman was authorised by the inhabitants,
meeting in God's House Chapell, (the then pro-parish
Church) to superintend the disbursements of the monies
raised, and to keep a strict account in a book. And in 1694,

---

* Cartulary of Southwick Priory.
† Borough Records.

A Prospect of Gods House from Wimbleton's Bastion at Portsmouth 1716

to pay up debts upon account of the Church, it was agreed that a book of rates shall be made, which shall amount unto and comprise six poor-books, after the rate of the said parish." Thomas Heather, good dear simple vicar, in his private notes, December 10, 1694, writes thus— "Our Parish Church is become a beauteous structure, I heartily wish I could see the chancel answer it."

Although the close of the 17th century was a time of thick darkness as regards Gothic architecture and Church order, it possessed, at least in Portsmouth, a bright and glowing gratitude ; for on the monument erected by the inhabitants to the memory of Ambrose Stanyford, we find the following words—"Beneath this stone lyes the earthly remains of Ambrose Stanyford, Esq., who, *by the good providence of God, was the happy instrument of contriving, framing, and finishing the inside beauty of this House, for the glory of God and to the joy and comfort of his people assembling here to His worship.*" This family of Stanyford continued in the Borough as leading burgesses until the middle of the seventeenth century, and then the name disappeared. Curiously enough, in the year 1794, we find a pue in the Garrison Church the property of a Mr. Stanyford. It is marked K on Plan No. 9, and this explanation is given," K seat formerly granted to Mr. Stanyford, and built at his own expense."

Among the treasures of the " Domus Dei " is a set of massive Communion plate ; consisting of two immense flagons, two chalices, two pattens, and a large alms dish. They were presented by Queen Anne, but when, and on what particular occasion, I have not been able to discover. It is very probable that Her Majesty made the offering when she visited Government House with her Consort, Prince George of Denmark. At the same time it is only fair to state, that some maintain that the plate was given when the King of Spain embarked at Portsmouth, on His Majesty's return from Windsor, "where all the great ladies of Queen Anne's court had received costly gifts."

In the reigns of the 1st and 2nd Georges, Portsmouth appears to have received no royal attention; but George III. was on several occasions a visitor, inspecting the Garrison and Dockyard, or giving honour to the heroes who so nobly fought the battles of their country. On May 2nd, 1778, His Majesty and the Queen arrived at Portsmouth, and on Sunday morning went to the Royal Garrison Chapel, where the Rev. George Cuthbert, Vicar of Portsmouth, Chaplain to the King, and afterwards Mayor of the Borough, preached, taking his text from the 6th chapter of Deuteronomy and the 13th verse. And again in June, 1794, a few days after the arrival of the victorious Howe at Portsmouth, the King and his Queen came to the renowned arsenal to do honour to the great Admiral, accompanied on this occasion by six of the Royal children. "The Royal Family reached the Governor's House about 7 o'clock, when the band of the Gloucester Militia played on the Parade. The Queen and the ladies sat on the balcony for some time, and then joined the King and Prince Ernest on the Queen's battery, where, with a host of nobility, they continued to promenade." A grand Levée took place on Friday the 27th, at Government House. It is only right to record that the king attended Divine Service in the Dockyard Chapel. His Majesty seems at all times to have borne in mind, that a nation's well being depends upon its holy recognition of the God of Forces.

The old "Domus Dei" is of interest in the Borough of Portsmouth, as being intimately connected with the Volunteer Forces of the last and present centuries. On the 29th May, 1799, the Royal Garrison Volunteers of Portsmouth, under the command of Major William Garrett, were assembled in the Garrison Church previous to the presentation of Colours to that loyal and devoted Corps. The sermon was preached by the Rev. John Davies, B.A., St. Mary's Hall, Oxford, who took for his text, Psalm XVIII, verse 39. "Thou hast girded me with strength unto the battle, Thou shalt throw down mine enemies under

Drawn by J. Armstrong.
about 1430.

Engraved by W.H. Toms

CALCOTT, LITH PORTSEA.

Nº 12.

me." The words of the preacher were plain and stirring :—
" Embarked in the service of your king-and country,
as the inscription on your banner denotes, *Honoured by the
express approbation of your Sovereign*, to *you* belongs the
distinguished and exalted privilege of bearing on your
consecrated standard the ensigns of *royalty.* So high a
token of pre-eminence and favour can only be considered
as the suitable reward of strict and soldier-like conduct,
without which the purpose of enrolment would be defeated.
Indeed, the uniform regularity of your deportment, and
the undisturbed harmony which has, on all occasions, pre-
vailed through your ranks, whilst they reflect the highest
lustre on the character of your officers, display most amply
the sincerity of your zeal, and claim from every description
of good and loyal men, the grateful tribute of confidence
and esteem.

" In thus augmenting the strength and promoting the
wise and salutary measures of government, you have not
even solicited, as a compensation for loss of labour, that
reasonable allowance of pay which you might fairly and
equitably have claimed. Aware too of the serious inter-
ruption which every branch of commerce must occasionally
sustain from the necessity of your frequently appearing in
the military school, the inconveniences, to which not only
yourselves, but many of your respective *employers* cheerfully submit at this momentous crisis, demand particular
notice and commendation.

" Thus brought into the field from the most patriotic
and disinterested motives; furnished with every regimental
requisite at the sole expense of your liberal and zealous
commander; trained under the auspices of men equally
independent and respectable, you may become, in the
absence of regular forces, not merely a *local* safeguard and
defence, but to your vigilance may be entrusted the important charge of defending a Garrison, whose consequence
to the Empire is no less the subject of deserved than
universal admiration ; and whose spacious docks and

immense magazines for the ready equipment of our vast
naval bulwark stand unrivalled in the annals of the world.

"It is here within our view that the great maritime
force of the country is collected; and we have seen the
adjoining harbour crowded with the spoils of vanquished
squadrons.   It is here too, that we have been eminently
honoured with the presence of. Majesty: here in person has
He celebrated the triumphs of His Fleet: *and here within
these walls* has He offered up the pious incense of His
gratitude and thanks to Him who giveth victory unto
kings; the great and glorious God, the Lord strong and
mighty, even the Lord mighty in battle, who girdeth with
strength of war."

On leaving the Church, the Volunteers were formed beneath the balcony of the Governor's House, which, with the
small square tower at its west end, hid entirely the south
side of the Chancel, and the Ensigns received the Colours
from the hands of Mrs. William Garrett, who addressed
the Major in the following words :—

"Sir,—I have very great pleasure in presenting to
your corps these emblems of loyalty and attachment to your
king and country.   From the known zeal and patriotism
of yourself, your officers, and men, I have no doubt but
you will defend them at the hazard of your lives.   In
protecting them you will, I trust, secure for your country
the happiness it enjoys under its present constitution.   It
is my most sincere and ardent prayer to the Almighty
Disposer of events that the cause, which you and your
brethren in arms have so nobly stood forward in defence
of, may be crowned with success; and that the blessings of
peace may be speedily restored to these kingdoms."

To which Major W. Garrett returned the following
answer:—

"Madam,—I cannot but feel infinite gratification in
returning to you my own thanks and those of my officers
and men, for the honour you have conferred upon us in
presenting to us these consecrated Banners.   It will indeed

be most satisfactory to us hereafter to reflect, that, in following the laudable example of our brother volunteers, we may have in any degree contributed to the permanent security and welfare of our country against its foreign or domestic foes."

"To you, gentlemen (turning to the Ensigns) I have the honour to deliver these sacred pledges of our fidelity and attachment to our king and country, confidently relying, that in your hands they will never be disgraced; and from the frequent instances I have experienced of the zealous and spirited conduct of the corps I have the honour to command, I need only observe to them that these are the true rallying points, and to remind them, that the cause they have engaged in is for the preservation of all that Englishmen hold most dear—their wives, their children, their country, and their laws."

"I beg leave to offer you, Sir, (the Reverend R. Davies) our best thanks for the very excellent discourse you have been good enough to give us. The sentiments it contained will, I trust, make a deep and lively impression upon the minds of those to whom it immediately applied; and I have no hesitation in declaring in the face of Heaven, and before you, Sir, our respected Governor, (Sir William Pitt) that being animated with the most zealous ardour for the defence of our King and country, we will, to the utmost of our abilities, whenever called upon, perform the duties of faithful soldiers and good citizens."

When Major Garrett delivered that soldierly address it was little thought that, within three quarters of a century, a Volunteer Drill Shed would occupy a part of the then Governor's garden, and Volunteer Corps be drilled from Penny Street and Green Row to the eastern and western ramparts. While the name of Garrett will be handed down in the story of Portsmouth as honourably connected with the old Government House and the gallant old Volunteers; that of Colonel Richards will long be

remembered, as representing the 3rd Hants Artillery
Volunteers, who proved such generous friends to the Garrison by providing it gratuitously, for nearly two years,
with a most convenient temporary place of worship.

I may mention here that, at the end of the last
century, three handsomely bound Prayer Books were
presented to the Garrison Church by George III. The
exact date when the royal gift was made does not appear,
but we may fairly suppose that it was shortly after the
occasion when His Majesty there publicly thanked God
for His merciful watchfulness over our nation.

But the old "Domus Dei" was destined to receive a
gathering more distinguished far than any it had ever
known in the days of which I have already told; for, on
Wednesday, the 22nd day of June, 1814, it was announced
by telegraph to H. R. Highness the Duke of Clarence, the
Port Admiral, that the Prince Regent had left London and
would, with the Emperor of Russia, Frederick, King of
Prussia, Marshal Blucher, Prince Platoff, and a crowd of
distinguished personages, pay a formal visit to England's
great arsenal. The Royal party left London about nine
o'clock, and arrived at Portsmouth at four o'clock the same
day. On reaching the Landport gate, His Royal Highness
was received by Lieut.-General Houston, Lieut.-Governor
of the Garrison, who presented His Royal Highness with the
keys of the town, which were forthwith returned to the
Lieut.-Governor. On entering the town a salute with a triple
discharge of all the artillery on the ramparts and the lines
was given, and all the vessels fired a royal salute. These
salutes were repeated when His Royal Highness alighted
from his carriage at the Government House, where he was
received by the Secretary of State for the Home Department, the Board of Admiralty, the Commissioners of the
Navy, His Royal Highness the Admiral of the Fleet,
Lieut.-General Houston, and other high officers. The
Prince Regent proceeded at once to hold a Levée, at which
the Admiral of the Fleet presented Admiral Sir Richard

The "Domus Dei" as when visited by the Allied Sovereigns in 1814.

Bickerton, Commanding the Port ; Vice Admirals G. Martin and Sir Harry Neale, Bart. : Rear Admirals Sir F. Laforey, Bart., Foote, and T. B. Martin; and all the Captains and Commanders in commission at the Port. Immediately after the Levée His Royal Highness proceeded, with his attendants, to the balcony in front of Government House, where he was received by the people with the greatest enthusiasm. At seven o'clock a dinner of forty covers was served, and the " Domus Dei " rang again with the loyal shouts of the distinguished and honoured guests. Thousands of lamps lit up the buildings in a way that would have greatly astonished the simple Brothers and Sisters and their Prior, could they have risen from their graves and seen their home, once so calm and quiet, thus strangely changed. In the centre was the word ' Peace ' with a star blazing over it, and at the two angles of the house, the letters A and F in honour of the illustrious visitors. About eight, His Majesty the King of Prussia, accompanied by their Royal Highnesses the Prince Royal, Prince William, Prince William (His Majesty's brother) and Prince Frederick of Prussia, were received by a guard of honour ; and at a much later hour, the Emperor of Russia and the Duchess of Oldenburg arrived, attended by the Earl of Yarmouth, Count Lieven, and many noblemen of the imperial court. On Thursday, the 23rd, Prince Blucher joined the distinguished gathering ; and in the evening of that day the Prince Regent had a dinner of still greater brilliancy. Their Majesties, the Grand Duchess, the Princes, and their respective suites, with the Board of Admiralty, the Ministers, and leading naval and military officers, sat down to a sumptuous repast of one hundred and twenty covers. The Prince Regent and the royal visitors were pleased again to gratify the wishes of the people, by appearing on the balcony, and were received with a heartiness to be imagined, but not described.

During the evening of the 24th, the Iron Duke, the loved

and renowned of the nation, reached Portsmouth.   That immortal hero, ever actuated by a sense of duty, awaited at the old " Domus Dei " his Royal Master's return from the Naval Review, which had occupied the whole day.   The instant the Prince Regent saw him he hastened towards him, seized him by the hand, and for the moment was unable to speak ; but at once recovering himself he turned to the assembled Sovereigns and Generals and said—" England's glory is now complete ; it only wanted the presence of your Grace." That night, Government House, some parts of which were as old as the days of King John, saw the Prince Regent of England, with kings and nobles, and knights, and renowned officers, British and Foreign—a glorious company, gathered round a royal board rejoicing that God had in mercy given peace to Europe ; and once more the Royal Host and his guests presented themselves to the public, and received the warmest expression of joy and sympathy from a happy and contented people.   On the following day, June 25th, a Levèe was held.   High honours were conferred, the Mayor and Corporation did homage, and old " Domus Dei" witnessed a scene the like of which Portsmouth can never hope to see again.

It must be remembered that Government House had for some years been uninhabited, (save a few back buildings occupied by the Town Major) and was, on the visit of the allied Sovereigns, merely fitted up temporarily for the Prince Regent and his distinguished guests.   It was never used again.   Twelve years after that renowned visit not a trace of it was left.   Its demolition commenced January 21st, 1826, and was completed on March 18th of that year. The only remains of antiquity particularly noticed were some "low pointed early English arches, surrounded by modern brickwork," some groining forming the ceiling of wine cellars, and the lofty old chimney, so difficult to destroy ; but of this we may be sure, very much highly interesting to the antiquarian escaped the attention of busy, uneducated workmen.

Talbot Edwards 1716

The "Domus Dei" A.D 1716.

Nº 4.

We have now, as we enter upon the second quarter of
the nineteenth century, the Church and Infirmary of the
ancient Hospital of St. Nicholas and St. John the Baptist
standing alone ; the solitary, but truly sacred remains of an
institution which, in days of sad disease and much poverty,
had been to thousands a source of great comfort. This
will be a favourable moment for noticing the various
changes which took place from time to time in the appearance of the Hospital.

We have seen that, in the days of Elizabeth, it was
thoroughly repaired, a part having been given over for the
Captayne's or Governor's quarters ; while the remainder,
the church included, was converted into government
offices and storehouses. In course of time buildings incon-
veniently placed, and therefore little used, would be pulled
down, or, if not destroyed, greatly altered. Such is the
common course of things ; but, allowing for all this, we may
be certain, that the house which received Charles II. and
Catherine of Braganza, his affianced, on her arrival from
Portugal, was a portion of the old Hospital, not nearly so
much changed as many imagine. Evelyn writes of it thus
" The Hall of the Government House is artificially hung
round with arms of all sorts, like the hall and keep at
Windsor." In 1716 the "gate hewse and lodging hewse"
were still in existence, and they, be it remembered, were
standing alone and of comparatively little use, and therefore most liable to decay.

I have already suggested that possibly some extensive
changes were commenced, but not carried out about the year
1716. By examining the sketch taken in the time of Charles
II. and that of 1756 it will be seen that in neither are there
dormer windows. It is therefore clear that late in the 17th
or early in the 18th century alterations were made in the roof
of the church, for in the sketch by Talbot Edwards (1716)
and Armstrong (1730) we find four dormer windows. It is
equally clear that many additions were made about that
period to Government House. My belief is that Talbot
Edwards who occupied in the Garrison, I understand, the

position of Director of Public Works did very much to the buildings of the old "Domus Dei" and desired to do more. It is highly probable that he introduced the dormer windows. If so for some cause or other they were removed and the roof of the church lowered before the year 1756, for the drawing of Joseph Wakley "taken on the spot" is we may be sure an accurate and valuable representation of the Church and Government House towards the end of the reign of George II. A square tower is now found at the east end of the north aisle of the church but attached to the house. This is said to have been added in order that all shipping approaching the harbour might be seen. During the next fifty years further changes were made, but not affecting the extent of the building south-westward; an observatory was added, the roofs altered, the double flight of steps was removed, and a balcony, supported by five pillars, placed towards the centre, to which there was entrance by a double door from the great state room. But all that has now disappeared. On the 18th March, 1862, as I have already said, the Church and Infirmary of the old Hospital stood alone, the precious relics of a period when God fearing men gave largely and gladly for Christ's sake.

The Domus Dei." A.D. 1756.

CALCOTT, LITH, PORTSEA.

Nº 6.

No 8.

The Garrison Church (before restoration) A.D. 1866.

THE RESTORATION.

ALAS ! the ancient beauty of " Domus dei " had sadly departed. Externally and internally it offered every deformity which ages, ignorant of all laws of ecclesiastical architecture, could supply. The roof had been so frequently lowered that it was nearly flat ; a parapet of brick ran completely along the north and south sides of the nave and chancel ; eight long repulsive windows in the nave admitted a flood of light from the north and south, while at the west end was a curiously hideous window, which when designed was deemed, I doubt not, a marvel of talent. The windows of the chancel were equally bad, save those at the east end. These were a part of the original building, but unhappily had been so shortened that they looked stumpy and uncomfortable. Add to this a shabby hovel for a vestry attached to the north aisle at the west end, a huge box for a porch before the west entrance, and a lofty thick unseemly wall, effectually shutting out worship, save on Sundays ; and you will have some idea of the appearance of God's House outwardly, after well intentioned ignorance had for generations laboured to preserve it. Internally there had been many and grave alterations since the days when the sick and suffering lay along the side aisles, and, while their bodies were being cured, found food for their souls through the holy ordinances of the Church. What

those alterations were it is impossible to say, but the
accompanying plan gives a very vivid picture of the pues
and seats, and how they were appropriated at the close
of the last century. The entrance to the Governor's
elevated pue was from Government House by a door
fitted into one of the old windows; officers and officers'
wives occupied long seats against the walls on the north
and south sides of the west end of the chancel; the
Governor's servants were placed near the altar; but strange
to say two-thirds of the chancel and half the nave were
"disposed of to the inhabitants of Portsmouth." One pue
it will be observed, had in days past been granted to a Mr
Stanyford, it having been "built at his own expense."
Who this Mr. Stanyford was, I have not been able to discover; but certainly some leading inhabitant of the Borough,
as I observe that between 1715 and 1749 five Mayors of
Portsmouth bore that name. Possibly it was the renowned
Ambrose who so cruelly marred the beauty of the Parish
Church. As the water mark of the paper on which the
plan is drawn gives the year 1794, we may suppose that
about that date a gallery at the west end was built, for the
singers were then, we find, "removed to the west door." As
to the poor soldiers they were consigned to benches in the
far off part of God's House. Some slight alteration of the
above distribution took place to accommodate "the Engineers and respective officers of His Majesty's Ordnance;"
but beyond that I can discover no notice of any change,
save an addition to the pues, until 1846, when within
the church the appearance of everything had become
thoroughly repulsive.

Then, on entering the church, the great object which
at once attracted the eye, was two huge figures of Moses
and Aaron over the altar, holding up a frame work containing the ten commandments. In the chancel were
high pues backed by pannelling, which went entirely
round the walls up to the old string course. Over the
chancel door, which had been blocked up, stood an immense oblong pue elaborately, and I may say, beautifully,

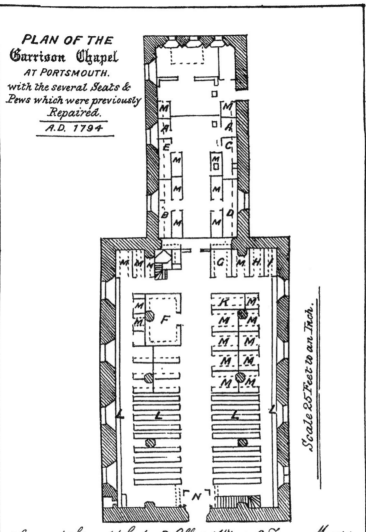

PLAN OF THE
Garrison Chapel
AT PORTSMOUTH.

with the several Seats &
Pews which were previously
Repaired.
A.D. 1794

Scale 25 Feet to an Inch.

A. Governor's Servants' Seats. B. Officers' Wives C. Town Majors
D. Officers' E. Commandants F. Late Singers, — removed over
West Door at N. G. Chaplains Family. H. Gunners' Wives' I. Gunners
K. Seat formerly granted to Mr. Hanyford & built at his own expense.
L. Benches for the Soldiers. M. Seats disposed of to the Inhabitants

Nº 9.

CALCOTT, LITH. PORTSEA.

carved, the work of the reign of Queen Anne. As this
was elevated on four square pillars, also richly carved, and
topped by lofty damask curtains, its appearance must have
been terribly oppressive. This pue of honour was that of the
Governor, the entrance to it being by a staircase close to
the altar rail, and also by the door already noticed. Marble monuments of every form, the black edged envelope
pattern prevailing, were fixed high and low in every
direction; not seldom, in beds cut out from the pillars or
walls; while at the east ends of the aisles they, together
with lath and plaster, blocked up two old windows of
great beauty. The pulpit, prayer desk, and clerk's pue!
formed a hideous combination, vast pues throughout the
nave received the troops for prayer or sleep, and over the
whole was a heavy whitewashed ceiling, which kept the
church comfortably warm in winter, and miserably close
in summer.

This was undoubtedly a sad state of things, for which
no one was responsible. It was the result of generations
which knew nothing of, and cared nothing for, church
architecture, and never required the shadow of a lecturer
to denounce ultra-ritualism. No change whatever took
place for twenty years; but at last, in the year 1846, much
attention seems to have been paid to the internal arrangements. All the pues in the chancel, except the Governor's,
were replaced by others more conveniently arranged; the
nave was entirely cleared, except a single row of pues
running partly across from the north and south aisles;
the stone floor was made good and covered with kamptulicon, and benches arranged throughout for the troops.
Further, a font was erected, the pillars made clean! with
yellow wash, and the covered out-door staircase into the
gallery changed to an open inside one. During 1850
and 1851 further alterations were made. The chancel was
completely cleared and re-pued; the Governor's gallery
with stairs leading to it taken away; the Communion rail
carried to the wall; the great picture of Moses and Aaron
was removed; the east windows lengthened; six new side

windows were introduced; two stoves with underground
flues were provided; new chairs and carpet placed within
the Communion rail; and subsequently a plain terry velvet
cover was presented for the altar   The pulpit and prayer
desk underwent several experiments but " nothing (notes
the then Chaplain) would take from them their heavy
appearance."

It may be thought by some that much of the money
expended during these latter changes was almost thrown
away, as little or no attempt was made really to restore the
ancient church.   Such a conclusion would be very unjust.
It is much to be rejoiced at that cleanliness and comfort
were more aimed at than restoration, as thirty years ago
the building would, by any such experiment have been
lastingly injured; whereas now it has happily passed
through the hands of one of the greatest architects of this or
any other age.   But the money was well spent if only as a
sanitary precaution, for, previous to the removal of the old
pues and repairing the old floors, the atmosphere of the
church must have been, not only very offensive, but highly
dangerous to health.   It is calculated that in some old
cathedral cities and many of our thickly populated towns,
in which churches and churchyards are very numerous,
the mortality of the inhabitants was, previous to the
days of church restoring, seriously increased by congregations assembling in old, musty, ill-ventilated buildings,
beneath and around which thousands had been buried.
The green reeking walls oozing from the piled earth without;
broken floors emitting impure gases from beneath; foul,
lofty, baized pues confining foul air; begrimed hassocks;
all this and much more, acting upon a congregation
breathing in a stove-heated, gas-lighted church, crowded
with galleries and devoid of all ventilation, brought many
a worshipper to a premature grave.   We have, therefore,
great cause for gratitude to those who made the first effort
to improve the old Garrison Church.   They purified it and
rendered it for a time at least clean and decent.

But alas! the cleanliness and decency did not last

Garrison Church before Restoration.

very long: fifteen years made the old God's House almost
as bad as ever. On the outside, the dingy cement covering
the fine old stone walls added to the ugliness of the
building, dwarfed as it was in length and height; while
within, the chocolate painted pues and seats had become
worn and unseemly; the kamptulicon had rotted; the
smoke had given the ceiling and yellow washed walls and
pillars a dismal appearance—in a word both chancel and
nave had returned to their former state of impurity. That
such was the common opinion is certain, for the "Portsmouth Times" in a leading article of August, 1865, thus
writes :—"We call the Garrison Church 'a large building'
for externally it might pass for a barn, or a drill shed, or a
brewhouse; and, without private information to the contrary, we should not be much the wiser after an internal
view, beyond acquiring the knowledge that it is a parallel-
ogram divided into partitions. Further we should find the
air pervaded by a thick, so to speak, fusty smell, consequent
upon villainously low-pitched roofs, aggravated by the
residuum of exhalations which we may call the essence of
closely packed humanity.

Mr. Street, in his report, dated as far back as the
4th December, 1861, speaks in equally strong language.
Having declared that "*the building is one of extreme architectural value and interest*," he describes its appearance in
these words :—"The exterior of the Chapel has been so
much modernized and mutilated that scarcely any original
feature now remains. The roofs have all been lowered to
a very flat pitch; The windows have been destroyed; and
the walls have been covered with plaster and whitewashed.
The appearance of the building is now unsightly in the
extreme, and, I think I may say, a disgrace to the conspicuous site on which it stands."

The opinion of so eminent an architect together with
his simple but beautiful design, showing to what the fast
decaying relic of antiquity might be restored, led, after
several years of delay, to active measures. A meeting
convened by circular was held in the Guildhall, on August

5th, 1865, W. G. Chambers, Esq., J.P., occupying the chair, the Mayor, R. W. Ford, Esq., being unavoidably absent, at which Colonel Shadwell, who (with the Reverend J. E. Sabin, senior chaplain of the garrison) had from the first been most active in furthering the restoration, was invited "to state what was proposed to be accomplished." Colonel Shadwell said, "that as far back as 1862 it was suggested that the Garrison Chapel should be restored, but at that time the proposition fell through, and nothing was done until the Secretary of State came down to Portsmouth in August last year. Lord William Paulet, who was then Lieutenant-Governor, showed him the chapel. Earl de Grey was not particularly impressed with the beauty of the outside, but he thought that with regard to the interior, the building possessed great capabilities for improvement. The matter went on till March, when a letter was addressed by the Secretary of State for War to the Quarter Master General, in which Earl de Grey said that if the garrison of Portsmouth and others would be willing to contribute to the fund, he should be prepared to consider the propriety of inserting in the estimates for 1866-67 a sum of £1500, provided such a sum was raised as would, with such grant, defray the cost of the restoration."

The following circular was subsequently issued :—

"RESTORATION OF THE GARRISON CHURCH."

"It is proposed to restore the chapel of Saints John the Baptist and Nicholas, now used by the troops of the Portsmouth garrison, so that it may become a seemly house of worship for the living, and a resting place not wholly unworthy of the brave men who lie within and around its walls.

"This chapel has been thoroughly surveyed by G. E. Street, Esq., the well known architect, and his designs for its restoration have met with general approval.

"The architect has separated his scheme into parts,

each of which can be executed in order, according to its importance as funds become available. They are as follows :—

1. New roofs to the chancel and nave, new windows, wall cleaned and repaired at a cost of £1620
2. Rebuilding of the west front adding one bay to the length, thereby increasing the internal accommodation .. 500
3. Renewing the floors and seats 700
4. Building a bell turret 500
5. Placing a fence of proper design round the graveyard .. 200

£3500

" The whole sum is larger than can be granted by the War Office, hence the necessity of an appeal to the Navy, to the Army, and to the public for contributions.

" A confident hope is entertained that many persons will come forward to aid in restoring its sacred appearance to the ancient place of worship, containing or overshadowing as it does the remains of General Sir Charles Napier and many other gallant soldiers and sailors."

Colonel Shadwell, having read the circular to the meeting, observed that " a provisional committee had been formed, a subscription list opened, and that a few persons had already contributed, Lord William Paulet having headed the list with £50 as his first subscription."

In order that matters might take an active form, Colonel Sir J. William Gordon, K.C.B, Commanding Royal Engineer, moved, and Admiral Sir Henry Chads, G.C.B. seconded, the first resolution, viz. :—

" That a vigorous effort be made by means of the combined action of the inhabitants of this town, of the members of the united services who have been and are resident therein, as also of those in any way interested in Portsmouth, to restore the ancient chapel of Saints John the Baptist and Nicholas, now used as a garrison chapel, to a state worthy of the site on which it stands, and of the memory of the brave men who lie interred therein."

This was unanimously agreed to. It was further determined to nominate a committee to carry out the resolution, and to request Lord William Paulet to remain chairman of the general committee.

The committee was formed in due season, and, on the 15th of August, met for the purpose of electing an executive committee. It was then decided that such committee should consist of twelve members, who were at once nominated. Between the 15th of August, 1865, and the end of January, 1866, nothing was done beyond arranging committees, corresponding with the War Department and the architect, and raising subscriptions by private effort; but on the 24th of the latter month, the names of the general and executive committee were "approved and ordered to be printed." They were as follows :—

CHAIRMAN : MAJOR-GENERAL LORD WILLIAM PAULET, K.C.B.
ADJUTANT-GENERAL TO THE FORCES.

The Bishop of Winchester.
Admiral Sir Michael Seymour, G.C.B.
Adml. Sir Thomas Pasley, Bt., K.C.B.
*Admiral Sir H. D. Chads, G.C.B.
Lieut-General Foster, R.E.
*Rear-Admiral Wellesley, C.B.
*Major-General Sir J. W. Gordon, K.C.B., R.E.
*Major-Gen. T. R. Mould, C.B., R.E.
*Major-General W. H. Elliott, R.A.
Major-General Tate.
*Colonel Shadwell, War Office.
Col. Sir A. Alison, Bart., C.B., A.A.G.
R. W. Ford, Esq. (Ex-Mayor)
*Colonel Wodehouse, C.B., R.A.
*Colonel Hadden, R.E.
*J. W. Miller, Esq., M.D.
*The Rev. N. H. McGachen, M.A.
*The Ven. Archdeacon Wright, M.A., Chaplain to the Forces.

*The Rev. J. E. Sabin, M.A., Chaplain to the Forces.
The Rev. H. St. George, Chaplain to the Forces.
The Rev. S. Beal, M.A., Chaplain to the Royal Marine Artillery.
*E. M. Wells, Esq., (Mayor of Portsmouth.)
*C. B. Hellard, Esq.
*Major-Gen. Alexander, C.B., R.M.A.
Colonel Longden, R.A.
Major-General H. Marriott, R.M.L.I.
Lieut.-Colonel Meehan, Staff Officer of Pensioners.
*Captain McCoy, J.P.
Colonel Boulderson.
Major-General Paynter, C.B., R.A.
Colonel Willis, Q.M.G.
Major Breton, Town Major.
*W. G. Chambers, Esq.

*Of which those marked * are the Executive Committee.*
HON. SECS. : Colonel G. A. Schomberg, C.B. and Captain Molesworth, R.E.

The executive committee, now in a position to work effectually, made every possible effort to begin the restoration; and so successful was that effort that on the 21st

of November, 1866, a contract was signed by the chairman
Lord William Paulet, for the execution of Parts 1 and 2,
at an outlay of £3135, together with an organ chamber
(£178) ; the latter sum being guaranteed by a member of
the committee. It will be at once seen that the cost of
the restoration had seriously increased. The total expense
estimated in 1865 for the complete restoration of the
church was £3500, but when tenders were called for, so
greatly had labour and material advanced in price, that
the money required reached £5000. Under these circumstances, the Minister of War increased the government
grant to £2000, and so enabled the committee to proceed
in their work with all confidence. On the 10th of February, 1868, when the builders, Messrs. Sims and Marten had
nearly completed their contract, a letter was received from
Sir J. William Gordon, stating, that a consultation had
been held between Lord William Paulet and himself, and
that, with the consent of the committee, they would jointly
advance and pay into Messrs. Grants' bank £450, the amount
required for completing the boundary wall and bell
turret. This was a most acceptable offer, as it not only
secured the execution of Parts 4 and 5 of the scheme, but
also necessitated the improvement of the churchyard,
which was in a most disgraceful condition. Any attempt
to describe its state would of necessity prove a failure, so
utterly had it been neglected for years. Brick graves
abounded ; some tottering, some in ruins; lofty iron rail-
ings covered with rust and sadly mutilated, stood round
begrimed tombs, of which much was hidden by accumu-
lated dirt and rank grass ; head stones were everywhere
and in every direction ; deep hollows and irregular mounds
alternated; and round all stood a thick, high wall, inviting
the thoughtless to use God's Acre as a receptacle of dead
animals and old kettles. The restoration of the fabric of
the church would have been seriously marred, had not the
opportune and generous offer of Sir J. William Gordon,
enabled the committee to proceed at once with the
boundary wall, while the equally kind consideration of

Lord William Paulet, allowed them to build, without further delay, an elegant bell turret.

In order that the churchyard might be duly cared for, and everything done with a becoming caution, a sub-committee was appointed; and to its prudent exertions must be attributed, the well arranged walks and generally neat appearance of the ground. That which before was a disgrace became by degrees an ornament.

A sum of four thousand guineas had now been expended. Let us see what it had produced. The west front of the church had been rebuilt, and one bay added to the length of the building, thereby affording further internal accommodation; new roofs had been put to the chancel and nave, and new windows; an organ chamber built, and all the walls and pillars thoroughly repaired. Further, a handsome bell turret had been raised, and a substantial stone wall, supporting an appropriate iron railing, had been carried round the churchyard. The restoration had been a dissolving view; the ugliness of the old deformity had gradually disappeared, and the beauty of God's House gradually developed; until at length the Garrison Church commanded the admiration of all who examined it.

But, internally there was yet much to be done. The floor from one end to the other was of earth, and in several places there were large holes opening into deep vaults. It was therefore necessary at once to lay a concrete foundation throughout the building, to tile the chancel, to flood the nave with cement, and then to provide temporary fittings, which included 800 chairs. The estimate for all this was much smaller than expected. The whole cost would amount to only £325. Still this outlay, together with the then existing debt, would involve the committee in a responsibility of nearly £850. Sir J. William Gordon once more came to the rescue, and removed every impediment to progress. At a meeting, held on the 19th of June, 1868 a letter was read from him stating "that he was very willing to forego his claim for repayment of the loan lent by him to the Restoration Fund, until money had been collected for completing the chancel and nave, and supplying the chapel with chairs. He hoped that by such arrangement, the chapel might be opened to the troops for Divine Service on the 1st of November, 1868.

Every exertion was made to meet the wish of Sir J. William Gordon, and with such success, that on Friday, the 30th of October, 1868, a bright and happy day, the old Garrison Church of Portsmouth received a crowded congregation, to offer to the God of Forces grateful thanks for having permitted them so thoroughly to restore their holy building. The sermon, which was deeply heart stirring, was preached by the Right Reverend The Lord Bishop of Winchester. His Lordship was received at the gate of the church by a large body of the local clergy, together with many chaplains of H. M. Forces. The offerings amounted to £75 1s. 8d.

The building was now out of the hands of the contractors, and the committee being in a position to request the War Department to appoint a Board of officers to survey the work, the secretary wrote a letter to that effect, and also informed the War Department, that, as the building had been prepared for service, the committee wished to give it over as temporarily fitted, until such time as they were in a position to resume and complete the restoration. A letter was also written to Mr. Street, asking him to name a day when, with the officials appointed by the authorities, he could inspect the works.

After a short delay, the Board of survey was appointed, and the work examined. Mr. Street expressed himself thoroughly satisfied. The only objection made, and certainly a very reasonable one, was that of the officer of engineers, Captain Keith, who recorded on the face of the report, that, as there was no porch at the southwest end of the south aisle, the means of ingress and egress were too limited. In all other respects the restoration was declared a great addition to the beauty of the town, and to the convenience of the garrison.

As this is a special æra in the restoration, it may be well here, for the information of subscribers and all interested, to give a brief statement of monies received and monies expended, up to the time when the War Department took over the building from the contractors:—

	£	s.	d.		£	s.	d.
Received from War Department	2000	0	0	Contract for general work	3135	0	0
do. „ Lords of the Admiralty	50	0	0	do. Organ Chamber	178	0	0
By sale of old lead	9	12	2	do. Bell Turret ..	135	0	0
Subscriptions to 27th of January, 1869	1577	5	3	do. Boundary Wall	304	13	4
do. unpaid ..	57	3	0	do. Concrete, Tiles, and Marble steps for Chancel ..	185	13	0
Grant for Gas, War Department	98	0	0	Extras in interior, including Concrete and Cement for Nave & Floor	102	16	3
Balance unpaid ..	944	3	0	Gas Fittings, including Metre and Standards..	113	14	4
				Exterior of Chapel (extras) and Grave Yard	63	5	8
				Chairs for Chancel &Nave	97	0	9
				Fitting up Chancel, &c.	39	7	1
				Books for Church ; Printing, Postage, Carriage, Stationery, &c., &c. ..	78	16	4
				Extras to foundation of New Wall, West End	39	8	8
				Mr. Street, Architect, his account ..	263	8	8
	£4736	3	5		£4736	8	8

H. B. TUSON, Capt. R.M. Art., Hon. Sec.

N.B. Full details are given in the audited account.

The debt, on February 9, 1869, was £927 16s. 5d. an amount which would have daunted some committees But, throughout this work of years, there never was for a single moment any doubt as to money coming in when required. Ever confident, the committee held on courageously, and the public seemed grateful for their unflinching resolution. They were also greatly supported in their appeals by the following flattering official communication.

War Office, March 4th, 1869.

My dear Archdeacon,

I ought long ago to have told you how much I was delighted, during my recent official visit to Portsmouth,

with all that I saw in your restored Church. Your
committee deserves great praise for the knowledge,
as well as the perseverance, which has been displayed in
planning and carrying into effect such a plan of perfect
restoration. The work, as now completed, will bear comparison with anything of the kind that has ever been
attempted in this country ; and the Government, not less
than the Army, ought to feel (and must feel, if the matter
be seriously looked into) the most profound gratitude for
the exertions which all of you have made. I wish that it
were in my power to congratulate the committee on being
free from debt. But it is hardly possible to believe, if the
case be brought fairly before the public, that gentlemen,
who have exhibited such rare liberality, not less than patience, should be left for any length of time burthened
with the responsibility comparatively so insignificant as
that of a few hundred pounds.

Believe me,
Yours very sincerely,
G. R. GLEIG.

To the Venerable Archdeacon Wright,
    Chaplain to the Forces, Portsmouth.

Subscriptions continued to flow in freely. On the 5th
June, 1869, the debt was reduced to £685 1s. 3d., and, on
the 30th June, 1870, there remained only a small deficit of
£278 7s. 5d.

It was now that the War Department determined to
carry on Part 4, the reseating of the church, by means of
a committee composed entirely of military men ; Heads
of Departments and officers commanding corps being *ex-
officio* members. This change was announced by letter,
dated August 13th, 1870, which ended with the following
passage :—

"In making this communication to you, Lt.-Gen. Lord
Templetown requests you to be good enough to convey to
the executive committee the thanks of the Secretary of
State for War for its past labours, and for the manner in

which the restoration has been carried out. He congratulates the members on the great improvement to the building which has resulted from their untiring efforts."

A reply to Lord Templetown's official cómmunication was drawn up, and in due time the honorary secretary to the new committee forwarded an official statement, that the responsibility for the debt to Lord William Paulet and to the trustees of the late Sir J. William Gordon would be taken over from the old committee. Upon this, a full and complete statement of accounts was prepared by Captain Tuson, R. M. A., and sent, with all the bank-books, subscription lists and papers, to Major Barker, for the use and information of the new committee.

It is only right that the almost last act of the old committee should be placed before the public ; as it speaks of those whose names will long be remembered in the story of the restoration of the " Domus Dei " of Portsmouth.

"This committee cannot separate without recording their high sense of the valuable labours of Major-General Schomberg, C B., Colonel Shadwell, C.B., the late Captain Molesworth, R.E., Lieut.-Colonel Chads, and Captain Tuson, R.M.A. ; who, as honorary secretaries, so zealously exerted themselves. They would also offer their grateful thanks to Captain Tuson, for the accuracy with which he has kept the records connected with the restoration, as well as for the admirable manner in which he has attended to the accounts, which now cover a period of five years."

The new committee began its labours on the 31st of October, 1870, having on it one member who had throughout worked with the old committee. This proved convenient, as there was always one at hand, who could give information of all previous proceedings, and also state what had been found the best modes of obtaining assistance from the public. The debt was now only £261 11s. 0d.

During the first year of the new regime, the attention of the committee was chiefly confined to obtaining money, and the erection of the memorial stalls, for which the old committee had collected nearly £400. By means of a bazaar, held in

August, 1871, all debt was paid off, a tender for erecting forty-two handsome stalls was accepted, and in so promising a condition was the restoration fund, in October 1871, that the committee considered it might confidently provide the long desired south porch and a vestry. The vestry had become absolutely necessary, as an organ had been presented to the church, and would soon occupy the organ chamber, which had been used as a temporary vestry. The porch had from the beginning been delayed solely through the want of funds. When the plans for the porch and vestry were submitted to the Secretary of State for War, his approval was communicated in terms of unmeasured approbation. The following letter from the Chaplain General, conveying that approbation, will be as satisfactory to the subscribers as it was encouraging to the committee.

War Office, September 28th, 1871.

My dear Archdeacon,.

The official application for leave to act upon Mr. Street's plan in building a porch, and otherwise bringing to a close the great work of church restoration in Portsmouth, has just been submitted to me   I do not lose a moment in begging you to express to the committee of management the high sense I entertain of the patience, perseverance, and excellent spirit, which they have displayed in carrying forward towards its happy completion an undertaking from which most men would have shrunk. The Church in the Army is greatly indebted to them for work done from first to last so wisely and so well.

I assure you,—and I request that you will make this statement to the committee,—that, in the admiration which I experience, the Secretary of State fully shares. The restored church will be an enduring monument in a righteous cause of the gentlemen who have taken a leading part in making it what it is.

Ever yours sincerely,

G. R. GLEIG, Chaplain-General.

To the Ven. Archdeacon H. P. Wright, M.A.,
    Chaplain to the Forces, Portsmouth.

E

It now only remained to floor and seat the nave to complete the compact originally made with the War Department. This part of the restoration, the committee determined to carry out, by doing a bay at a time. A resolution was therefore passed, to proceed with the tiling of the first bay at once, and to place seats in it as money was forthcoming. On the 20th of June, 1872, designs were supplied by G. E. Street, R.A., for the tiling, and for simple but handsome and substantial open oak seats; and early in July a tender was accepted for tiling the church from the chancel steps to the first pillar, and constructing benches as required. It is confidently expected that by the assistance of departments, corps, and friends the few hundred pounds (£700) required for finishing the nave, in other words for completing the restoration, will be speedily forthcoming. Funds have as yet always been provided as wanted, and, now that the end is so near at hand, it would be folly to despond.

But it may reasonably be said, while all must admit the skill of the architect and generosity of the public, which together have so thoroughly restored one of the most consistent and interesting examples of early English; what proof is there that the army has by such restoration been spiritually benefitted. It is not always easy, but generally very difficult, to measure spiritual influences. I can simply say that the soldiers now speak of their church with pride, and many of them find it a true house of peace to them. At the voluntary services thousands of soldiers and civilians now worship together (thanks to the liberality of the government) in a free church—a freedom which gathers Sunday after Sunday crowded congregations. As a testimony of the great usefulness of the restored church to the army, I will ask the reader to receive the witness of a true soldier, one who at home and abroad, in the field and in days of peace, has been a marked and honoured member of his great profession. When, in December last, the committee determined to make a general appeal to the army for funds, I wrote to Lieut.-Colonel Kent, commanding

the 77th Regiment, the following letter; and received from
him an answer, which will, I trust, lead all friends of the
soldier to help the committee complete a work, which has
now been actively going on over a period of seven years.

Portsmouth, December 26th, 1871.

My dear Colonel,

As the Government and general Public have
been very liberal, and enabled us to produce so satisfactory
a restoration of the ancient and, I may now say, beautiful
Garrison Church, the committee are about to ask every
officer in the service to contribute. The sum so raised
will we trust enable us to complete our work. Many regiments on foreign stations know nothing of Portsmouth
Garrison Church, and desire before they give, to be quite
sure that the money provided will be wisely expended.
As you are about to leave this garrison will you kindly
say how far the restored church has been of use to you
and your corps. Officers require not merely the appeal
of the chaplain, which may or may not be judicious,
but also the testimony of some one of themselves. You
and the 77th have had a long experience of the restored
Garrison Church and its services, and what you say will I
am sure be considered fairly and generously by other
regiments.

Yours faithfully,

H. P. WRIGHT.

To Lieut.-Col. Kent, Commanding
    77th Regiment, Portsmouth.

Portland, 5th January, 1872.

My dear Archdeacon,

I had not time before leaving Portsmouth to
answer your letter, and since I came here I have been too
busy; but I had not forgotten it, and have no hesitation in
saying that the beautifully restored Garrison Church was
of the greatest benefit and advantage to my regiment
during the year and a half that we were quartered in the
old Clarence barracks. In proof of which I may mention

that whereas it was a rare sight to see a soldier at the
voluntary services, when I was last quartered in Portsmouth some years ago, you may now see scores and scores.
And not only has the church been so beautifully restored
as to render it one of the finest examples of ecclesiastical
architecture in the kingdom, but, I assure you, until I went
there some eighteen months ago, I had no idea it was
possible to make the military service so cheerful and
attractive. I shall always take the deepest interest in it,
and don't know anything that would afford me greater
satisfaction than to see the work of restoration carried out
to a successful completion, *à propos* to which I shall feel
obliged by your bringing to the notice of the committee,
that it is our wish to present one of the windows on the
north side of the nave, if there is no objection to our doing
so. It will be a lasting memorial of our very pleasant
stay at Portsmouth, and will serve to hand down the
names of our dear brother officers, Orpen and Weigall, to
future generations.

Yours very sincerely,
HENRY KENT.

To the Venerable Archdeacon H. P. Wright, M.A.,
        Chaplain to the Forces, Portsmouth.

I need say no more upon this matter as I am sure the
letter of such an officer will persuade every reasonable
mind, and secure the help of every generous heart.

As I look upon the fine old Garrison Church, which,
for nearly 700 years, has been a blessing to generation
after generation ; as I walk up its noble, lofty nave ; as I
enter its deep, beautifully groined chancel ; I feel grateful
indeed to the holy, and skilled, and generous men, who produced the Hospital, of which now our Garrison Church is
the sole remain. And this will be the feeling of all who
visit the valuable relic. Well did one dear to the Church,
a leader in everything high and heavenly ; one who, alas !
was so suddenly and so early taken from us ; one from
whose lips it was my privilege to receive many a learned

lesson, well did he write when he thus pleaded with us :—

"Let us reverence the spirit of self-sacrifice of the
dark ages (as we contumeliously term them); and see with
what a noble ardour the men of those days devoted *all*—
money, time, thought, hope, life itself—to raising for God
and man shrines as worthy of God as human hands could
raise, and fit and able to lift man's thoughts and hopes
beyond earth, and lead them on heavenward. They did
not sit down to sum up the exact cost of glorifying God ;
they did not calculate exactly how many the holy roof
would cover ; they knew with their hearts, if their tongues
never uttered, the truth—

> 'High Heaven disdains the love
> Of nicely calculated less or more.'

And in the spirit of that higher philosophy, they gave all
they could, knowing that they gave not in vain. And
vain it has not been. No. As year by year the pealing
anthem has fallen on the charmed ear ; and nave, and
choir and aisle have unfolded their awful perspective to
the astonished eye : if a human, as well as a heavenly
register could have been kept, to tell what transports of
love, of devotion, of heartfelt penitence, of rapture, and of
tears, the holy walls have witnessed, and sent up in memorial on high ; the lowest of all the low, the utilitarian
himself, if he believed that there is another world beyond
the grave, would be constrained to allow, that the riches
lavished on the Abbey, the Cathedral, the Parish Church,
(and the "Domus Dei") were always spent wisely and
well."*

---

* The Reverend Hugh James Rose, B.D.

THE RESTORED CHURCH—ITS GIFTS
AND ITS MEMORIALS.

N order that any one, visiting the Garrison Church, may at once learn something about it on the spot, I will now act as guide, and draw attention to the chief objects of interest in the restored building. The story of the "Domus Dei" as told in the early part of this book, will then be read with greater interest. Let us first study it from the outside. Remember that you are not looking upon an old church, formed of chancel and nave, but upon an ancient "House of the Sick and Infirm" now called the nave, and their chapel; in other words upon a Hospital for the cure of the bodies and souls of destitute sufferers—a true "Domus Dei." The building is throughout well proportioned. This is the result of the skill of the great architect, G. E. Street, R.A., who extended the nave one bay, and so brought it to its original length, his corner stone and that of the old Infirmary falling on precisely the same spot: a great triumph on the part of Mr. Street, as when he formed his plan, nothing whatever was known of the destruction of the western bay in the time of Elizabeth. The porch, charming in design and thoroughly well built, is a recent addition; but you will observe that there is, as it were, a continuous buttress running from the porch

along the south aisle, and rising suddenly about two feet at
the east end. This has evidently been at one period all
equally high, as the marks of the upper weathering can be
easily traced. Many archæologists have examined this
wall, and strange have been the conjectures about it. A
walk to the east end of either aisle will help, I think, to remove the difficulty. It will there be seen that the roof of
the aisles originally came down at a much steeper pitch,
terminating at the weathering of the thick wall. The line
of the old roof is quite distinct, the stone work above it
being palpably of a much later period. There were therefore no two light windows as at present, but in the thick
wall, low down, there were narrow Early English piercings
about six in number; of which one fortunately remains
perfect, a second presents its lower half, while further west-
ward we find only the sill; all plainly indicating that the
sick within received light by a succession of small, narrow
windows. But why, it may be asked build the south wall
so thick? Because at first it was designed to make the side
aisles broader than they now are. The south wall was
built to such design, and so were the east ends with a window in each; but when the work had proceeded thus far it
was determined, for some wise reason we may suppose, to
narrow the aisles. A second wall was therefore necessary
on the south side, which at once accounts for the seemingly
continuous buttress and its weathering; while, on the north
side, the wall, which had not been commenced, was brought
in to reduce the width of the aisle, and a splay left at its
east end so as not to interfere with the beautiful three-
light window already completed. The idea that the small
window still existing in the south wall was a squint, by
which the chantry altar could be seen, is evidently worth-
less, as the chantry is of a date much later than that of
the window. This is the only explanation I can suggest
with respect to the curious north wall which has been so
frequently examined and discussed, and the suggestion is
supported by the fact, that, when the Church was extended
the workmen found two walls, one within the other.

The Corbel Table, which is commonly given as a beautiful example in the more important works on Gothic architecture, is well worthy of attention ; but, beyond it, I am not aware that there is anything more connected with the exterior of the church calling for special remark.

Let us now enter the building. As the door is opened the stranger is at once surprised and impressed. The lofty arches, and their broad space, give a grandeur to the interior which was little expected·; and so does the simple substantial roof carrying the eye far above heavenward. Along the narrow aisles you can picture the sick pilgrims stretched on their wooden bedsteads, kindly ministered to by the brothers and sisters ; and, if you walk to the east end of either aisle, you will at once perceive that the window is not in the centre, but was evidently pierced for a width which would have been secured had the first design for wider aisles been carried out. Many of the corbels in the nave are remarkable, indeed almost unique. They seem as it were to bud gracefully out from the capitals, and show exquisite taste and ingenuity on the part of the architect. The two aisle windows toward the east were, before the restoration, covered by lath and plaster and mural tablets. Their original form has been strictly preserved.

Generally speaking, the *Capella Infirmorum*, the chapel of the infirmary, was separated from the *Domus Infirmorum*, the hall of the infirmary, by a wall rising to the roof, and having a door in the centre. This was certainly the case with the Portsmouth "Domus Dei," the doorway being marked on the Henry VIII. Plan, No. 16, but the partition was for convenience pulled down, when the hall was taken into use for public worship. The change was far from a disfigurement, for it opened out a deep and handsome chancel, to which the hall became an equally handsome nave.

The chancel is 53 feet long and 22 feet broad, with a noble groined vaulting chastely bossed at the intersections, the ribs supported by delicate vaulting shafts with plain, foliaged, and grotesquely headed corbels. Above the vaulting is a spacious false roof, giving the proper pitch to the roof of the building. The three lancet windows at the east end with trefoiled head, are exactly what they were when the church was first built, but those on the north and south sides, while filling the old openings, are new in design and greatly admired. Each is ornamented by two Purbeck marble shafts.

The pavement of the chancel is throughout a union of encaustic tiles and marble; that of the altar space having a very rich appearance from the introduction of bands of green glazed tiling. The old sedilia were found nearly destroyed, but fortunately just sufficient remained to secure the design, which has been carefully copied. The piscina is close to the east wall, and near it a credence table, divided by a Purbeck marble shaft. On the north side of the altar, in the east wall, is a spacious almery running in deeply southwards. The altar rails are perfectly plain, but supported by wrought iron standards of exquisite pattern. Before the restoration the two doors in the chancel were concealed by pannelling, That at the west end is the entrance to the belfry, which in old hospitals and monastaries, was commonly placed without the west end of the south side of the church.* Many ask if this door did not formerly lead to a rood-loft, forgetting that rood-lofts are rarely (I fancy never) found so early as the beginning of the thirteenth century. In the belfry hung the two bells mentioned in the Deed of Amicable Settlement, A.D. 1229. If the chancel has a failing it is in height; but, as a whole, it is of its kind rarely surpassed. We will now proceed to examine its gifts and memorials.

THE ALTAR

Is the gift of the Reverend John E. Sabin, M.A., Chaplain to the Forces, 1st class, to whom Portsmouth is greatly indebted for its now beautiful Garrison Church. He was

---

* Archœologia Cantiana Page 201. No. 39.

one of the very first movers in the work (they so often are
forgotten while others get the credit) and has been a
generous subscriber.   The altar was designed by G. E.
Street, R.A., and made by Messrs. Bramble Brothers, Portsea.   The dimensions are as follows :—length, 9 feet ;
height, 3 feet 9 inches ; breadth, 2 feet 9 inches.   It is of
the finest oak and handsomely pannelled.

THE ORGAN,

Occupying a spacious Organ Chamber which runs back
from the centre of the north side of the chancel, is an
offering made by the Sunday evening congregation and
friends.   The builder was Mr. A. Hunter, of 379, Kenning-
ton Road, Lambeth, whose skill as an organ builder is well
known throughout Portsmouth ; and, especially so, for the
brilliant instrument constructed for Mr. J. D. Antill, of
Portsea, which is one of the largest organs in the county.
Indeed it may justly be said, that Mr. Hunter, by his
genius and perseverance, has secured a reputation which
places him among the very foremost in his profession.
The synopsis of the Garrison Church Organ is as follows:—

GREAT ORGAN—Compass Double C to G.

1	Double Diapason	..	CC to G	6	Flute	..	..	CC to G
2	Open Diapason	..	CC to G	7	Twelfth	..	..	CC to G
3	Dulciana	..	Ten. C to G	8	Fifteenth	..	..	CC to G
4	Stopped Diapason	..	CC to G	9	Mixture Four Ranks			CC to G
5	Principal	..	CC to G					

SWELL ORGAN—Double C to G.

10	Double Diapason	.	CC to G	14	Mixture Three Ranks		CC to G
11	Open Diapason	.. Ten. C to G		15	Cornopian	..	CC to G
12	Stopped Diapason	..	CC to G	16	Oboe	.. ..	CC to G
13	Principal	.. ..	CC to G				

PEDAL ORGAN.

| 17 | Open Diapason | .. CCC to F | 19 | Coupler Swell to Pedals |
| 18 | Coupler Great to Pedals | | 20 | Coupler Swell to Great |

Three composition Pedals acting on the Great Organ and two on the
Swell Organ.

THE STALLS,

Forty-two in number, of the finest oak, are all memorials telling of England's gallant soldiers and sailors. They were made after the beautiful design of G. E. Street, R.A., by Mr. G. W. Booth, of 21, King William Street, Charing Cross. The carving, which is of the highest order, was executed by Mr. Earp, of London.. Each stall has an appropriate brass prepared by Messrs. Clayton & Bell. The following are the officers to whose memory the stalls have been dedicated :—

IN MEMORY OF	PRESENTED BY
1 Admiral Viscount Nelson, G.C.B. ..	..H.R.H. The Duke of Edinburgh, K.G.
2 Field Marshal The Duke of Wellington, K.G.	H.R.H. The Duke of Cambridge, K.G.
3 Alfwine, Bishop of Winchester, (A.D. 1032)	Bishop of Winchester.
4 General Sir John Moore, K.C.B. ..	..Lieutenant-General Viscount Templetown, K.C.B.
5 General Viscount Hill, G.C.B. ..	..Viscount Hill.
6 Field Marshal Lord Raglan, G.C.B. ..	..Friends.
7 Field Marshal Sir Alexdr. Woodford, G.C.B.	Lieutenant-General Viscount Templetown, K.C.B. and the Viscountess Templetown.
8 Admiral Sir Henry Ducie Chads, G.C.B.	..Sons and Daughters.
9 General Sir John Macdonald, G.C.B. ·	..The late Lieut. Gen. the Hon. Sir J. Yorke Scarlett, G.C.B.
10 Sir James McGrigor, Bart. ..	..Army Medical Department.
11 General Sir Alexander Dickson, G.C.B.	..12th Brigade Royal Artillery.
12 General Sir Hercules Pakenham, G.C.B.	..Mrs. Thistlethwayte.
13 General Sir George Brown, G.C.B. ..	..Colonel Willis, C.B.
14 General Sir Charles Napier, G.C.B. ..	..Lady C. Napier.
15 General Sir William Napier, K.C.B. ..	..His four daughters.
16 General Sir George Napier, K.C.B. ..	..Major-Gen. W. C. E. Napier.
17 General Sir James Outram, Bart., G.C.B.	..Friends.
18 General Sir George Charles D'Aguilar, K.C.B.	Mj.-Gen. D'Aguilar, R.A.,C.B.

19 General Sir George Cathcart, G.C.B. ..   ..Earl Cathcart.
20 Lieutenant-General Sir Henry Barnard, K.C.B. Colonel Barnard.
21 General Sir Harry Jones, R.E., G.C.B.   ..Friends.
22 Lieutenant General The Hon. Sir J. Yorke
        Scarlett, G.C.B.   ..   ..   ..The Hon. Lady Yorke Scarlett
23 Major General Sir J. W. Gordon, R.E., K.C.B. Lieut.-General Lord William
                                                        Paulet. G.C.B.
24 Major-General Strangways, R.A., C.B.   ..Officers of Royal Artillery.
25 Major-General Sir Henry W. Adams, K.C.B. Officers 49th Regiment.
26 Major-General F. Adams, C.B.   ..   ..Officers 28th Regiment.
27 Colonel Wodehouse, R.A., C.B.   ..   ..Widow and daughters.
28 Officers (Etonians).   ..   ..   ..Eton College.
29 Officers (Harrovians).   ..   ..   ..Harrow School.
30 Officers (Rugbeians).   ..   ..   ..Rugby School.
31 Colonel Carpenter, C.B. 41st Regiment.   ..Major Carpenter.
32 Officers of Army Medical Department.   ..Army Medical Department.
33 Colonel J. Hinde King, C.B. Gren. Gds.   ..Brothers and Sisters.
34 Colonel Egerton, C.B.   ..   ..   ..Officers, 77th Regiment.
35 Officers, 49th Regiment   ..   ..   ..Officers, 49th Regiment.
36 Major Butler, Cey. Rif. (killed at Silistria) ..Captain Butler.
37 Captain Butler 55th Regt. (killed at Inkerman) Officers 55th Regt.
38 Captain Cassan, Knight of Windsor.   ..His Widow.
39 Twelve Chaplains who died during the   Army Chaplains.
        Crimean War
40 Captain Sir Robert Newman, Bart. Gren. Gds. Sir Lydston Newman, Bart.
41 Rev. Pierce Butler, Crimean Chaplain.   ..His Widow.
42 Captain Hatchell, 43rd Regt. L. Inf.   ..Officers 43rd Regt. L. Inf.

ADMIRAL VISCOUNT NELSON and Field Marshal THE DUKE OF WEL-
    LINGTON need no record of services here.   Their deeds are written on
    the heart of every patriot, and are told of in the brightest pages of
    England's history.   The story of each graces volumes.

3 ALFWINE, Bishop of Winchester, was a renowned and successful
    warrior against the Danes.   He held the See from 1038 to 1047.

4 GENERAL SIR JOHN MOORE, G.C.B., entered the Army when only 15,
    and served with distinction in Corsica, as Colonel; in the West Indies
    as Brigadier-General; in Ireland during the rebellion of 1798, and in
    the expedition to Holland as a General of Staff.   He was in Egypt
    with the army under Abercromby, and obtained the order of the Bath

for his services in command of the reserve. When war again broke out in 1802 Moore served in Sicily and Sweden. In 1808 he was sent with a corps of 10,000 men to strengthen the English army in the Peninsula, and at the close of that year was instructed to co-operate with the Spaniards. The apathy of the Spaniards and the overwhelming numbers of the French compelled him to retreat after the fall of Madrid. In December he began his disastrous march from Astorga to Corunna some 250 miles. On his arrival at Corunna with an army worn by hardships, he was compelled to fight. On the 16th January, 1809, the battle was fought. While leading the 42nd Regiment in a brilliant charge he was struck by a cannon-ball on the left shoulder and died in the moment of victory. A monument was erected to his memory in St. Paul's Cathedral.

5 GENERAL VISCOUNT HILL, G.C.B., second son of Sir John Hill, Bart., of Hawkstone, entered the army at the age of fifteen, and obtained a Captaincy before he was twenty. He was with Moore at Corunna. He also served in the campaigns of 1809, 1810, and 1811, under the Duke of Wellington, and displayed great gallantry and great talent as a Commander. When the army returned home the fame of General Hill was second only to that of Wellington. He was created Baron Hill, of Almarez and Hawkstone, received a parliamentary grant of £2000 a year; and both title and annuity were granted to his nephew in remainder. He was also made a G.C.B. He commanded a division at Waterloo, and remained with the army of occupation, as second in command, until it quitted the French territory. He was Commander-in-Chief of the army from 1821 to 1842. After his resignation, he was created a viscount. He died December 10, 1842, in his seventy first year.

6 FIELD MARSHAL FITZROY JAMES HENRY SOMERSET LORD RAGLAN, G.C.B., eighth son of the fifth Duke of Beaufort. He entered the army in his 16th year, and in 1807 served on the staff of the Duke of Wellington in the expedition to Copenhagen. As Lord Fitzroy Somerset, his name became a household word. He was present at all the great actions of the Peninsular campaign. He was among the first to mount the breach at the storming of Badajoz, and it was to him the Governor gave up his sword. On the return of Napoleon from Elba, he served under the Duke in Flanders, and lost his sword arm at Waterloo. From 1827 to 1852, he was military secretary to the Commander-in-chief. On the death of the Duke, in September of

that year, was made Master-General of the Ordnance, and in October was called to the House of Peers as Baron Raglan of Raglan. In 1854 he was appointed commander of the English forces which were despatched to Turkey. The victory of the Alma, the flank march to Balaklava, the battle of Balaklava, the sanguinary struggle at Inkerman, (which obtained for him the baton of Field-Marshal) and the siege of Sebastopol, will ever be closely connected with the name of Raglan. Early in June, 1855, he suffered from a slight attack of cholera, which became at last violent and carried off the great soldier on the 28th of June, 1855. Having been present at the death of Lord Raglan, the following extract from my note-book may not be uninteresting. "The room was small and with little furniture in it. Colonel Somerset and Lord Burghersh stood on one side of the neat, narrow, camp bed, Dr. Prendergrast at its head, Colonel Steele and General Airey on the other side. I stood next, close to the dying hero. As I uttered the words ' peace to this house and all that dwell in it,' all fell on their knees. At the close of the heart searching service, I placed my hand upon the broad, handsome forehead of the noble soldier, and commended the departing soul to the keeping of God. A few minutes after the great man went to his rest. Colonel Steele then asked me to pray that those present might be strengthened. I did so, and heavy grief sat upon the hearts of all who joined in that solemn appeal to heaven for aid." May England have many such sons, and when afflictions like those of 1854 threaten her armies, may she have as devoted and as able a servant as Lord Raglan ! His Lordship received the gold cross and five clasps for Fuentes d'Onor, Badajoz, Salamanca, Vittoria, Pyrenees, Nivelle, Nive, Orthes and Toulouse; and the silver war medal and five clasps for Roleia, Vimiera, Talavera, Busaco, and Cuidad Rodrigo. He also received the Crimean medal and clasps for Alma, Balaklava, and Inkerman, and a large number of foreign orders.

7   FIELD MARSHAL SIR ALEXANDER WOODFORD, G.C.B., son of Colonel John Woodford formerly of the Grenadier Guards, and of Susan Gordon, eldest daughter of Cosmo George 3rd Duke of Gordon, and Widow of John 9th Earl of Westmoreland, was born in 1782, and entered the army in 1794, as Cornet in the 14th Light Dragoons. In 1795, was appointed a Lieutenant, and in 1799, joined the 9th Foot, from Winchester School, and was present in the campaign in North Holland in 1799. Was severely wounded in the action of the 19th September that year at

St. Morel, and was gazetted killed. In 1800 was exchanged and returned to England, and promoted by purchase to a Captain Lieutenancy in the 9th Foot in the same year. Exchanged into the Coldstream Guards as Lieutenant and Captain in 1800. Appointed to the Staff as Aide de Camp to Major General The Honorable James Forbes, afterwards Lord Forbes, and was stationed at Ashford and Dover, forming part of the army assembled on the coast to repel the threatened Invasion in 1803. In 1807, Sir Alexander rejoined the Coldstream for the Expedition to the Baltic, and was present at the capture of Copenhagen, and served with a detachment of his regiment, under the command of Col. Spencer, 40th Regiment, in assisting to fit out the Danish Fleet in the dock yard. In 1808, he resumed the Staff-appointment as Aide de Camp to Lord Forbes, and served with him in Sicily in 1808, 1809, and 1810. In that year he was promoted by purchase to be Captain and Lieutenant-Colonel Coldstream Guards, and joined the 2nd Battalion the same year. In 1811, he joined the 1st Battalion serving under the Duke of Wellington in Portugal, and was present at the Siege and Capture of Ciudad Rodrigo, and with the corps covering the Siege of Badajoz ; he commanded the Light Companies of the Guards at the Battle of Salamanca, in the defence of the Arapiles, was present at the Capture of Madrid, and the Siege of Burgos. Commanded the rear-guard of the army in the retreat from Burgos. In 1813 succeeded to the command of the 1st Battalion Coldstream Guards, and was present at the battle of Vittoria, and during the operations before San Sebastian, and in the Pyrenees. Was present at the passage of the Bidassoa, and entry into France, and at the crossing of the Nive and Nivelle, and at the affair before Biarritz in December, 1813. Was also present at the crossing of the Adour, and the investment and sortie from Bayonne, and at the entry into Bordeaux. In 1814, embarked in the Gironde for England, and was promoted to 2nd Major Coldstream Guards, having been previously appointed Aide de Camp to the Prince Regent. In 1815, took the command of the 2nd Battalion Coldstream Guards at Brussels, and was present at the action at Quatre Bras, 16th June, and at the battle of Waterloo. Was engaged as senior officer in the defence of Hougomont, by the Duke of Wellington's special order, from mid-day until night. Entered France a 2nd time at the head of the Coldstream, at Malplaquet, and was present at the Capture of Paris, and remained during the winter in garrison in that city. Served with the Army of Occupation for three years at

Cambray, and embarked for England from Calais in 1818. In 1820 was promoted to be Lieutenant-Colonel Coldstream Guards. In 1825, was made Major General, and appointed Lieut-Governor of Malta in that year, and as Major General on the Staff in the Ionian Islands in 1827 and second in command, Acting Lord High Commissioner in 1832. Was appointed Lieut.-Governor of Gibraltar in 1835, and succeeded Lord Chatham as Governor in 1836, and remained in command until 1842. Appointed Colonel of the 40th Regiment, and was President of the Clothing Board for several years. Was President of the Crimean Inquiry. Was appointed Lieut.-Governor of Chelsea in 1856, and Governor in 1868. Appointed Colonel of the Scots Fusileer Guards in 1863, and Field Marshal in the army in 1868. The Field Marshal had received the Peninsular and Waterloo Medals. The Gold Medal for Salamanca, Vittoria, and the Nive, as well as the cross of Maria Theresa, and St. George of Russia, and was Knight Grand Cross of the Military Order of the Bath, and of St. Michael and St. George.

8 ADMIRAL SIR HENRY DUCIE CHADS, G.C.B., entered the Royal Naval Academy at 12 years of age, and in 1803 embarked on board the Excellent, 74, and shared in the defence of Gaeta and the capture of Capri; promoted 5th November, 1806, and employed in the Illustrious, 74. In July, 1808, joined the Iphigenia, 36 guns, and was actively engaged in attacking the Isle Bourbon, and particularly distinguished himself at the capture of l'Isle de la Passe leading the storming party. On the recapture of Bourbon by an overwhelming French squadron, Lieut. Chads was made prisoner, but relieved from a wretched captivity on the subsequent reduction of the Mauritius, and re-appointed first of the Iphigenia. In August, 1812, as senior Lieutenant of Java, 46 guns, miserably manned, fought the renowned action with the powerful and ably equipped American ship, Constitution, 56 guns and 485 veterans. Captain Lambert having been mortally wounded, Lieut. Chads (himself severely wounded) gallantly continued the struggle, until compelled to strike to his giant antagonist after a contest of three hours and forty minutes, the Java having become a sinking hulk. This action secured promotion and the command of the Columbia, sloop of war. Commander Chads afterwards distinguished himself at Guadaloupe in 1815. In 1823, he joined the expedition against Rangoon, and there his exertions were so conspicuous and effectual that he was advanced to Post rank, created a C.B., and received the thanks of the supreme Government of India, and high commendation of the

House of Commons at home. Captain Chads was next engaged in forcing the passage of the Bocca Tigris, September, 1834, commanding the Andromache from 1834 to 1837. In 1841 he again proceeded to China in command of the Cambrian, returning home in 1845, and from August, 1845, till he attained Flag rank in 1854, was Captain of the Excellent, Gunnery ship, and Superintendent of the Royal Naval College. In 1846, he was awarded the Captain's good service pension. Captain Chads reformed the whole system of gunnery, both as regards weight of metal and rapidity of fire. In the war with Russia, Rear Admiral Chads hoisted his Flag on board the Edinburgh, and distinguished himself at the capture of Bomarsund. He struck his Flag in 1855, and as a reward for his services, was created a k.c.b. From 1856 to the end of 1858, he held the command-in-chief in Ireland, and in 1865, was created a g.c.b., and received the Admiral's good service pension. Sir Henry Ducie Chads, as sailor, citizen, friend, and father, was honoured and beloved by all who knew him.

9 GENERAL SIR JOHN MACDONALD, G.C.B., Colonel Commandant of the 42nd Highlanders (The Black Watch) served with the 89th in Ireland during the Rebellion of 1798, and was present at the battles of Ross, Vinegar Hill, and other principal actions.

In 1799 and 1800 he was at the siege of La Valetta and capture of Malta. He served in Egypt the three following years, and was present in the action when landing on the 8th March, and also in the two other general actions fought on the 13th and 21st March, 1801.

In 1807, he was employed as Military Secretary to Lord Cathcart, whilst his Lordship commanded the King's German Legion as a distinct army in Swedish Pomerania, as well as during the subsequent attack upon, and capture of, Copenhagen and the Danish Fleet. In 1806, he served in the Walcheren expedition, and had charge of the Adjutant General's Department of the reserve commanded by Sir John Hope. The following year he was employed as Deputy Adjutant General to the force allotted to the defence of Cadiz, under Lieut-General Graham, and was present at the battle of Barossa. In 1813 and 14, he was employed in charge of the left wing of the Peninsular army, and in that capacity was present in the actions upon the Nive, and in the affairs which attended the closing of the blockade of Bayonne, and at the action brought on by the general sortie from that fortress. Sir John received a medal for services in Egypt, and the gold medal and one clasp for Barossa and the Nive.

F

10 SIR JAMES McGREGOR, BART., entered the service in September, 1793. He served in Holland and Flanders in 1794 and 5; in the West Indies in 1796; in the East Indies 1798; in Egypt, as superintending surgeon of the Anglo-Indian army in 1801; with the army at Walcheren in 1809, and in the Peninsula from 1811 to the end of the war. Sir James has received the war medal with four clasps for Badajoz, Vittoria, Pyrenees and Toulouse. In 1815 he was placed at the head of the Medical Board. Knighted 1814—created a Baronet in 1831, received rewards for long and brilliant services in the field, and for many works of high talent bearing upon the health and well-doing of the soldier.

11 MAJOR-GENERAL SIR A. DICKSON, G.C.B., K.C.H. entered the Royal Artillery on the 6th November, 1794.

It is not possible to do justice to the services of an officer who was preeminently the first artilleryman of his day, and one of the most distinguished of the many celebrated officers who served under the great Duke of Wellington.

As a Lieutenant he was present at the capture of Minorca in 1798, and and at the blockade of Malta, and surrender of La Valetta in 1800. Here, as subsequently at Monte Video, he served as acting engineer.

As a Captain he commanded his company at the seige and capture of Monte Video, and the attack upon Buenos Ayres in 1807. He proceeded to Portugal in 1809, and served as Brigade-Major to the Royal Artillery under Colonel Howorth at the affair at Grigo, the capture of Oporto, and subsequent expulsion of Soult from Portugal in 1809. Shortly after this time he was given the command of the Portuguese artillery, with the local rank of Lieut-Colonel, and by this arrangement Lord Wellington was enabled to overcome the technical difficulty arising from the regimental seniority of other officers, and to treat Dickson as virtual chief of his artillery.

He commanded the Portuguese artillery in the battle of Busaco, and at the Lines of Lisbon (Torres Vedras) in 1810, at the affair of Campo Mayor, the siege and capture of Olivenca, and the battle of Albuera in 1811.

He commanded the artillery operations in 1811, at the first and second sieges of Badajos, under Lord Wellington's immediate orders; also at the siege and capture of Ciudad Rodrigo, the siege and capture of Badajos, the attack and capture of the forts of Almaraz, the siege and capture of the forts of Salamanca, and the siege of Burgos in 1812;

and he commanded the reserve artillery of the army at the battle of Salamanca, and at the capture of the Retiro, Madrid, in the same year. Colonel Sir W. Robe, who commanded the Artillery of Lord Wellington's army, having been severely wounded at Burgos, was obliged to return home, and the chief command of the artillery was then conferred by Lord Wellington upon Dickson, who, by virtue of his rank in the Portuguese artillery, was the senior officer of that arm in the Allied army.

He commanded the Allied artillery at the battle of Vittoria, 1813; the siege and capture of St Sebastian, the passage of Bidassoa, battle of Nivelle, and battle of Nive in 1813; and at the passage of the Adour, and battle of Toulouse in 1814.

The next campaign of Lieut-Colonel Dickson was the inglorious one of New Orleans in 1814—15. He commanded the artillery of the expeditionary force and was present in the attack on that place and at the capture of Fort Bowyer, Mobile.

Returning from America early in the year, he was present and engaged in the battles of Quatre Bras and Waterloo, and subsequently commanded the battering train with the Prussian army at the sieges of Maubenge, Landrecies, Phillippeville, Marienbourg, and Rocroy, in July and August, 1815.

To record the occasions on which this distinguished officer was honourably mentioned in public despatches would be to recapitulate nearly the whole of the foregoing actions.

Captain Dickson was promoted to Brevet-Major and Brevet-Lieutenant Colonel in 1812, but, almost incredible to relate, he received no further promotion until 1825, when he attained the same rank regimentally, and was also aide-de-camp to the King, with rank of Colonel in the army, on the 27th May, in the same year.

In September, 1822, he was appointed Inspector of Artillery, and Deputy-Adjutant-General, Royal Artillery, on 10th April, 1827, in succession to Lieut-General Sir J. Macleod, upon whose decease in January, 1833, he was appointed Master-Gunner, St. James's Park.

In 1838 upon the death of Lieut-General Millar, he succeeded that officer as Director-General of Artillery (Field Train Department), which appointment was combined with that of Deputy-Adjutant-General during his life. Sir A. Dickson was also a Commissioner of the Royal Military College, Sandhurst, and Public Examiner at Addiscombe·

He was created a Knight Commander of the Bath in January, 1815, and on the 28th June, 1838, was made a Grand Cross of the same Order.

He was also a Knight Commander of the Guelphic Order (K.C.H.), and was in receipt of a good service pension of £365 per annum.

The following medals and Foreign Orders were conferred upon Sir A. Dickson, viz :—

(1) The gold cross and six clasps for the following battles and sieges in which he held a command of Artillery :—Albuera, Busaco, Ciudad Rodrigo, Badajos, Salamanca, Vittoria, St Sebastian, Nivelle, Nive, Toulouse,

(2) Medal for Waterloo.

(3) The Prussian Order of Merit.

(4) Knight of the Tower and Sword of Portugal.

(5) Portuguese medal for Peninsular War.

(6) Spanish gold and enamel cross for Albuera.

At the conclusion of the Peninsular War a most gratifying testimonial to his great merits was presented to him by his brother officers of the Royal Artillery (many of whom were his seniors in the Regiment) in the shape of a handsome sabre, on the blade of which is the following inscription :—

" This sword is presented to Sir Alexander Dickson, K.C.B. and K.T.S by the Officers of the Royal Artillery, who had the honour to serve under his command in the memorable campaigns of 1813-14, as a lasting mark of their gratitude to him for that zeal which added so much to the reputation of his Corps, at the sieges of St Sebastian, and in the battles of Vittoria, Nive, Nivelle, Orthes, and Toulouse, the latter of which so successfullly terminated their long and arduous services in Spain and France, under the Duke of Wellington."

Major-General Sir Alexander Dickson died in London 22nd April, 1840, aged 63, and was buried in Plumstead Churchyard, with military honours.

Among the celebrated artillerymen whose names and deeds add lustre to the annals of the corps, there is no name greater or more deserving of remembrance than that of Sir Alexander Dickson.

12 GENERAL THE HONOURABLE SIR HERCULES PAKENHAM, G.C.B. served at the siege and capture of Copenhagen in 1807, also the Peninsular Campaigns of 1808-9-10-11 and 12, including the battle of Roleia, Vimiera (wounded), Busaco, and Fuentes d' Onor, siege and

storm of Badajoz (severely wounded at the assault), he was also wounded in the action of Obidos, 15th August, 1808. Sir Hercules has received the gold medal for Busaco, Fuentes d' Onor, Ciudad Rodrigo, and Badajoz; and the silver war medal with two clasps for Roleia and Vimiera.

He was eight years Governor of Portsmouth commanding the South Western District.

13 GENERAL THE RIGHT HONOURABLE SIR GEORGE BROWN, G.C.B. served at the siege and capture of Copenhagen in 1807; in the Peninsula from July 1813 to May 1814, including the battle of Vimiera, passage of the Douro and capture of Oporto, with the previous and subsequent actions; battle of Talavera (severely wounded through both thighs), action of the Light Division at the bridge of Almeida, battle of Busaco, the different actions during the retreat of the French army from Portugal, action at Sabugal, battle of Fuentes d' Onor siege of San Sebastian, battles of the Nivelle and Nive, and the investment of Bayonne. Sir George served afterwards in the American War, and was present at the battle of Blandensburg and capture of Washington, was slightly wounded in the head and very severely in the groin at Blandensburg. This hero of a hundred fights commanded the Light Division throughout the Crimean War. He received the war medal with seven clasps for the Peninsula, and a medal and four clasps for service in the Crimea, was made G.C.B. and presented with the highest French service and Turkish decorations. After the Crimean War, Sir George commanded the troops in Ireland.

14 GENERAL SIR CHARLES JAMES NAPIER, G.C.B. The three Napiers, Charles, William, and George—were known in the Peninsular War as ' Wellington's Colonels.' Charles the eldest, before he was twelve years old, received a commission in the 22nd foot. His first service was in the Irish rebellion, 1798, and in the insurrection, 1803. Commanded the 50th throughout the campaign terminating with the battle of Corunna, when he was taken prisoner after receiving five wounds, viz. leg broken by a musket shot, sabre cut on the head, in the back by a bayonet, ribs broken by a cannon shot, and several severe contusions from the butt end of a musket—returned to the Peninsula the latter part of 1809, where he remained until 1811, and was present at the action of the Coa (had two horses shot under him), battle of Busaco (shot through the face, also jaw broken and eye injured), battle of Fuentes d' Onor, second siege of Badajoz, and a great number of

skirmishes. In 1813 he served in a floating expedition, on the coast of the United States of North America; served also the campaign of 1815 and was present at the storming of Cambray.

Commanded the force employed in Scinde, and on the 17th February, with only 2800 British troops, he attacked and defeated, after a desperate action of three hours' duration, 22,000 of the enemy strongly posted at Meeanee. On the 21st February, Hydrabad surrendered to him, and on the 24th March, with 5000 men he attacked and signally defeated 20,000 of the enemy posted in a very strong and difficult position at Dubba, near Hydrabad, thus completing the entire subjugation of Scinde. Early in 1845, with a force consisting of about 5000 men of all arms, he took the field against the mountain and desert tribes, situated at the right bank of the Indus to the north of Skiharpore, and after an arduous campaign, he effected the total destruction of the hill robbers. He was in due time Commander-in-Chief of the army in India. Sir Charles received the gold medal for Corunna, and the silver war medal with two clasps for Busaco and Fuentes d' Onor. He was G.C.B. and Colonel of the 22nd foot. He was the first English general who ever recorded in his despatches the names of private soldiers. Never lived a truer soldier than Charles James Napier.

15 LIEUTENANT-GENERAL SIR WILLIAM FRANCIS PATRICK NAPIER, K.C.B., served at the siege of Copenhagen and battle of Kioge in 1807; Sir John Moore's campaign of 1808-9; the subsequent Peninsular campaigns from 1809 to the end of the war in 1814, and was present in many of the soul stirring scenes which he has described with so much ability in his admirable " History of the Peninsular War," including the action of the Coa (wounded), battle of Busaco, actions of Pombal, Redinha, and Casal Nova—was severely wounded at the head of six companies supporting the 52nd; action of Foz d'Arouce, battle of Salamanca, passage of the Huebra, action of Vera, when Soult attempted to relieve San Sebastian; and again, when the Allies passed the Bidassoa; battles of the Nivelle and Nive—wounded in defending the churchyard at Arcangues; battle of Orthes; served also in the campaign of 1815.

Sir William received the gold medal and two clasps for Salamanca, Nivelle, and Nive, at which battles he commanded the 43rd Light Infantry, and the silver war medal with three clasps for Busaco, Fuentes d' Onor, and Orthes. He died February 12, 1860, aged 74.

16 LIEUTENANT-GENERAL SIR GEORGE NAPIER, K.C.B. accompanied the expedition to Sweden and from thence to Portugal in 1808, when

he became Aide-de-Camp to Sir John Moore, in which capacity he served the Corunna campaign, and was at the battle of Corunna, and the actions which preceded it, served afterwards with the 52nd in the campaigns of 1809-10 and 11, when he was made Brevet Major—he and his brother William being two out of eleven chosen by Lord Wellington on the occasion of Massena's retreat. He gained the brevet of Lieutenant-Colonel for leading the storming party at the smaller breach of Ciudad Rodrigo, where he lost his right arm, having had the same arm broken at the action of Casal Nova, and again wounded during the siege of Ciudad Rodrigo, two days before he lost it in the breach.

He was also wounded at the battle of Busaco, while in the act of striking with his sword a French Grenadier at the head of the enemy's attacking column.

In 1813 he rejoined the 52nd, and was present at the battle of Orthes, the action of Tarbes, and the battle of Toulouse. Sir George was made K.C.B. and received the gold medal for Ciudad Rodrigo ; and the silver war medal and three clasps. He was Governor and Commander-in-Chief of the Cape Colonies.

17 LIEUTENANT-GENERAL SIR JAMES OUTRAM, G.C.B. went to India as a cadet in 1819, and was made lieutenant and adjutant of the 23rd Bombay Native Infantry. From 1835 to 1838 he was engaged in re-establishing order in the Matie Kanta. He went under Lord Keane to Afghanistan as aide-de-camp, and his ride from Khelat through the dangers of the Bolan Pass will long be famous in Indian annals. He became political agent at Guzerat and commissioner at Scinde. He was afterwards resident at Sattara and Baroda, and on the annexation of Oude, was made resident and commissioner by Lord Dalhonsie. He was also commissioner with diplomatic powers during the Persian war. Landing at Bombay in July 1857, he went to Calcutta and was placed by Lord Canning in charge of the forces for the relief of Lucknow. His career during the mutiny was of the noblest kind, and upon him greatly depended the success of our arms. For his eminent services, he was made Lieutenant-General in 1858, and received the thanks of Parliament in 1860. He took his seat as a member of the Supreme Council of India, but his failing health compelled him very soon after to resign and return to England. A statue was voted to him in Calcutta and noble gifts bestowed upon him. In England his numerous admirers erected a statue to his honour in London, and

presented him with a valuable dessert service. He spent the winter of
1861 and 1862 in Egypt, and after a short residence in the south of
France, died in Paris, March 11, 1863. His services in the East as a
soldier and diplomatist extended over a period of forty years, and never
did hero set a brighter example of moderation, humanity, and practical
christianity in all his dealings with the natives of India.

18 MAJOR-GENERAL SIR GEORGE CHARLES D'AGUILAR, K.C.B., served
eight years in India during the wars of Scindia and Holkar, and was
present at the siege and storm of Baroach in Guzerat, in August,
1803; at the reduction of Powenghar in Malwa in 1804; the capture
and occupation of Ougein, the capital of Scindia, in 1805; also at the
several assaults upon the fortress of Bhurtpore in 1806, in the last of
which he was wounded. Served subsequently in Walcheren at the
siege of Flushing. Also in Sicily, the Greek Islands, and the coast of
Spain, where he was present in 1813 at the action of Biar, and defeat
of Marshal Suchet at Castalla. Joined the army in the Netherlands
under the Duke of Wellington in 1815, and was present at the capture
of Paris.

Major-General D'Aguilar served twenty six years on the general staff,
of which eight were as Assistant Adjutant-General (principally under
the Duke of York) and twelve as Adjutant-General of the army in
Ireland.

He commanded the expedition which in 1847 assaulted and took the
Forts of the Bocca Tigris in the Canton river, those of the staked
barrier and those of the city of Canton, spiking 879 pieces of heavy
ordnance.

19 LIEUTENANT-GENERAL THE HONOURABLE SIR GEORGE CATH-
CART, K.C.B., son of William, Earl Cathcart, was born in 1794,
joined the 2nd Life Guards when he was 16 years of age and fought
with the grand army in the campaigns of 1812 and 1813 as Aide-de-
Camp to Lord Cathcart; was engaged at Lutzen 3rd May, Bautzen 20th
and 21st May, Dresden 28th August, Leipsic 18th and 19th October,
1813; Brienne 1st February, Bar-sur-Aube 21st March and Fère
Champanoise 25th March, 1814.

Served also the campaign of 1815 as Aide-de-Camp to the Duke of
Wellington, and was present at the battles of Quatre Bras and
Waterloo. In 1837, he proved himself an energetic and efficient
officer in quelling the outbreak in Canada. In 1852, he was made
Governor of the Cape of Good Hope with command of the forces, and

brought to a successful end the harassing Kafir war. He returned to England in time to take command of a division during the Crimean war, and was deemed one of the ablest and most active of the generals of the army in the East. His bravery was ever conspicuous, especially so at the battle of Inkerman, when he fell a hero, beloved and respected by all who knew him. I well remember that early in the evening of the day our army reached the heights above Sebastopol, Sir George Cathcart sent my friend to Lord Raglan, offering to take Sebastopol at once with the 4th Division. It was my melancholy duty to bury this true nobleman and deep was the sorrow of our army at the loss of so gallant a soldier. His work entitled *Commentaries on the War in Russia and Germany in* 1812 *and* 1813 has always been deemed a master-piece.

20 MAJOR-GENERAL SIR HENRY BARNARD, K.C.B., entered the Guards at the age of 15, was with the army of occupation and acted as Aide-de-Camp to his uncle, Sir Andrew Barnard, G.C.B.; served in Jamaica as Aide-de-Camp to Sir John Keene, and with the Guards in Canada during the rebellion. He commanded a Brigade in the Crimea, was afterwards Chief of the Staff and in command of the 2nd Division when peace was made. In February, 1857, he proceeded to India and was appointed to command the Umballa Division. Almost immediately after his arrival. there, the mutiny broke out, and he was actively employed in organizing the Delhi field force. On the death of Major-General Anson, he succeeded to the command of the army before Delhi, and after much successful fighting, died July 5th, 1857, worn out by toil, constant exposure to the sun and anxiety. Medal and clasp for the Crimea, K.C.B., Commander of the Legion of Honour, Commander 1st class of the Military Order of Savoy, and 3rd class of the Medjidhe.

21 GENERAL SIR HARRY JONES, R.E., G.C.B., served in the expedition to Walcheren in 1809. Also the campaigns of 1810, 11, 12, 13, and 14, including the actions and sieges of Cadiz, Tarragona (1811,) Badajoz (1812,) Vittoria, St. Sebastian, passage of the Biddasoa, Nivelle, Nive, Bayonne.

Was wounded leading the forlorn hope at the first assault of St. Sebastian. He received the silver war medal with five clasps. Was appointed commanding engineer of the fortifications on Montmartre after the entrance of the English troops into Paris, in 1815. Appointed a Brigadier-General for particular service in the Baltic in

1854, and commanded the British forces during the siege operations against Bomarsund, in the Aland Isles, and for his services in the Baltic, was made Major-General. Appointed to command the Royal Engineers in the Eastern campaign in 1855, which he retained until the fall of Sebastopol; was wounded in the forehead by a spent grape shot on the 18th June. Medal and clasp, K.C.B., Commander 1st class Military Order of Savoy, &c., &c. Formed one of the Council of War held in Paris in January, 1856, when he received the Cross of Commander of the Legion of Honour. Was made governor of the Military College, Sandhurst, and created G.C.B.

22 MAJOR-GENERAL SIR JOHN WILLIAM GORDON, R.E., K.C.B., served in the Crimea, and was at the battles of the Alma, Inkerman, and at the siege of Sebastopol. He greatly distinguished himself throughout the war, was severely wounded, a ball passing through both arms while he was directing the siege operations ; received brevet rank of Major, Lieutenant-Colonel, and Colonel, C.B., fourth class of the Medjidhe, Officer of the Legion of Honour, and medal with three clasps for Alma, Inkerman, and Sebastopol; was afterwards created K.C.B.

23 LIEUTENANT-GENERAL THE HONOURABLE SIR JAMES YORKE SCARLETT, G.C.B., served the Eastern campaign of 1854-55, in command of the Heavy Cavalry Brigade, and afterwards of the Cavalry Division; greatly distinguished himself at the battle of Balaklava, also at Inkerman and the Tchernya, and the siege and fall of Sebastopol. Medal with three clasps, K.C.B., Commander of the Legion of Honour, Sardinia and Turkish medal and 2nd class of the Medjidhe, was afterwards Adjutant General and while in command of the troops at Aldershot Camp was created G.C.B.

24 BRIGADIER-GENERAL THOMAS FOX STRANGWAYS served as a young subaltern with the Rocket Troop of the Royal Horse Artillery, sent to Germany and placed under the orders of the Crown Prince of Sweden in 1813, and was engaged at the battle of Goerde, 15th September, and the actions around Leipzig, 16th-19th October, 1813, during which he succeeded to the command of the troop, his immediate commander, Major Bogue, having been killed. For his services on that occasion he received the order of " St. Anne" from the Emperor of Russia, and the order of the " Sword" and a gold medal for " bravery and good conduct" from the Crown Prince of Sweden, both of whom were eye-witnesses of his gallantry during that short but eventful campaign. He served in the campaign of 1815, and was dangerously wounded at Waterloo.

On the outbreak of the Crimean War, he embarked with the Army for the East as a Lieut-Colonel of Horse Artillery, and succeeded to the command of the whole of the Artillery (on General Cator's resignation through sickness) with the rank of Brigadier-General. He landed with the army in the Crimea, and was present at the battles of Alma and Balaklava, and the first bombardment of Sebastopol. On the morning of the 5th November, 1854, at the great battle of Inkerman, General Strangways was on horseback at Lord Raglan's right hand, when a shell from the enemy burst among the staff, and carried away his left leg. The shock was so great that he died about an hour afterwards. Lieut.-Colonel Adye, the Assistant Adjutant-General to the Artillery, was with him when he fell, and received his last words. He was buried the following day on Cathcart's Hill, deeply lamented as a brave, chivalrous officer, and a kind friend. A nobler soldier never breathed.

25 MAJOR-GENERAL SIR HENRY WILLIAM ADAMS, K.C.B. commanded the 18th Royal Irish in the following operations—in China, 1840-1842, (medal) viz., the first taking of Chusan, storming and taking the heights above the city of Canton, capture of Amoy, second capture of Chusan, storming and taking the fortified heights of Chinhae and capture of the city of Ningpo. Was Brigadier-General with the Army of the East, commanded a brigade of the 2nd Division at the battles of the Alma and Inkerman, and died in Scutari Barracks, Dec. 19th, from wounds received in the latter action, before his well earned honours reached him.

26 MAJOR-GENERAL FRANK ADAMS, C.B. commanded the 28th Regt. throughout the Eastern campaign of 1854-55, including the battles of Alma and Inkerman, siege and fall of Sebastopol, and action of 18th of June in the cemetery. Succeeded to the command of the Brigade on Sir William Eyre being wounded, and brought it out of action. Medal and three clasps, C.B., Officer of the Legion of Honour, Sardinian war medal and 3rd class of the Medjidhe.

27 COLONEL WODEHOUSE, R.A., C.B. served the Eastern campaign of 1854-55, including the affairs of Bulgaria and McKenzie's Farm, the battle of Alma, Balaklava, and Inkerman, (horse killed) siege of Sebastopol and repulse of the sortie on the 26th October, 1854. Medal and clasps, C.B. Knight of the Legion of Honour, 5th class Medjidhe and Sardinian medal, and afterwards Aide-de-Camp to the Queen. A model soldier, without fear and without reproach.

28   ETONIANS who were killed or died of disease during the Crimean War:—

JAMES HUNTER BLAIR was M.P. for Ayrshire and Lt-Col. Scots Fusiliers Guards; killed at the battle of Inkerman, November 5th, 1854.

THE HON. JOHN WILLIAM HELY HUTCHINSON, Captain 13th Light Dragoons; died at Scutari, 1855.

LIEUT. KEKEWICH, 20th Regiment, was at the battles of Alma, Balaklava and Inkerman, slightly wounded in the last battle; died at Corfu, February 16th, 1855, aged 18.

LIEUT. FRANCIS RICHARD HUNT, killed at the attack on the Redan, June 18th, 1855.

FREDERICK LUXMOORE, Lieutenant 30th Regiment, killed at the battle of the Alma, September 20th, 1854.

FREDERICK HENRY RAMSDEN, Captain Coldstream Guards, killed at the battle of Inkerman.

LEONARD NEILL MALCOLM, 2nd Lieutenant Rifle Brigade, killed in the Crimea.

JAMES CHARLES MURRAY COWELL, Lt.Col. Coldstream Guards, killed at Inkerman.

THE HON. GREY NEVILLE, 5th Dragoon Guards, died of wounds received in the Cavalry Charge at Balaklava.

HENRY LANGHORNE THOMPSON, C.B., one of the gallant defenders of Kars, formerly 68th N. Infantry, died a few days after his return home in 1856.

HENEAGE WYNNE, Major 68th Light Infantry, killed at Inkerman.

HORACE WILLIAM CUST, Captain Coldstream Guards, A.D.C. to General Bentinck, killed at the battle of the Alma.

WILLIAM WHITAKER MAITLAND, died of disease contracted in the Crimea.

ASHTON SAMUEL YATE BENYON, Lieut. 53rd Regiment, died from exposure in the Crimea, 1855.

ROBERT HENRY PAYNE CRAWFURD, Captain in the 96th Light Infantry, died in the Crimea.

HERBERT WILLIAM WILBERFORCE, Lieutenant R.N., eldest son of the Bishop of Winchester, died at Torquay, 1856, on his return from the Baltic.

CHARLES FRANCIS SEYMOUR, Lieut-Colonel Scots Fusilier Guards, served in the Kafir War, and fell at Inkerman.

CHARLES AUGUSTUS PENRHYN BOILEAU, Lieutenant Rifle Brigade, died at Malta, 1855, of wounds received before Sebastopol.

ARTHUR FERDINAND PLATT, Major 49th Regiment, died at Scutari, 1855.

EDWARD ROWLAND FORMAN, Captain Rifle Brigade, was killed in an assault on the Redan in 1855.

LACY WALTER YEA, Lieut.-Colonel 7th Royal Fusiliers, was killed at the storming the Redan, 1855.

HON. SIR GEORGE CATHCART, K.C.B., Lieut-General, killed at Inkerman, while in command of the 4th Division of the British Army in the Crimea, 1854. (See Stall No. 19, P. 72.)

EDWARD JOHN WELLESLEY, Major 73rd Regiment, Assist-Quar-Mast-General, died of cholera after the battle of Inkerman.

JAMES MOLESWORTH, 7th Royal Fusiliers, died at Malta on his return from the Crimea.

HENRY ASTLEY SPARKE, Lieutenant 4th Dragoons, killed in the Balaklava Charge, 1854.

JOHN BARRY MARSHALL, Captain 4th Light Dragoons, died of fever in the Crimea.

GEORGE HENRY PROCTOR, Balliol College, Oxford, Assistant Chaplain in the Crimea, died of fever at Scutari, 1855.

GEORGE DUCKWORTH, Captain 5th Dragoon Guards, died in Varna Bay, on board the 'Bombay,' in 1854.

JOHN ARTHUR FREEMAN, Captain Scots Greys, died at Balaklava, 1854.

CORNELIUS GICHAN SUTTON, 23rd Fusiliers, died the night the troops landed in the Crimea, September 18th, 1854.

AUGUSTUS COX, Lieut-Colonel Grenadier Guards, died at the Alma on the arrival of the Army there, September 21st, 1854.

AUDLEY LEMPRIERE, Captain 77th Regiment, killed before Sebastopol.

JAMES BIRDSHARPE, Major.

CHARLES LUKE HARE, Captain 7th Royal Fusiliers, died 1854 of wounds received at the battle of the Alma.

HENRY MONTOLIEN BOUVERIE, Captain Coldstream Guards, killed at Inkerman.

HENRY TOWNSEND, Captain.

FRANCIS BYAN DAVIS, Lieutenant Grenadier Guards, died at sea of wounds received before Sebastopol, 1854.

Hon. Granville Charles Cornwallis Eliot, killed at Inkerman.

Herbert Millingdamp Vaughan, 95th Regiment, wounded and taken prisoner in attack on Redan, died in Hospital.

Hon. Francis Grosvenor Hood, Lieut-Colonel Grenadier Guards, killed in the trenches before Sebastopol, 1854.

John Henry Upton Spalding, Midshipman, was killed in the trenches before Sebastopol.

Owen Gwyn Scawden Davies, Lieutenant 38th Regiment, killed in the Crimea, 1855.

Duncombe Frederick Ball Buckley, Captain Scots Fusilier Guards, killed in the trenches before Sebastopol, 1855.

Henry Thorold, Ensign 33rd Regiment, was shot through the heart while serving out cartridges at Inkerman.

29 HARROVIANS who fell in action, or died of disease, during the Crimean War.

Major-General James Bucknall Estcourt, Adjutant General of the Army in the East, died of cholera in the Crimea on the 24th of June, 1855, aged 53 years.

Lieut-Colonel The Hon. Thomas Vesey Dawson, Coldstream Guards, fell at the battle of Inkerman on the 5th of November, 1854, aged 35 years.

Lieut-Colonel James Brodie, C.B., 30th Regiment, fell mortally wounded in the attack on the Redan, on the 8th of September, 1855, aged 32 years.

Captain Hylton Jolliffe, Coldstream Guards, died of cholera in the Crimea, on the 3rd of October 1854, aged 28 years.

Captain George Lockwood, 8th Hussars, Aide-de-camp to the Earl of Cardigan, fell in the Light Cavalry Charge at Balaklava on the 25th of October, 1854, aged 36 years.

Captain William Kent Allix, 1st Royal Regiment, Aide-de-camp to General Sir de Lacy Evans, fell at the battle of Inkerman, aged 32 years.

Captain The Hon. Charles Welbore Herbert Agar, 44th Regiment, fell at the assault upon Sebastopol on the 18th of June, 1855, aged 31 years.

Captain William Henry Cecil George Pechell, 77th Regiment, fell in the trenches before Sebastopol, on the 3rd of September, 1855, aged 24 years.

CAPTAIN JAMES AUGUSTUS LOCKHART, 41st Regiment, fell in the advanced trenches before the Redan on the 8th of September, 1855, aged 21 years.

CAPTAIN JAMES ERNEST KNIGHT, 77th Regiment, died of fever before Sebastopol on the 2nd of October, 1855, aged 19 years.

LIEUTENANT HENRY ANSTRUTHER, 23rd Regiment, fell in the battle of the Alma on the 20th of September, 1854, aged 18 years.

LIEUTENANT THE HON. ROBERT ANNESLEY, 11th Hussars, died of cholera in the Black Sea on the 28th of September, 1854, aged 20 years.

LIEUTENANT HENRY CHARLES DAWSON, Enniskillen Dragoons, died of fever in Balaklava Bay on the 5th October, 1854, aged 19 years.

LIEUTENANT CAVENDISH HUBERT GREVILLE, Coldstream Guards, fell at the battle of Inkerman, 1854, aged 19 years.

LIEUTENANT PERCIVAL HART DULKE, Rifle Brigade, died of fever in Balaklava Harbour on the 9th of April, 1855, aged 18 years.

LIEUTENANT ROBERT JOHN BROWN CLAYTON, 34th Regiment, died in camp on the 12th of July, 1855, of wounds received at the assault on the Redan on the 18th of June, 1855, aged 20 years.

LIEUTENANT HENRY CHARLES EVANS, 55th Regiment, fell mortally wounded in the trenches before Sebastopol on the 4th of August, 1855, aged 18 years.

LIEUTENANT HENRY STUART RYDER, Rifle Brigade, fell within the Redan in the assault of the 8th of September, 1855, aged 20 years.

LIEUTENANT EDWARD SHUTTLEWORTH HOLDER, 23rd Welsh Fusiliers, fell mortally wounded at the assault on the Redan on the 8th of September, 1855, aged 18 years.

CORNET HUGH MONTGOMERY, 13th Light Dragoons, fell in the Light Cavalry Charge at Balaklava on the 25th of October, 1854, aged 24 years.

ENSIGN JAMES HULTON CLUTTERBUCK, 63rd Regiment, fell at the battle of Inkerman, aged 19 years.

30   RUGBEIANS who fell during the Crimean War and the Indian Mutiny.

SIR HENRY WILLIAM ADAMS, K.C.B., (See Stall No. 25, P. 75.)

THOMAS UNETT was Lieut.-Colonel of the 19th Regiment at the battle of the Alma, September 20th, 1854. His horse was severely wounded. At the battle of Inkerman, employed in the trenches and honourably mentioned. Mortally wounded while leading the assault of the Redan, September 8th, 1855, died of his wounds, September 15th.

DOUGLAS JOHN THOMAS HALKETT, Major 4th Light Dragoons, killed in the Balaklava Charge, October 25th, 1854. In the retreat after the Charge of the Light Cavalry Brigade, he was seen to fall wounded, but the pursuing Russians soon swept over the spot, and nothing more is known.

ROBERT MURRAY BANNER, Major 93rd Regiment, present at the battle of the Alma; died at Balaklava, a few days after the battle, of disease aggravated by constant exposure to damp and cold.

SAMUEL TOOSEY WILLIAMS, Captain Scots Greys, was at the battle of Balaklava on the morning of the 25th of October, 1854. The Russian Cavalry advanced against the Scots Greys and Enniskillens, in the proportion of three to one. The Scots Greys dashed forward, and were received into the midst of the enemy, who closed in upon them. For several minutes the red-coats disappeared, but soon were seen driving before them in headlong flight, the routed Russian Cavalry. Captain Williams escaped unhurt, but was taken ill shortly afterwards and died at Pera, November 23rd, 1854.

JOHN PRATT WINTER, Captain of the 17th Lancers. On the flank march to Balaklava, his troop were ordered to charge the Russian rear-guard, at Mackenzie's farm, where they took several prisoners and a quantity of baggage. On the 25th of October, 1854, in the heroic charge of the Light Cavalry at Balaklava, he led the second squadron of his Regiment, and was seen to fall close to the enemy's guns just as the retreat was sounded. His horse, severely wounded by grape shot, galloped back to the English lines.

ARTHUR WATKIN WILLIAMS-WYNN, son of the Right Hon. Sir H. Watkin Williams-Wynn, Captain of the 23rd Royal Welsh Fusiliers, killed at the battle of the Alma. I find in my notes as follows :—" A few yards from the ditch in front of the earthwork, English and Russians were lying one on the other. I counted eight officers of the 23rd Fusiliers, including poor Chester, their gallant Colonel; a calm expression was on their faces, which seemed to say, 'Grieve not for us—we died doing our duty.'

Captain Watkin Williams-Wynn had gone close up to the Russian gun, and was lying with his face heavenwards.

> "When from grim Alma's blood-stained height
>   There came the sound of woe,
> And in the first and latest fight
>   That noble head was low ;
> Fond hearts that writhed beneath the blow
> Were tortured with keen thirst to know
> How, ere their loved and lost one bled,
> By fate's cold hand the gloomy thread
>   Of the last hour was spun :
> And yearnings from their English home
> Bounded across the ocean foam,—
> "Where did ye find my son ?"
> The answer from that fatal ground
> Came pealing with a trumpet sound,—
> "Close to the Russian Gun."
> With many a gallant friend around him,
> In one proud death—'t was thus we found him !"

WILLIAM HALSTEAD POOLE, Captain 23rd Welsh Fusiliers was at the battles of the Alma, and Inkerman. He was mortally wounded at the storming of the Redan, September 8th, 1855, and died on the 24th of September.

GEORGE CHARLES WIDDRINGTON CURTOIS, Lieutenant 63rd Regiment, killed at the battle of Inkerman.

EDMUND CORBETT, Captain 88th Regiment, on the 17th June, 1855, while gallantly attacking the Quarries, received a ball through the head. His last words were " Come on men."

LAWRENCE BLAKISTON, Captain 62nd Regiment, was engaged before Sebastopol from the latter end of 1854. He was killed at the attack of the Redan on September 18th, 1855, while in the act of passing through an embrasure of the parapet.

JOHN GEORGE DON MARSHALL, Captain 92nd Highlanders, served in the Burmese War of 1852-3, including the storming and capture of Rangoon, Bassein, and other minor affairs; also in the Crimea at the seige of Sebastopol.

JAMES WEMYSS, Lieutenant 92nd Highlanders, was at the battle of the Alma, and at Balaklava, October 25th, where the Regiment two deep, repulsed a large body of Russian Cavalry. Died on the 15th June, 1855, of Crimean fever

JOHN HENRY THOMPSON, Lieutenant 17th Lancers, was killed by a round shot while taking part with his Regiment in the heroic charge of the Light Cavalry Brigade at Balaklava.

G

CHARLES HOWE PROBY, Lieutenant First Royals, died at Malta, September 10th, 1855, from an illness brought on by exposure in the trenches before Sebastopol.

REGINALD CYRIL GOODENOUGH, Lieutenant 97th Regiment, was mortally wounded at the storming of the Redan, September 8th, 1855, and died September 20th.

CHARLES AUGUSTUS PENRYN BOILEAU, Lieutenant Rifle Brigade, was mortally wounded at the assault of the Redan, June 18th, 1855. His gallantry had been especially commended by the Commander-in-Chief, Lord Raglan. Died of his wound at Malta, August 1st, 1855.

ARCHIBALD CLEVELAND, Cornet 17th Lancers, was at the battle of the Alma, charged the rear-guard of the Russians, and took several prisoners ; shared in the glorious charge of the Light Cavalry at the battle of Balaklava, where his horse was mortally wounded. At the battle of Inkerman he was struck by a shell and died of his wound on the following morning.

WILLIAM OWEN, 23rd Welsh Fusiliers, was mortally wounded before Sebastopol by a shell on the night of the 29th June, 1855.

HENRY WINCHCOMBE HARTLEY, Lieut-Colonel of the 8th Regiment, served at the siege of Delhi, 1857, and was afterwards Brigadier at Umballah. Died at Jullunder, June 24th, 1858.

GEORGE BIDDULPH, Lieut-Colonel 45th Native Infantry, served during the campaign on the Sutlej and with the army of the Punjaub ; was present in 1848 at Chillian Wallah, Goojerat, Sadoolapore and passage of the Chenab. When proceeding to join his Regiment, Tait's Irregular Horse, he was surrounded and taken prisoner by a party of Sikhs near Ferozepoor, early on the morning of the battle of Moodkee, December 18th, 1845. He was conveyed up and down the Sikh Camp, mounted behind a trooper, to be shown as their first prisoner. Many of the enemy struck and abused him, and he was then chained to a gun, and a guard watched him for three days and nights. His undaunted bravery, however, under these circumstances, and his tall figure (six feet four inches) elicited much admiration, and the Sikhs exclaimed that he was a true Englishman. Two days afterwards he was released, and allowed to join the British army at Moodkee. After a short absence in England, 1856, he returned to Bengal on the breaking out of the Sepoy mutiny. At the siege of Lucknow, November 18th, 1857, he had to take the command of a division, when Brigadier Russell was wounded, and as he was explaining plans, and organizing a column to storm the hospital, a bullet, after passing through another officer's hat, struck him dead, passing through his brain.

THOMAS ONSLOW WINNINGTON INGRAM, Lieut-Colonel of the 97th Regiment, received the Order of the Legion of Honour, medal and clasp, and Turkish medal for highly distinguished service before Sebastopol; employed in 1857 in suppressing the Sepoy mutiny. On the 14th of March, was killed in the Kaiserbagh in Lucknow, a ball passing through the head.

CHARLES WILBRAHAM RADCLIFFE, Captain 7th Regiment Bengal Light Cavalry, served during the campaign on the Sutlej, present at Sobraon, (Medal); was constantly engaged during the siege of Lucknow. While commanding a detachment of 600 men at Chinhut, to oppose 16,000 mutinous Sepoys, he was mortally wounded on the night of the 24th of September, at Lucknow, and died October 1st 1857, shortly before the relief by Lord Clyde. Had he lived, he would have been recommended for the Victoria Cross, by Sir James Outram, for his gallant conduct at Chinhut.

GEORGE SNELL, 64th Native Infantry, Bengal, murdered with his wife and child during the Mutiny, at Seetapoor, Oude, June 3rd, 1857.

WHALEY NICOLL HARDY, Royal Artillery, served at the siege of Sebastopol, 1855, was killed at Secunderabagh near Lucknow, on November 16th, 1857. His death was mentioned with regret by the Governor-General in Council.

WILLIAM STEPHEN RAIKES HODSON, Brevet-Major of the First European Bengal Fusiliers, and Commander of Hodson's Horse; was present in 1845 at the battles of Moodkee, Ferozeshur, wounded at Sabraon; present also at several affairs with the enemy, including the battle of Goojerat.

Conmanded the corps of Guides in the attack upon the Affredies, on the heights above Bareedee, 1853, and was engaged in repulsing the rebels from the English lines at the siege of Delhi, with his newly-raised Regiment of Irregular Horse. When Delhi was taken, the next day he started with Lieutenant Macdowell and fifty of his own men for Humayoon's tomb, about six miles from the city, where the King of Delhi was. The King surrendered on condition that his life should be spared. The next day he started again for Humayoon's tomb, where the three Princes were, the heirs apparent to the throne, and murderers. They surrendered unconditionally and were sent off to Delhi in a cart drawn by bullocks. There appeared every probability of a rescue from an increasing hostile crowd, when Hodson addressed his men, and informed them that these were the wretches who murdered helpless women and children. He then shot the three Princes, one after another, and their bodies were exposed in the city in the same place where they had outraged the European women. On the 11th of March, 1858, at Lucknow, after the Begum's Palace had been stormed, he received a mortal wound, of which he died the next day. Had he lived he would have received the Victoria Cross. Hodson's Horse is to remain permanently a brigade of two regiments as a memorial of his gallantry.

CHARLES AYSHFORD SANDFORD, Brevet-Major, was engaged in the suppression of the Bengal mutiny, 1857; he obtained the command of the Guide Cavalry at the siege of Delhi, and took part in every action of importance, and was repeatedly mentioned in despatches as an excellent officer. On the advance to Lucknow he was appointed to the 5th Punjaub Cavalry, and while reconnoitring a village, on the 10th of March, 1858, was killed by some men concealed in a tower.

ARTHUR AUSTEN MOULTRIE, Lieutenant H. M. 90th Regiment, was mortally wounded at Lucknow, September 25th, 1857, whilst gallantly charging a battery of the mutinous Sepoys. Died the next day.

WILLIAM TATE GROOM, Lieutenant First Madras European Fusiliers, was engaged with his Regiment under General Havelock, July 29th, 1857, when the guns of the Mutineers were taken and they were put to flight; present the next day at Busserct Gunge, when the enemy were driven out and guns again seized; also at Boorseeke Chowhi, on the 11th of August. On the 1st October, he led the advance on Phillip's battery, near Lucknow, was wounded October 9th, and died at Lucknow, October 21st, 1857.

ALEXANDER KEY, Lieutenant 28th Native Infantry, was murdered with seven other officers of his Regiment by the Mutineers, between Mahomdie and Aurungabad, June 5th, 1857.

CHARLES JAMES SALMOND, Adjutant 2nd Cavalry Gwalior Contingent, during the Sepoy mutiny of 1856-7 was constantly engaged under Sir Hope Grant, and took part in all the proceedings for the relief and withdrawal of the garrison of Lucknow ; was wounded and mentioned by Lord Clyde as having greatly distinguished himself. After the action of the 6th of December, 1857, he was unable through illness to join in the pursuit of the rebels, and was shortly afterwards found killed near Cawnpore.

PATRICK ALDOURIE GRANT, Lieutenant, 7th Bengal Native Infantry, was murdered by the Mutineers at the cantonment, Lucknow, when the first rebellion broke out, May 30th, 1857.

THOMAS GEORGE POULDEN, Lieutenant, Royal Artillery. While engaged in the suppression of the Sepoy mutiny, received sunstroke and died at Tasseram on the 3rd of May, 1858.

LEONARD REDMAYNE, Lieutenant 14th Light Dragoons, was present at the capture of Dhai, Central India, October, 1857, and was killed in action with the rebels, November 23rd, 1857.

EDWIN FELL HAIG, Lieutenant and Adjutant 5th Fusiliers, was killed in action in the city of Lucknow, while effecting the relief of the garrison, September 26th, 1857.

PHILIP LOVELL COLLIER PHILLIPS, Lieutenant 4th Battalion Rifles, on his voyage to Bengal to put down the Sepoy Mutineers, stemmed and quelled a serious mutiny on board ship. On the 9th August, 1858, the ship unfortunately grounded in the river, and exposure to cold and wet brought on illness of which he died August 22nd, 1858.

EDWIN STEPHEN SALE, Ensign 37th Regiment, was killed July 30th, 1857, in the unfortunate night expedition to relieve Arrah.

31 COLONEL CARPENTER, C.B. commanded the 41st (the Welsh) Regt., at the battle of the Alma, and fell while gallantly leading it at the hard fought battle of Inkerman.

32 OFFICERS OF THE ARMY MEDICAL DEPARTMENT. The severe demands made by the Crimean War upon the Medical Departmen told heavily upon its Officers, as is testified by the following long list of casualties :—

DEPUTY INSPECTOR GENERALS.—Thomas Spence, M.D., Alexander McGrigor, M.D.

STAFF SURGEONS 1ST CLASS.—John Mitchell, M.D., Chilley Pine, Nicholas O'Connor, M.D., George Kincaid Pitcairn, M.D., John Marshall.

SURGEONS.—Francis Cornelius Huthwaite, Peter Mackey, M.D., Daniel Anderson, M.D., William Browne, William Abbott Anderson, John Newton, Francis Smith, Michael Allen Lane, Edward LeBlanc, Christopher Macartney, M.D., James Alexander Wishart, M.D., Walter Simpson, M.D., Christopher Bakewell Bassano.

ASSISTANT SURGEONS.—Ebenezer Alfred Jenkin, Frederick York Shegog, M.D., Philip Giffard Martel, James Allyosius Shorrock, James Thomson, M.D., Alexander Rothney Reid, M.D., John Francis O'Leary, Henry Beckwith, John James Norris, Edward Patrick Boyle, James Lamont, M.D., Edmund Sidney Wason, M.D., John Phillipson Langham, Frederick Arthur Macartney, John Grabham, William Renwick, Malcolm Currie Ancell, John Henry Gilborne.

ACTING ASSISTANT SURGEONS.—Frederick Graham, Harvey Ludlow, Robert Thomas Simons, John Horsley White, John Longmore, Harry William Wood, Joseph Mayne, Thomas Oak Mitchell, Alexander Struthers, M.D.

PRINCIPAL APOTHECARY.—George Hume Reade.

DISPENSERS OF MEDICINE.—James Martin Beveridge, John H. Whitwell.

DRESSERS.—Harry Harrison, Thomas Fell.

33 COLONEL JOHN HINDE KING, C.B., Grenadier Guards, served with the 49th Regt. the Eastern Campaign of 1854-55, including the battles of the Alma and Inkerman, and seige of Sebastopol; was present at the sortie on the 26th October, capture of the Quarries and assault of the Redan on the 18th June and 8th September; was severely wounded, left hand amputated. Medal and three clasps, Brevet-Major and Lieut-Colonel, Knight of the Legion of Honour, and C.B.

34 COLONEL THOMAS GRAHAM EGERTON, C.B., 77th Regiment, was present at the affair of the Bulganak, at the battles of the Alma and Inkerman, and the seige of Sebastopol. His gallant conduct was at all times the admiration of the Army. He fell in the brilliant capture of the Rifle Pits on the 19th April, 1855, deeply lamented by a regiment to which he had been so noble an example.

35 OFFICERS, 49th REGIMENT:— No regiment was more distinguished during the Crimean War than the 49th. Officers and men

were ever among the foremost A large number of the survivors bore
home with them honourable marks of their gallantry :—

Maj. Gen. Sir H. W. Adams, k.c.b., died of wounds Dec.	19th, 1854
Major Thomas Dalton	killed Nov. 5th, 1854
Major C. T. Powell	killed Oct. 26th, 1854
Major C. S. Glazbrook	killed Dec. 18th, 1854
Captain W. W. Maitland	ague Nov. 15th, 1856
Captain W. R. Corbet	fever Mar. 19th, 1855
Captain C. Rochfort	killed Sept. 8th, 1855
Lieut. and Adj. A. S. Armstrong	killed Nov. 5th, 1854
Ensign C. Michell	killed Sept. 14th, 1855
Ensign A. F. Platt	fever Aug. 11th, 1855
Asst. Surgeon Beckwith	cholera Oct. 18th, 1854

36 Major James Armar Butler, the "Hero of Silistria," served
during the Kafir war 1846-7, in the 90th Light Infantry (medal)
and afterwards in the Ceylon Rifle Corps; died 13th June, 1854, aged
27, from a wound received while engaged in the glorious defence of
Silistria. His skill and heroism commanded the admiration of the
world.

37 Captain Henry Thomas Butler, 55th Regiment, served in China
(medal) at Amoy, Chusan, Chinhae, (including repulse of night
attack) Chapoo, Woosing, Shanghae, and Ching Kiang Foo; also
served with the Army of the East, and was present at the battles of
the Alma and Inkerman ; at the latter battle he was Deputy Assistant
Quarter Master General to the First Division, and fell while actively
engaged in his important duties, aged 42.

38 Captain Arthur Wellesley Cassan, 65th Regiment, lost left
arm by a grape shot when leading the attack at the escalade of the
Fortress of Dwarka in the East Indies; mentioned in general orders
by Lieut-General the Hon. Sir Charles Colville for his gallant conduct on the occasion, was made a Knight of Windsor for distinguished
services—died at Portsmouth, 23th July, 1870, aged 75.

39 Twelve CHAPLAINS who fell during the Crimean War :—

The Rev. G. Mockler	died	29th September, 1854
The Rev. J. J. Wherle	„	— December, 1854
The Rev. M. Canty	„	2nd February, 1855
The Rev. W. Whyatt	„	23rd February, 1855
The Rev. D. Shehan	„	10th March, 1855
The Rev. G. H. Proctor	„	10th March, 1855

The Rev. H. J. Whitfield	died	17th June, 1855
The Rev. J. Doyle	,,	— July, 1855
The Rev. J. Sheil	,,	15th August, 1855
The Rev. J. Freeman	,,	19th August, 1855
The Rev. R. Lee	,,	14th October, 1855
The Rev. G. Strickland	,,	26th April, 1856

It is a remarkable fact, that considering the number employed, far more Chaplains died during the Crimean War, than in any other branch of the service. In my note book I find the following touching story of George Mockler, the first who nobly fell "The cholera was still with us, and poor Mockler, the Chaplain of the 3rd Division, was carried off by it just after our arrival on the Heights. At Gallipoli and in Bulgaria he had been a loved and respected minister of God, labouring with his wonted faithfulness among the sick, until at last he himself was attacked by a serious fever, which left him sadly enfeebled just at the time the army was embarking for the Crimea. Nothing would induce him to remain on board a transport: 'No,' he said, 'my soldiers may want me, and I feel that it is my duty to share their trials and dangers.' He landed, and dragged his fever-worn frame from Old Fort to Balaklava, where stricken by cholera, he laid himself down to die. As soon as I heard of his illness, I hastened to him, and arrived a little before his end. I asked him if he knew me; he said, 'Yes, well.' I then told him that I would commend him to God's keeping; and as I read the almost inspired service for the Visitation of the Sick, the poor fellow, with his eyes fixed steadily heavenwards, softly breathed out his last words, 'Beautiful prayers, beautiful prayers,' and shortly after went to his rest."

40 Capt. Sir Robert Newman, Bart., Grenadier Guards, gallantly shared in the brilliant attack of the Guards on the thirteen gun battery, at the battle of the Alma, and fell at Inkerman while bravely leading his Company against a Russian column.

41 Capt. Christopher Hore Hatchell, 43rd Light Infantry, was engaged in the suppression of the mutiny 1857-8. Medal; also highly distinguished himself by his gallantry during the New Zealand War, 1864-5 Medal. Accidently drowned in Cork harbour, October 11th, 1870, Aged 33.

42 Pierce Butler, Rector of Ulcombe, served as Chaplain to the Forces in 1854-5 at Scutari and with the 2nd Division before Sebastopol; was present at the taking of Kertch. He was the first promoter of

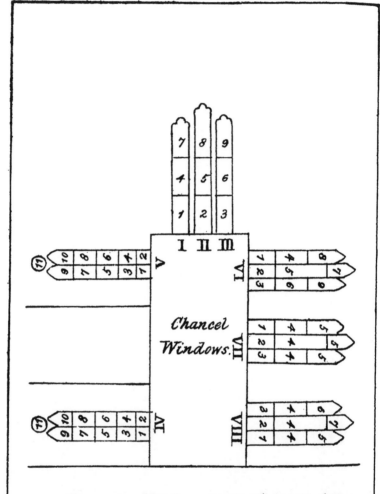

Plan of the Windows in the Chancel of the Garrison Church to which the description refers.

№10.

the recent and already renowned Survey of the Sinaitic Peninsula; died February 8th, 1868. Gentle and brave, able and lowly, calm and adventurous, holy and cheerful, Pierce Butler was honoured and beloved by all who knew him.

MEMORIAL WINDOWS.

The windows of the church are twenty three in number, eight in the chancel and fifteen in the nave. They are all memorial windows by the eminent firm of Clayton & Bell, and are considered remarkably fine examples of modern stained glass. In order that there might be no violent contrasts, as so often found in our cathedrals and large churches, the Restoration Committee decided, that all the memorial glass should be supplied by one Firm, and further that the subjects in the chancel should present the history of the New Testament, while those in the nave should give that of the Old Testament. This arrangement has afforded great satisfaction. The accompaning plan will assist the visitor while examining the windows.

THE CHANCEL.

THE THREE WINDOWS OVER THE ALTAR.

(SEE NOS. I. II. III. IN THE PLAN).

These windows, each divided into three compartments, represent the Passion of our Lord.

1. *The Agony.* 2. *The Betrayal.* 3. *The Lord before the High Priest.* 4. *The Scourging.* 5. *The Ecce Homo.* 6. *Our Lord bearing the Cross.* 7. *The Stripping.* 8. *Jesus Crucified.* 9. *Taking down from the Cross.*

No. I. is in memory of General Sir C. J. Napier, G.C.B.

No. II.   ,,   ,,   Field Marshal Lord Raglan, G.C.B.

No. III.   ,,   ,,   Field Marshal Lord Clyde, G.C.B.

THE TWO WINDOWS ON THE NORTH SIDE OF THE CHANCEL.

(SEE NOS. IV. AND V. IN THE PLAN).

Each of these windows is divided into ten compartments, six containing Apostles, and four subjects taken from the Gospel.

NO. IV.

1. *St. Philip.* 2. *St. Bartholomew.* 3. *Our Lord's Baptism.* 4. *The Temptation.* 5. *St. James.* 6. *St. John.* 7. *Call of St. Peter and St. Andrew.* 8. *Nicodemus going to Christ by night.* 9. *St. Peter.* 10. *St. Andrew.*

This window was an offering from the Officers of the 67th Regt. In the circle is the device of the 67th Regt., and on a brass beneath is the following inscription:—

"To the memory of 11 officers and 361 noncommissioned officers and men of the 67th (South Hampshire Regt.) who died on foreign service during the years 1858 to 1865 in India, China, and the Cape:—

Paymaster J. A. Popo,	13th Oct., 1860	Home.
Ensign & Adjt. C. V. Killeen	23rd May, 1862	Tien Tsien.
Lieut. C. H. B. Turner	17th Nov., 1867	Tien Tsien.
Captain W. S. Arnold	10th Aug., 1859	Barrackpore.
Lieut. C. U. Creyke	9th Nov. 1862	Aden.
Captain C. U. Coxen	28th Feb., 1864	Home (on leave)
„ A. F. Robertson	24th July, 1863	Shanghai
„ M. Nugent	20th Oct., 1862	Taku
Ensign F. T. Blake	27th Sept., 1862	Hong Kong
„ J. H. A. Routledge	not known	On passage Home
Captain G. F. H. Atchison	21st July, 1861	Tien Tsien "

NO. V.

1. *St. Jude.* 2. *St. Matthias.* 3. *Sermon on the Mount.* 4. *The Centurion pleading for his Slave.* 5. *St. James.* 6. *St. Simon.* 7. *Raising Jairus' Daughter.* 8. *Raising Lazarus.* 9. *St. Thomas.* 10. *St. Matthew.*

An offering from Colonel Willis, c.b. On the glass is inscribed:—

"To the Glory of God, and in memory of Eliza Angelina, wife of Colonel George Harry Willis, c.b., q.m.g. Southern District, who died 5th August, 1867."

THE THREE WINDOWS ON THE SOUTH SIDE OF THE CHANCEL.

(SEE NOS. VI., VII. AND VIII. ON THE PLAN.)

These windows, architecturally of great beauty, are filled with brilliant glass, and the drawing here as throughout the church is highly artistic. They represent the Burial, Resurrection, and Ascension of our Blessed Lord; the Coming of the Comforter; and the Conversion ;of Paul, and Acts of the Holy Apostles.

NO. VI.

1. *Joseph begging the body of Jesus.* 2. *Preparation for the Tomb.* 3. *The Entombment.* 4. *The Three Maries.* 5. *The Angel.* 6. *St. Peter and St. John.* 7. *Our Lord rising from the Tomb.* 8. *Noli Me Tangere.* 9. *St. Thomas convinced.*

This window was presented by the 46th Regt. The brass is inscribed thus:—

" To the Glory of God, and in memory of Arthur George Vesey, commanding 46th (South Devon) Regt. who died at Suez on his return to England, October 18th, 1861, aged 49. This window was given by the Officers of the Regiment as a mark of their kindly feeling and respect."

Colonel Vesey joined the 46th Regiment on the 29th May, 1836. He embarked with the service companies for the Crimea on the 12th October, 1854, and for his services at the siege of Sebastopol, received the Crimean medal and clasp, the Turkish medal and the 5th class of the Medjidhe.

NO. VII.

1. *The walk to Emmaus.* 2. *The Supper at Emmaus.* 3. *Feed my Sheep.* 4. *The Ascension.* 5. *The Day of Penticost.*

This was also given by the 46th Regt. The words below the window are as follows:—

" To the Glory of God and in memory of Colin Frederick Campbell, Major of the 46th Regiment and Colonel in the Army, who died at Simla 24th Sept. 1868, aged 44 years. This window is given by the officers of the Regiment as a mark of their kindly feeling and respect."

Colonel Campbell joined the 46th Foot on the 1st May, 1840. He embarked with the service companies for the Crimea, on the 12th October, 1854, and served at the siege of Sebastopol from that date to the conclusion of the war. When employed as Assistant Engineer, he was wounded in the trenches on the 28th July, 1855. He received the Crimean medal and clasp, the Turkish medal, the Sardinian war medal, the French decoration of Knight of the Legion of Honour, and the 5th class of the Medjidhe. Colonel Campbell was an officer of distinguished bravery and worth, noted for cool daring and high professional attainments. His early death in the very prime of life was a loss to the service generally.

NO. VIII.

1. *Stoning of St. Stephen.* 2. *Raising of Dorcas.* 3. *Healing at the Beautiful Gate.* 4. *Conversion of St. Paul.* 5. *St. Paul preaching at Athens.* 6. *Philip baptising the Eunuch.*

This window tells of a family which will ever be honourably named in the history of England's army:—Lt.-Gen. The Hon. H. D. Butler and his four sons. The words on the brass are very touching:—

" To the Glory of God and in pious memory of Lieut.-General The Honourable Henry David Butler, who served in Egypt and the Peninsular War, died in Paris, December 7th, 1856, and his four sons:—Henry Thomas, Captain 55th Regt. fell at Inkerman, Nov. 5, 1854, Aged 42. Charles George, Captain 86th Regt. died of Fever at Bombay, Dec. 17, 1854, Aged 31. Pierce, Rector o Ulcombe, Kent, some time Chaplain to the Forces in the Crimea, died Feb. 8th, 1868, Aged 42. James Armar, Capt. Ceylon Rifle Regt., died from wounds received at the gallant defence of Silistria, June 21, 1854, Aged 27.

This window was given by numerous friends and relations."

THE NAVE.

There are fifteen windows in the Nave. Two at the East end, three at the West, five on the North side, and five on the South. This will appear from Plan No. 11, to which the reader is referred.

NO. IX.

1. *Annunciation.* 2. *Salutation.* 3. *Nativity.* 4. *Adoration of Magi and Shepherds.* 5. *Presentation in the Temple.* 6. *Jesus with the Doctors.* 7. *Jesus subject at Nazareth.*

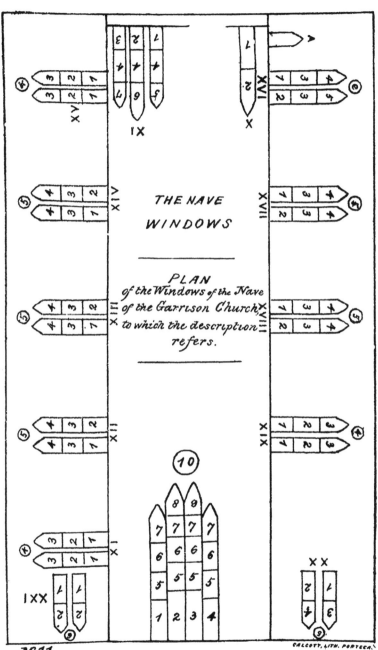

THE NAVE
WINDOWS

PLAN
*of the Windows of the Nave
of the Garrison Church,
to which the description
refers.*

Nº 11.

CALCOTT, LITH. PORTSEA.

This window was presented by friends of Captain Molesworth, R.E., a very promising officer, who was suddenly called from a life of great usefulness. No one laboured harder than he to further the restoration of this Church, and, when taken to his rest, it may truly be said, that the Garrison and Borough of Portsmouth felt deeply the loss they had sustained. The words on the brass are few but forcible:—

"The above window is dedicated to the Glory of God, and in memory of Morgan Crofton Molesworth, 2nd Captain Royal Engineers, who died July 10th, 1867. He was highly distinguished in his profession, and greatly esteemed in the garrison and by the community. He laboured for the restoration of this church with a fervent spirit serving the Lord, and during the progress of the work, at the early age of 30, was himself called to his rest."

"Be ye also ready."

NO. X.

1. *Jonathan.* 2. *David.*

This memorial was a gift by one who deemed it a privilege to pay respect to the memory of his two brothers, good men and true. On the glass are the following words:—

"In memory of my brothers, Captain C. M. M. Wright, R.N., and Lieut. E. Dirke Wright, 59th Regiment. They bled for their country. H. P. Wright, Chaplain to the Forces, 1st Class, September, 1867."

Captain Charles Mayson Moncrieffe Wright, after thirty three years afloat, reached Post rank, in days when to be a good first Lieutenant was to be far from promotion. He was severely wounded (1819) in the Persian Gulf when attacking the Pirates at Ras-al-Khyma, their head quarters, and also was greatly distinguished (1832) while suppressing piracy in the Straits of Malacca.

Lieutenant Edmund Dirke Wright, led the forlorn hope at the taking of Bhurtpore in 1826, when he was severely wounded in the arm and hand.

NO. XI.

1. *Lot taken prisoner.* 2. *Abraham's battle with the Kings.* 3. *Melchizedek and Abraham.* 4. *Abraham.*

The offering of a sorrowing widow. On the brass is thus inscribed:—

"To the Glory of God, and in loving memory of Edwin Wodehouse, Colonel Royal Artillery, C.B., Aide-de-Camp to the Queen, eldest son of Vice-Admiral the Honourable Philip Wodehouse, who died at Portsmouth, on the 6th Oct., 1870, Aged 53, this window is dedicated by his widow."

"O Lord ! eternal rest, and light perpetual."

(See Page 75)

NO. XII.

1. *Jacob's Dream.* 2. *Jacob and Rachel.* 3. *Meeting of Jacob and Esau.* 4. *Joseph in Egypt.* 5. *Jacob.*

This beautiful window was given by the 77th Regiment, a farewell offering on leaving the Garrison. (see Page 52)

The inscription on the brass is as follows:—

" To the Glory of God, and in Memory of

COLONEL R. J. STRATON, C.B.
MAJOR H. A MACDONALD.
    „   R. B. WILLINGTON.
    „   W. N. M. ORPEN.
CAPTAIN W. GAIR.
    „   H. S. WEIGALL.
LIEUT. AND ADJUTANT G. COOK.
LIEUT. A. T. BUTTS.
    „   A. BISHOP.
ENSIGN A. L. HENNING.
    „   C. J. ARNOLD.
    .,   F. P. FERGUSON.
    „   H. N. MOORE.

who died in the service of their country, between the years 1856 and 1871, the Officers of the 77th (East Middlesex) Regiment have erected this window."

NO. XIII.

1. *Moses Avenging the Israelite.* 2. *Moses before Pharaoh.* 3. *Passage of the Red Sea.* 4. *Manna.* 5. *Moses Striking the Rock.* 6. *Moses.*

The brass tells of the loss endured by the Reverend James Stuart Robson, Chaplain, R.M.A., who dedicated this window to the memory of those he tenderly loved. On the brass are the following words:—

"To the Glory of God, and in memory of Lieut. Charles Rufus Robson, R.N. only brother, and of Ensign William James Stuart Robson, 17th Regt., only son of the Reverend J. Stuart Robson."

Lieut. C. R. Robson, was actively engaged in the Baltic as 1st Lieutenant of H.M.S. Cruiser, and was present at the bombardment of Sweaborg. He also greatly distinguished himself on the Coast of Africa, and, while employed on the Pacific Station, received the thanks of the American Government for assistance rendered to their ships, when in imminent danger.

NO. XIV.

1. *Balaam's Journey.* 2. *Balaam's Prophecy.* 3. *Victory over the Midianites.* 4. *Passage of the Jordan.* 5. *Aaron.*

Offered by the Chaplain Department in memory of their Brethren. On the brass are these few words:—

" To the Glory of God, and in memory of the twelve Chaplains who fell while striving to do their duty during the Crimean War, this window is dedicated by the Chaplain Department of the Army."

(See Page 87)

NO. XV.

1. *Burning of Ai.* 2. *The Fall of Jericho.* 3. *The Sun and Moon standing still.* 5. *Joshua.*

Beneath this window are three brasses. One on the splay, on which is beautifully engraved the device of the 82nd Regiment, by which Corps the window was presented. On the second brass are the words:—

" To the Glory of God, and in memory of the undermentioned Officers, 250 non-commissioned Officers and soldiers of the 82nd Regiment (Prince of Wales' Volunteers) who have been killed in action or died since the regiment embarked for the Crimea in 1855. This window is erected by the Officers now serving in the regiment."

On the third, the names of the Officers.

CAPTAIN D. S. COLLINGS	Jan. 1855.
LIEUT. R. HAYWOOD	Feb. 1855.
„ H. ASPREECE	June, 1855.
„ A. P. HENSLEY	Nov. 1857.
ENSIGN W. THOMSON	Nov. 1857.
CAPTAIN J. GORDON	Jan. 1858.
LIEUT. S. DOUGLASS	Mar. 1858.
CAPTAIN S. SLATER	Sept. 1861.
ENSIGN J. CARROLL	Feb. 1863.
LIEUT. H. A. ELLIS	May, 1863.

CAPTAIN J. GORE	Mar. 1864.
„ J. H. PILKINGTON	Aug. 1865.
LIEUT. S. PITT	Dec. 1865.
„ J. N. TANNER	June, 1866.
CAPTAIN C. SPENCER	July, 1866.
LIEUT. T. RYAN	Sept. 1869.
„ C. NEVILLE	Feb. 1870.
LIEUT.-COL. C. T. V. BUNBURY,	Jan. 1871.

XVI.

1. *The Appeal of the Israelites to God.* 2. *Judah and Simeon agree to go up together.* 3. *Caleb's conquest of Hebron.* 4. *Jael and Sisera.* 5. *Deborah praising God.* 6. *Caleb.*

The brass states full particulars as to the donors :—

" To the Glory of God the above window was given by the Officers, Non-commissioned Officers and Privates of the 46th (South Devon Regiment) and in memory of comrades who died during the foreign service of the Corps in the Crimea, Corfu, and the three Presidencies of Bengal, Madras, and Bombay, during the years, 1854-1868."

Names of Officers.	Date of Death.
LT-COL. & BT-COLONEL A. G. VESEY	Died at Suez on passage home, 18th October, 1868.
MAJOR & BT-COL. C. F. CAMPBELL	Died at Simla, 14th September, 1868
CAPTAIN W. H. O. TOOLE	Died on March from Alma to Sebastopol, September 1854.
CAPTAIN T. J. CONNELL	Died at Mooltan, 31st August, 1858.
CAPTAIN C. B. SPEKE	Died at Poona, 31st August, 1868.
LIEUTENANT E. MESSENGER	Killed at Sebastopol by explosion of a mine.
LIEUTENANT F. COUCHER	Died at Mooltan, 19th August, 1859.
LIEUTENANT V. DALY	Died at Cawnpore, 26th April, 1862.
LIEUTENANT A. K. MALCOLMSON	Died at Calcutta, 7th February, 1867.
LIEUTENANT E. G. SERLE	Died at Poona, 20th June, 1868.
ENSIGN H. A. WHITMORE	Died at Corfu, 14th September, 1857.
SURGEON A. G. MONTGOMERY	Died at Lucknow, 27th June, 1857.
QUARTER-MASTER G. SANDERSON	Died at Jullundur, 13th January, 1861.
QUARTER-MASTER W. G. STREET	Died at Shalyehanpore, 8th May, 1864.

XVII.

1. *Gideon Threshing.* 2. *The Fleece.* 3. *Trial of Gideon's Army.* 4. *Destroying Peniel.* 5. *Gideon.*

This window is in memory of the Duke of Wellington's great friend, Sir James McGrigor, Baronet, K.C.B., &c., whose long and valuable services are noticed in Page 66.

XVIII.

1. *Samson killing the Lion.* 2. *Carrying away the gates of Gaza.* 3. *Defeating the Philistines.* 4. *Samson's Death.* 5. *Samson.*

No hero whose name is found in this Church deserved better a noble memorial than the gallant officer, Major Thomas Oldfield, R.M., to whose memory this window is dedicated. Honoured ever by his enemies in whose front he fell, he sacrificed that life, which he had so often hazarded in the defence of his country, at the siege of Acre in Syria, aged 43.

XIX.

1. *David introduced to Saul.* 2. *David killing Goliath.* 3. *Cave of Engedi.* 4. *David.*

This window is dedicated to the Glory of God and in memory of Lieut-General Lord Frederick Fitz-Clarence, G.C.H., son of King William IV., born 1799; married, 1821, Lady Augusta, daughter of the 4th Earl of Glasgow; entered the army in 1814; became a Lieut-General and Colonel of the 36th Regiment in 1851; appointed Commander-in-chief at Bombay in 1851; was raised to the rank of a Marquis's son in 1831; appointed Deputy Lieutenant of Northumberland; was Grand Master of the Freemasons of Scotland. Lord Frederick was Lieutenant Governor of Portsmouth from 1847 to 1851, and so endeared himself to the inhabitants, that, on his appointment as Commander-in-Chief in Bombay, they erected a monument to him, as an expression of their gratitude. On the west side of it are the following words:—

"To Lieut-General Lord Frederick Fitz-Clarence, G.C.H., this Column is erected by the inhabitants of Portsmouth, to mark their sense of the many services rendered to the Borough during his command of this Garrison."

H

XX.

1. *The Creation.* 2. *The Temptation.* 3. *Driven from Paradise.*
4. *Tilling the earth.* 5. *An angel.*

This window tells of an officer who saw long and active service, and was of a distinguished corps, one of the most distinguished. On the brass are the following words :—

"To the Glory of God and in memory of General Sir Charles Menzies, K.C.B., K.H., Knight Charles 3rd, Colonel of the Royal Marine Artillery, and formerly Aide-de-Camp to the Queen. Died August 22nd, 1866, aged 83. The above window is given as a mark of love and respect by his widow, Maria Wilhelmina Menzies."

General Sir Charles Menzies was attached to Lord Nelson's squadron off Boulogne, where he participated in all the desperate cutting out affairs on the French coast against Buonaparte's flotilla. Commanded a detachment of Royal Marines, and landed at Port Jackson, during an insurrection of convicts in March 1804; by his promptitude and exertions the town of Sidney, and indeed the Colony, was in a great measure preserved, and tranquillity restored. On the 22nd of June, 1806, he was in one of the boats of H.M.S. Minerva, cutting out five vessels from under Fort Finisterre, and on the 11th of July following, he was in the barge, which, when 50 miles from where the frigate lay at anchor, captured by boarding the *Buena Dicha*, Spanish Privateer of three times the force of the boat, after a sharp conflict: this attack was planned by General Menzies. Commanded and landed the Marines at the storming of Fort Finisterre, being the first who entered the Fort. In boats cutting out the Spanish vessel of war *St. Joseph* from the Bay of Arosa, where he landed and made prisoner the Spanish Commodore, who delivered to him his sword. Commanded the Marines at the capture of Fort Guardia. Slightly wounded cutting out the French corvette La Moselle from under a battery in Basque Roads. Taking of Fort Camerinus and gun-boats from under its protection. Repeatedly engaged in severe boat actions and against batteries. Right arm amputated. Received a sword of honour from the Patriotic Fund. Commanded the Royal Marine Artillery from 1837-44. Is a Knight of Charles III. of Spain, and a Knight of the Tower and Sword of Portugal, was created K.H. and K.C.B.

XXI.

1. *The Sealing of the Saints.* 2. *The Saints sealed directed Heaven-wards.*

This much admired window is dedicated to the Glory of God and in memory of Major-General Sir John William Gordon, R.E., K.C.B., by friends who deeply respected that true servant of God and his country. Sir J. William Gordon took from the beginning the liveliest interest in the restoration of this Church ; indeed it may be said that, had he not united with the Lieutenant Governor Lord William Paulet, the General of the District, and as Commanding Engineer supported his Lordship in his strong appeal to the War Department, the work would never have been done. (See Stall 22, Page 74).

XXII.

THE GREAT WEST WINDOW.

This window is a gift by the officers of the 43rd Light Infantry in memory of their brother officers who were killed during the New Zealand War, 1864-5. It is considered as a work of art of the highest merit.

1. *The reception of the Blessed.* 2. *The resurrection of the Blessed.* 3. *The resurrection of the wicked.* 4. *The condemnation of the wicked.* 5. *Angels and Archangels.* 6. *Prophets.* 7. *Apostles.* 8. *The Blessed Virgin Mary.* 9. *St. John the Baptist.* 10. *Majesty with the four Evangelists.*

This window resembles very closely the much admired east window of Castle Combe Church, save that the lancets are not trefoiled. Scrope in his "History of Castle Combe" writes thus of the "four narrow slightly trefoiled lancet lights with a quatrefoil opening above," "Its form, though very effective and beautiful, is extremely rare—perhaps unique."

XXIII.

1. St. George.

A Thankoffering from Alfred Smith, builder, he having been mercifully preserved during the restoration of the church.

FUNERAL TABLETS

Before the restoration of the church, Funeral Tablets, the
generality of them poor in design, were found all over the
walls—behind the gallery, let into the pillars, blocking up
windows, crowding the chancel; indeed it seemed as if the
most accomplished bad taste had from generation to generation been occupied, first in designing the tablets, and
afterwards in placing them.   The Committee wisely acted
upon the architect's advice as to the removal, as far as possible, of all black backings, and then arranged the marble
slabs in such a manner, that they should in no way vio-
lently disturb the architectural beauty of the building.
In order that the wording may not be entirely lost, for it
is on many of the slabs scarcely legible, I have given an
exact copy from each monument, and the position it occu-
pies in the Church.

CHANCEL—NORTH SIDE.

GREY.

Sacred to the memory of The Hon. Sir George Grey, Baronet, K.C.B.,
third son of Charles, 1st Earl Grey, 22 years Commissioner to His Majesty's
Dockyard of this Port.

He departed this life in the Faith and Hope of the Gospel, after a painful
and protracted illness, which he bore with exemplary christian patience and
resignation. Born October the 10th, 1767, died October the 3rd, 1828.

"The wages of sin is death, but the gift of God is eternal life, through
Jesus Christ, our Lord." Rom. vi. 23.

FISHER

Sacred to the memory of Benjamin Fisher, Esquire, Major-General on the Staff, and Commanding Royal Engineer in the South West District, who died in this garrison on the 29th of September, 1814, in the 62nd year of his age His abilities, zeal and integrity, were for 43 years faithfully devoted to his country's service in situations of great responsibility. His public conduct secured to him the approbation and respect of his superiors, his private virtues the ardent love of his family and attachment of all who knew him.

GUISE.

Sacred to the memory of Christopher William Guise, fifth son of the late Sir John Guise, Bart., of Highnam Court, Gloucestershire, and Lieut. in the North Gloucester Regiment. An unfortunate accident in the execution of his duty terminated his earthly career, the 13th day of October, 1803, in the 21st year of his age. He was highly esteemed and regretted by his brother officers, and died sincerely lamented by his afflicted relations. This monument is erected by his much distressed mother, in token of her love and affection.

CHANCEL—SOUTH SIDE.

CAMPBELL.

Sacred to the memory of Sir George Campbell, G.C.B., Admiral of the White Squadron of His Majesty's fleet. He was the son of Pryse Campbell, Esq., of Cawdor Castle, county of Nairn, N. B., and brother of Lord Cawdor, He married Eustatia, daughter of J. H. Campbell, Esq., Lord Lyon King at Arms for Scotland, brother of Pryse Campbell. He died Commander-in-Chief at Portsmouth, January the 23rd, 1821, aged 59, having served 49 years in the Royal Navy, in which he eminently distinguished himself in most arduous and essential services. In consideration of which and his high character, His present Majesty, in the most gracious manner, appointed him Groom of the Bed-chamber, and conferred on him the most honourable Military Order of the Bath.

> " To him whose loyal, brave, and gentle heart,
> Fulfilled the hero's and the Christian's part,
> Whose charity, like that which Paul enjoined,
> Was warm, beneficent, and unconfined,

This stone is reared—to public duty true,
The seaman's friend—the father of his crew.
Mild in reproof, sagacious in command,
He spread fraternal zeal throughout his band ;
He led each arm to act, each heart to feel
What British valour owes to Britain's weal.
These were his public virtues, but to trace.
His private worth, fair purity and grace ;
To paint the traits that drew affection strong
From friends, an ardent and an ample throng ;
And more to speak his memory's grateful claim
On her who mourns him most and bears his name,
O'ercomes the trembling hand of widow's grief,
O'ercomes the heart unconscious of relief;
Save in Religion's high and holy trust,
While placing this memorial o'er his dust.

OLDFIELD.

Sacred to the memory of Major Thomas Oldfield of the Marines, who from early youth distinguished himself under several commanders, and especially in America under Lord Cornwallis, until, honoured even by his enemies in whose front he fell, he sacrificed that life, which he had so often hazarded in the service of his country, at the seige of Acre in Syria, April the 7th, 1799, aged 43.

This monument was erected as a testimony of sincere affection and gratitude, by the widow and son of Lieutenant John Nicholson Oldfield of the Marines, the loving and loved brother of the above, who died April the 9th, A.D. 1793, aged 41, and was interred at Alverstoke.

IN THE TRANSEPT.

LEGGATT.

To the memory of the Rev. Samuel Leggatt, A.M., upwards of 26 years Chaplain to the Forces in this Garrison. Obiit March 7th, 1848. Ætat 74.

MONCREIFF.

In memory of Colonel Robert Moncreiff, formerly Commandant of the Portsmouth division of Royal Marines, in which corps, for a period exceeding 50 years, he was distinguished by valour and energy in service, and by a high sense of honour and justice in command. Died 24th of January, 1844, aged 36 years.

HAY.

Sacred to the memory of John Baker Hay, Esquire, Captain of H.M.S. " Queen Caroline." He died most deeply lamented on the 13th of May, 1823.

MCBEAN.

In memory of Captain William Frederick McBean, of the 31st Huntingdonshire Regiment, who died at Tien-Tsin, North China, the 21st April, 1862, in his 38th year. This tablet is erected by his brother officers, in token of their high regard for his upright and amiable character during the period he served in the regiment (upwards of seven years), and their deep regret at his untimely death.

HODGSON.

In memory of Christopher Hodgson, Lieut. 84th Regiment, son of Robert Hodgson, Esq., Prince Edward's Island. Obiit 26th December, 1838, ætat. 33.

HUME.

Sacred to the memory of John Hume, Surgeon, of His Majesty's 59th Regiment, who departed this life the 12th of August, 1828, in the 48th year of his age.

FETHERSTON.

Sacred to the memory of Lieut-Colonel Thomas Fetherston, of the Bengal Establishment, who departed this life the 13th August, 1832, aged 77 years.

KAY.

In memory of Lieut. Robert Kay, of the 7th Royal Fusiliers, who died at Manchester on the 1st of April, 1851, in the 31st year of his age. This tablet is erected by his brother officers as a token of their esteem.

MARSHALL.

Sacred to the memory of Captain George Marshall, of Her Majesty's 31st Regiment, eldest son of Lieut-Colonel Marshall, of the Royal Marines. He died on the 24th of August, 1842, in the 33rd year of his age, in Affghanistan, on his march to Cabool, of fever, brought on by over exertion and fatigue in action with the enemy on the 26th of July, 1842.

HARRISON.

Sacred to the memory of Major T. J. Harrison, late in the Royal Artillery, and of Weard House, Cornwall, who departed this life the 10th December, 1820, aged 58 years. This tablet was erected by the widow of the deceased, as a tribute to his many excellencies and virtues, and as a memorial of her devoted attachment. Also Charles James Henry Harrison, second son of the above, who died at Malta on the 6th January, 1839, aged 28 years. His loss will be ever deeply mourned by his family for his many virtues. He was a dutiful son, an affectionate brother, and a sincere friend.

ROBERTS.

Sacred to the memory of Paymaster Roberts, 59th Regiment, who died of fever at Antigua, on the 16th of December, 1841, aged 38 years. Also to the memory of Ensign Prior, 59th Regiment, who died on the 5th of February, 1844, aged 22 years, from the effects of a wound caused by the accidental discharge of his gun whilst shooting near this place. This tablet was erected by their brother officers as a token of their esteem.

WEMYSS.

Sacred to the memory of Lieut. Henry Wemyss, 21st Royal North British Fusiliers, youngest son of the late Colonel Wemyss, of Wemysshall, Fifeshire, N.B., who died on the 27th October, 1832, aged 19 years. Brief and lovely was his span of life, his youth was full of fair promise, he was beloved by all who knew him, and to his mother, by whom this sad monument is raised, he never caused grief until his death.

BUCK.

In memory of Brevet Major Henry Buck, who died at Portsmouth on the 21st December, 1862, after having served for 18 years in the 53rd Regiment. Aged 36 years. Erected by his brother officers in token of their esteem.

BULLOCK.

Near this place are deposited the remains of Miss Hannah Bullock, who departed this life 24th January, 1790, aged 44 years.

WILLIAMS.

Sacred to the memory of Lieut-Colonel Samuel Williams of the Royal Marines, who served his king and country with honour and fidelity forty-two years, and died the 16th day of December, 1824, highly respected, in the 59th year of his age.

CAMPBELL.

Sacred to the memory of Pieter Laurentz Campbell, Esquire, A.C.E., late Lieutenant in the Royal Scots Fusiliers, eldest son of Colonel Ronald Campbell, the 72nd Highlanders, born 31st March, 1809, died 4th October, 1848. He was successively appointed to various offices of confidence and authority under the government at the Cape of Good Hope, and New South Wales, in the department of H.M. Board of Trade, and in the Manchester and Leeds, and South Western Railways; and was in all conspicuous for superior ability, and for an energy and zeal to which at length he fell a sacrifice at the age of 39.
" By grace are ye saved through faith,
" And that not of yourselves, it is the gift of God."

ANDRAE.

In memory of H. G. Andrae, Esquire, late Bandmaster of the 4th (King's Own) Regiment, who died February 11th, 1850, aged 49 years. This tablet was erected by the Band of the Regiment, as a testimony of their sincere respect for their departed Master. " Requiescat In Pace."

SINCLAIR.

This tablet is erected in memory of John Sinclair, M.D, late Assistant Surgeon of H.M.S. " Excellent," by the officers of that Ship, as a token of their great regard and esteem. He died October the 25th, 1840, aged 26 years.

BYRON.

This tablet is erected as a token of sincere affection, to the memory of Rear Admiral Byron, C.B., who departed this life September the 2nd, 1837; also to that of his son, Commander Byron, who died February the 23rd, 1843, off Mazatlan, on the West Coast of Mexico, while in command of Her Majesty's Sloop of War " Champion."

KNATCHBULL.

Sacred to the memory of Ensign Wyndham Knatchbull, late of the 1st Regiment of Foot Guards, second son of Wyndham Knatchbull, Esq. of London, by Catherine his wife, daughter of the late Sir Edward Knatchbull, Bart. of Mersham Hatch, in the county of Kent. He was compelled to quit his regiment on service in Spain for the recovery of his health. He died on board His Majesty's Ship " Dictator" the 14th day of October, 1813, being the day on

which the ship arrived at Spithead. Having at the early age of 18 paid the last
tribute of the soldier, his remains were interred with military honours in the
burial ground adjoining to this chapel. A sorrowing father caused this tablet
to be placed here in sad remembrance of his irreparable loss, and in testimony of
the mournful regret of the numerous friends and relatives of the deceased.

HOVENDEN.

Sacred to the memory of Major Nicholas Hovenden, 59th Regiment,
who died at Leeds, on the 30th September, 1845, aged 52 years; 36 of which he
passed in the 59th Regiment, having served with it in the Peninsula, at Waterloo, and Bhurtpore. This tablet was erected by his brother officers as a token
of their esteem.

NORTH AISLE—EAST END.

O'CONNOR.

SOLI DEO GLORIA.

Siste gradum mortalis et hujus quem tenet urna hœc
Collige virtutem, quo duce disce mori,
Justitiam, regem, patriam, Christumque secutus
Moribus, officio, corde, et amore pio.

Hic jacet Daniel O'Connor (vulgò Cornelius dictus) ex antiquâ et
illustri O'Connorum prosapiâ ortus, in Momoniâ Hyberniæ provinciâ, qui,
per decem annorum curriculum, serenissimis nostris regibus Carolo primo,
piœ memoriœ, et Carolo secundo ter maximo, glorioso, jam fæliciter regnanti,
Equestris Turmœ Dux, fideliter, prudenter, fortiter, inservivit; consilio pru-
dentissimus, expertissimus in bello, quietissimus in pace, stetit, vicit, vixit,
neque elatus in prosperis neque dejectus in adversis, ut eum nec tumidè nec
timidè vixisse meritò dicas, (uno varbo) semper idem, toti patriœ totus, unicus
amicis amcissimus, pauperibus pater perpetuus, vir singulari patientiâ, vigilan-
tiâ, sobrietate, ornatissimus; uxorem duxit Dominam Annam Whaley, eximiœ
modestiæ, pietatis, charitatis fœminam, Londini in Parochiâ Stæ. Mariæ
Magdalenæ, ex quâ nullam habuit prolem, cum quâ per decem annorum spatium
unanimiter vixit, depositâ tandem (prop dolor) hujus mortalitatis sarcinâ, vitam
cum morte quietè, piè, religiosè commutavit, anno Regni Caroli Secundi XIV.,
et naturæ reparatæ MDCLXII. ÆTATIS SUÆ XXXXV., DIE X. SEPTEMBRIS.

Abi viator et refer, hujus interitu
cæterorum mortalium vitam solvi

TRANSLATION.

To the Glory of God alone.

Stay your step, thou mortal, and learn the virtue of him whom this urn contains, and, taking for your leader one who in morals, duty, heart and pious love, followed justice, his king, his country and Christ, learn to die. Here lies Daniel O'Connor (commonly called Cornelius), sprung from the ancient and illustrious race of the O'Connors, of the Province of Munster, in Ireland; who, for a period of ten years, as Captain of the Horse Guard, faithfully, prudently, and gallantly served our most Serene Sovereigns Charles I. of pious memory, and Charles II. thrice most great and glorious, now happily reigning. Most prudent in council, most expert in war, most gentle in peace, he stood, he conquered, he lived, neither elated in prosperity nor dejected in adversity; so that you may deservedly say, that he lived neither boastfully nor timidly. In a word, he was a devoted patriot, the warmest of friends and ever a father to the poor, one adorned in a remarkable manner with singular patience, vigilance, and sobriety. He married Dame Anna Whaley, a woman of eminent modesty, piety, and charity, of the Parish of St. Mary Magdalene, London; by whom he had no family, and with whom he lived in perfect concord for a period of ten years. The burden of this mortality having alas! been laid aside, he quietly, piously, and religiously changed life for death in the xivth year of the reign of Charles II, and of our Redemption 1662, on the 10th September, aged 45.

Go, traveller, and tell by the death of this man, how the life of other mortals should be spent.

BALL.

Sacred to the memory of Lieut-Colonel A. H. Ball, Royal Marines, who died 19th of April, 1829, aged 52 years, esteemed and regretted.

NORTH WALL—EAST END.

ASHHURST.

Sacred to the memory of Nathan Ashhurst, Esq., fourteen years Town-Major of this garrison, who, after a service of 44 years in various quarters of the globe, died here on the 19th of December, 1820, in the 60th year of his age. To a zealous and faithful discharge of his military duties in this garrison, he united in an exemplary degree the kind heartedness, benevolence, and friendly attentions of the citizen and good neighbour. To perpetuate their sense of those his estimable qualities, the military and naval officers and inhabitants of this town have caused this monument to be erected.

DESIMARETZ.

Near this monument lie interred the remains of Colonel E. Desimaretz, late His Majesty's Commissary for the demolition of the works at Dunkirk, who departed this life the 16th of September, 1768, in the 82nd year of his age. Though born a foreigner, he early adopted every generous sentiment of civil and religious liberty, and exerted his active abilities for the service of this nation, in quality of an engineer. An indefatigable zeal and unshaken integrity in the execution of several important works committed to his charge deservedly entitled him to the approbation of his superiors and the esteem of the public, while his social virtues in the sphere of private life endeared him to all his friends, by whom he is sincerely regretted. His affectionate daughter Mary Desimaretz Durnford hath caused this monument to be erected, as a testimony of filial piety to the memory of the best of fathers and of a tender mother, whose reliques were also deposited in this chapel on the 21st of July, 1761.

SOUTH AISLE—EAST END.

DAVIDS.

Sacred to the memory of Lieut-Colonel William Davids, Major in the Portsmouth Division of Royal Marines, who died November the 8th, 1803, aged 47 years. This stone is placed here by a sincere friend.

HAWKER.

Near this place lyeth the body of the Hon. Colonel Peter Hawker, late Lieut-Governor of Portsmouth, who departed this life the 5th day of January, 1732, in the 60th year of his age. The above tablet was repaired in 1838 by his great grandson, Colonel Peter Hawker.

HOWE.

In memory of John Howe, late Ensign in His Majesiy's 39th Regiment, who departed this life on the 3rd day of January, 1832, in the 21st year of his age, and whose remains are interred in the burying ground of this chapel.

SOUTH WALL—EAST END.

YEO.

Near his spot repose the mortal remains of Sir James Lucas Yeo, Captain

in the Royal Navy, Knight Commander of the Bath, Knight Commander of
St. Bento of Avis, who died on the 21st of August, 1818, in the 37th year of
his age. It was the enviable fortune of this able officer, living in times of high
enterprise, to meet with opportunities of distinction, of which he nobly availed
himself, adding essentially to the national renown, and by his personal prowess
winning for himself an imperishable name in the naval annals of his country.
This tablet was erected to his memory by his brother officers and personal
friends.

SOUTH AISLE—WEST END.

DURNFORD.

In memory of Charles Durnford, late Ensign in His Majesty's 65th Regiment, and fifth son of Colonel Durnford, of the corps of Royal Engineers,
who died at this place on the 7th of January, 1832, aged 20 years.

MARSHALL.

Sacred to the memory of second Lieutenant Charles Dudley Pater Marshall, son of Lieut-Colonel Marshall of the Royal Marines, who died on board
the brig "Annie," on his passage from Barbadoes to England, October the 14th,
1834, aged 21 years.

CAMPBELL.

In memory of Donald Campbell, Esquire, Rear-Admiral of the White,
Commander-in-Chief of H.M. Ships on the Leeward Islands Station. Died at
sea on board his Flagship "Salisbury," 11th of November, 1819, aged 67
years. Interred here 3rd of February, 1820. Also of Margaret Harriot, his
wife, who died the 17th of January, 1831, aged 65 years. This monument is
erected by their affectionate son H. D. Campbell. As also to Donald Campbell,
infant son of the above H. D. Campbell and Annie Maria, his wife, who died
the 14th of August, 1831, aged 11 months.

ROTTENBURG.

Sacred to the memory of Lieut-General Francis Baron de Rottenburg,
K.C.H., who departed this life, April 25th, 1832. This tablet is erected as a
mark of respect by his affectionate daughter, Lady William Paget.

FOSTER.

Near this spot are deposited the remains of Martha Foster, wife of Colonel Thomas Foster, who departed this life on the 3rd of May, 1825.

SOUTH WALL—WEST END.

COOKES.

Sacred to the memory of George Cookes, Esq., late Lieutenant in the South Gloucester Militia, who died 7th of February, 1795, aged 27 years, eldest son of the Rev. Thomas Cookes, of Barbourne House, Worcester. The deep regret which is still experienced for his most irreparable loss by his surviving friends will best express his unequalled worth and rare endowments. This tablet was erected 14th December, 1820, by a surviving friend.

YOUNG

To the memory of George James Young, Lieut. 17th Regiment, Bombay N. Infantry, who died at "Ootacamond," on the 23rd June, 1844, in the 21st year of his age.

Also Charles Edward Young, Lieutenant 50th Regiment, killed at the battle of "Moodkee" on the Sutlej, 18th of December, 1845, in the 20th year of his age. This tablet is erected by Major and Mrs. Young, late of the 38th Regiment, the sorrowing parents of the above young officers cut off in the morning of life in their country's service.

MAC GREGOR.

Sacred to the memory of Lieut-Colonel George MacGregor, c.b., of His Majesty's 59th Regiment, obiit 7th August, 1828, ætat 48. This monument was erected by his affectionate and disconsolate widow.

GIBBS.

In memory of Major-General Sir Samuel Gibbs, k.c.b., who gloriously fell in the service of his country at New Orleans on the 9th of January, 1815, in the forty-fourth year of his age.

MAUGHAN.

In memory of Mary, the beloved wife of Major I. Maughan, R.M.; she died July the 19th, 1835, aged 43, also of Cecilia Barbara Harriett, their eldest daughter, who died July the 17th, 1835, aged 24. To record his deep sorrow, but in humble submission to the Divine Will, the mourning father and husband dedicated this tablet.

MC BEAN.

Sacred to the memory of Amelia Harriotte, only daughter of Major Frederick McBean, of H.M. 84th Regiment, who died sincerely beloved and regretted by her parents and friends, 14th February, 1842, aged 5 years and 3 months.

ROBINSON.

Sacred to the memory of Thomas Robinson, Sergt-Major of the Portsmouth Division of Royal Marines, who died June 1st, 1822, aged 40 years. This tablet is erected by the non-commissioned officers of that corps, as a mark of their esteem and respect for a brave soldier and a worthy man.

WHETHAM.

In memory of Lieut-General Arthur Whetham, First Gentleman of the Bed Chamber to His Royal Highness the Duke of Cumberland, Colonel of the first battalion of the 60th Regiment, Lieutenant Governor of this Garrison and Commander of the South West District. He died 18th May, 1813, in the sixtieth year of his age.

TIMINS.

In memory of Lieut-Colonel Thomas Timins, Royal Marines, who departed this life 25th October, 1828, aged 65 years. He was senior officer of his corps in the battle of Trafalgar, and served his country fifty years with zeal, honour and humility.

MADDEN.

To the memory of Major General Sir George Allan Madden, Knt. C.B., and Commander of the Order of the Tower and Sword, born January 3rd, 1771, died December 8th, 1828, aged 57 years. His earlier services were in Corsica and Egypt, subsequently he distinguished himself in the war of the Peninsula, particularly near Fuentes de Cantos in Estremadura, where, at the head of the brigade of Portuguese Cavalry under his orders, he gallantly charged and repulsed the French army of Andalusia, on the 15th September, 1810, commanded by Marshal Mortier; and by this brilliant exploit was the means of saving the Spanish Army under the Marquis de Romana from destruction.

MADDEN.

To the memory of Captain William John Madden, eldest son of James Madden, Esquire, of Colehill House, Fulham, Middlesex, and brother of Major General Sir G. A. Madden, born 26th October, 1757, died 3rd May, 1833; also in memory of Sarah, wife of Capt. W. T. Madden, and daughter of the Rev. Arnold Carter, M.A., Minor Canon of Rochester Cathedral, born the 21st June, 1759, died 8th May, 1833.

CROCKET.

Sacred to the memory of Lieut. John Crocket, R.M.A., who was killed leading his men in an attack on a band of Pirates in the river Teba, near the Gambia, on the coast of Africa, on the 12th December, 1849, aged 26 years.
He met a soldier's death, and rests in a sailor's grave.
Also to the memory of Michael Cairns, boatswain's mate, aged 35 years, and John Neale, Gunner R.M.A., aged 27 years, who died of wounds received on the same occasion. This tablet is erected by their messmates and shipmates in H.M. Steam Frigate "Centaur," who deeply lament their untimely fate.

TORRENS.

Remember Charles John Torrens, Captain, R.A.. and youngest son of Major-General Sir Henry Torrens, Adj-General, K.C.B., K.T.S. He died at Portsmouth, March 14th, 1847, aged 30 years.

BALCHILD.

Sacred to the memory of Brevet-Major Charles Elliott Balchild, of the Royal Marines, who died at sea on board H.M.S. "Queen," on the 15th Sept., 1846, aged 56. His remains are interred in the English cemetery at Cadiz. Entered the service on the 25th April, 1804.

H.M.S. "QUEEN."

Sacred to the memory of

			Years	months	days
James Napper,	Surgeon	aged	40	„	„
James Hislop	Schoolmaster		28	„	„
Young Green West	Midshipman		15	7	5
Arthur Bridgman Simpson	do.		12	7	10
Henry Smart Crawford	do.		16	0	25
Charles William Thornton	do.		14	11	0
John Augustus Aldham	do.		15	3	8

of His Majesty's Ship " Queen," who fell victims to an insidious brain fever which developed itself on board that ship, between the 14th day of October, and the 15th day of November, 1827, after leaving the Island of St. Jago, Cape de Verde ; on her passage from England to the Cape of Good Hope. This tablet is erected by Captain Lord Henry John Spencer Churchill, the gunroom officers, and midshipmen of H.M.S. " Tweed," as a tribute of their esteem and sincere regard.

NORTH AISLE—WEST END.

PELLEW.

In memory of the Hon. Pownoll Fleetwood Pellew, R.N., grandson of Admiral Viscount Exmouth. He died at Portsmouth on Christmas Day, 1851, first Lieutenant of the Royal Yacht " Victoria and Albert," after a short and severe illness, aged 28 years. " The beloved son of a widowed Mother."

PERSSE.

Sacred, as a tribute of sincere affection by Major William Persse, to the memory of his dear wife, Eliza, daughter of the Hon. Tudge Moore, who departed this life on board the " Roxburgh Castle," when within reach of the British shore, after an absence of 10 years, on the 26th May, aged 36 years.

LAFOREY.

Near this place are deposited the remains of Sir John Laforey, Baronet, Admiral of the Blue Squadron, who departed this life on board His Majesty's

Ship " Majestic " at sea, on his passage from the West Indies, on the 14th day of June, in the year of our Lord, 1796, aged 76 years.

BARNES.

In memory of Quarter-Master William Barnes, 2nd Royal Cheshire Militia, who died at Portsmouth on the 28th of December, 1858, in the 46th year of his age. This tablet is erected by his brother officers as a token of their esteem.

WOODHOUSE.

Sacred to the memory of Ann Maria, wife of Lieut-Colonel William Woodhouse, commanding the 20th Regiment M.N.I., born November the 10th, 1784, died at Quilon, on the coast of Malabar, November the 5th, 1826. Also of Ann her Mother, relict of the late Samuel Leggatt, Esq., of Norwich, born August the 12th, 1746, died August the 20th, 1827, who lies buried in this Church.

" Optimis et dilectissimis matrum et sororum, Samuel (hujus præsidii sacerdos) Horatius et Gerardus hoc monumentum posuere."

Also of Gerard Leggatt, Esq., Captain in the 41st Regiment M.N.I., born May the 6th, 1872 ; died at Madras, September the 16th, 1828.

NORTH WALL—WEST END.

CARDEW.

In memory of Caroline, the beloved wife of Colonel Cardew, Commanding Royal Engineer of the South West and Sussex District, who departed this life, deeply lamented, at Landport House, Portsmouth, after a long and painful illness, which she bore with christian fortitude and resignation, September the 19th, 1845, aged 61. " Our light affliction, which is but for a moment, worketh for us a far more exceeding weight of glory."

WILLIAMS.

Sacred to the memory of Anne Maria Williams, sister of the late Colonel Sir Richard Williams, K.B., and Colonel Samuel Williams, who died on the 7th day of February, 1844, in the 87th year of her age.

ARCHBOLD.

Sacred to the memory of Lieut-Colonel Archbold of the Royal Marines who, after a faithful and honourable service, died at Portsmouth on the III day of January, MDCCCIX, aged LXX years. Also of Mary his wife, who died on the XXIII day of March, MDCCCIII, aged LXIV years. Also of second Lieutenant Thomas Archbold, Royal Marines, son of the above Thomas and Mary Archbold, who died on the II day of January, MDCCLXXXVI, aged XV years, and of Harriett, their daughter, who died on the XXV day of February, MDCCLXXIV, aged IV years and IX months, and of James, their son, who died on the XVIII day of May, MDCCLXXV, aged II years and II months.

The above all deceased at Portsmouth, and are buried near this spot. This tablet is erected agreeably to the will of Mary Anne, the dutiful and affectionate daughter of the above Thomas and Mary Archbold, who died at Cheltenham, on the VII day of October, MDCCCXXII, aged LIV years, and was interred at Leckhampton.

MEIK.

In memory of Thomas Meik, M.D., 39 years Physician to the town and garrison of Portsmouth, who died on the 23rd May, 1811, aged 76 years, and was buried near this monument, as were also four of his sons who died in their infancy. Likewise of Margaret, daughter of the late James Lind, M.D., Physician to Haslar Hospital, and relict of the above Thomas Meik, M.D. She died on the 18th December, 1832, aged 82 years.

Maria Johnston, daughter of the above, obiit the 6th August, 1841, aged 68 years.

WILLIAMS.

Sacred to the memory of Colonel Sir Richard Williams, late Commandant of the Royal Marines, (formerly Commandant of the Royal Marine Artillery) and Knight Commander of the most Hon. Order of the Bath, an honor granted in recompense of long and meritorious services in defence of his country. Died June 1st, 1859.

GRANT.

In memory of Lieut. William Grant, who, after a service of nearly sixty years, died on the 30th September, 1806, Town-Major of this Garrison, in the

79th year of his age, and on the anniversary of the day on which he very honorably distinguished himself at the battle of Bucker-Muhl in Germany, in the year 1762. He was a brave soldier and, in his character as a man, strength of mind, probity, and benevolence were united.

BURNETT.

In memory of Captain William Burnett, R.N., 3rd son of the late Sir Robert Burnett, Bart. of Leys, who died in command of Her Majesty's Ship "Magicienne" at Portsmouth, on the 16th of April, 1840, aged 41 years.

BALLINGALL.

In memory of Colonel David James Ballingall, Colonel Commandant of the Woolwich Division of Royal Marines, who died the 31st March, 1846. Also of Mrs. Colonel Ballingall, widow of the above, who died 5th December, 1859.

JONES.

In memory of Mary Gerrish Jones, widow of Capt. Lewis Tobias Jones, of the county of Sligo, Ireland, (formerly of the 14th Regiment) who died in April, 1835, and was interred in a vault near this tablet. Also in memory of the above Capt. Lewis Tobias Jones, who died at Bishop-Wearmouth in September, 1822.

THE LECTERN.

The Lectern, of the purest oak, is much admired for its simplicity and elegance. It was given by the sons and daughters of Lieutenant Alexander Russwurm, to whose memory it is dedicated. On a small brass are the following words :—

A.D.M.G.

"In Memoriam Alexandri Russwurm hanc Lectrinam Deo et Ecclesiæ dedere piè recordantes Filii Filiæque."

Lieutenant Russwurm served in the attack on New Orleans as Lieutenant, 5th W.I. Regiment.

THE PULPIT.

The Pulpit, designed by G. E. Street, R.A., was presented, in memory of their gallant comrades, by the crew of H.M.S. " Penelope." Beneath a cross, around which are the words " Crux mihi anchora," is the following inscription :—

" To the glory of God and in memory of the Seamen and Marines of H.M.S. Penelope, who were killed at Bomarsund or died in the service of their country, between the 5th of April, 1854, and July 8th, 1858, this Pulpit was erected by their surviving shipmates. Stations—Baltic, Cape of Good Hope, and East Indies."

THE COLOURS IN THE CHURCH.

The Colours of three Regiments—the 7th Royal Fusiliers, the Scinde Camel Corps, and the 67th (South Hampshire) Regiment, stand out on each side from the pillars in the nave. On a brass beneath each flag is inscribed the Regiment to which it belonged.

The following words will be found on a tablet beneath the Colours of the Camel Corps :—

The Standards waving above this Tablet are consecrated to the memory of General Sir Charles Napier, G.C.B., the conqueror of Scinde, by whose genius the Scinde Camel Corps was formed. Happier than most conquerors, he secured the affections of the vanquished by a wise and beneficial rule of that noble Province, which his valour and military skill had won for his country. May his glorious name animate the hearts of British soldiers in the day of battle.

This tablet is put up by Captain Bruce, Commanding the Camel Corps."

The Colours of the 67th Regiment were first unfurled at Cork in 1845, and, after having been well rent by hard service during the war in China, were solemnly placed in the old "Domus Dei," on the 30th October, 1868.

WARDENS OR MASTERS OF THE "DOMUS DEI."

THE list of the Wardens of the Hospital of Saint Nicholas is nearly complete, and a very valuable list it is. No one but the painstaking archæologist knows how long a time it requires to gather together the interesting particulars contained in the few pages of this chapter of my story. I therefore gladly here acknowledge that I am indebted to F. J. Baigent, Esq., of Winchester, for all the information I am able to supply with respect to the Wardens of the "Domus Dei," except that relating to the first three. It is, I have every reason to believe, the substance or result of more than 20 years' investigation and hard work. The Bishops' Registers preserved in the Library of Winchester Cathedral, only commence with Bishop Pontissara. There was therefore a period of 70 years, during which Wardens of the Hospital existed, but their names could only be discovered by searching early documents, into some of which they had been introduced as those of witnesses to deeds, or of parties to agreements bearing upon the interests of the Hospital. In this matter I received help from one who is world-known as a learned archæologist, Sir Frederic Madden, K.H., so long the eminent Keeper of the Manuscripts in the British Museum. Indeed throughout my endeavour to tell the tale of the "Domus Dei," I have found him ever ready to guide me to what is trustworthy, and to warn me when my authority was weak.

The most common title for the head of a Hospital is *Custos* or *Warden*, and strictly speaking it is the most fitting designation, but *Prior* and *Master* are constantly met with in early documents. Curiously enough in the earliest document known connected with the "Domus Dei," (1214), and also in that by which it was surrendered, the Superior is termed 'Master.' I would here observe that its Masters were all men of mark, and the Wardenship was at all times considered a valuable piece of preferment. In days of tremendous pluralism, the value was undoubtedly increased by the fact, that the Head of the Hospital was seldom or ever called upon to be in residence.

With these preliminary remarks, I shall now proceed to give a list of the Wardens, and such particulars concerning them as I have been able to collect. After the rule of two or three, whose names have not yet been discovered, the Wardenship was held by

BENJAMIN, in 1248.* This we learn from the following grant made in that year. William de Clamorgan, son of Philip de Clamorgan gives to the Church of Blessed Mary of †Quarraria and the monks there 11s. of quit rent, which Fulco de Wymering has been accustomed to pay yearly to the said William for a tenement in Heleseye, &c, &c. " Witnesses, *Benjamin, Chaplain, then Prior of the Domus Dei of Portesmuwe,* &c."

NICHOLAS, before and in 1266.‡ This also we know from the witnesses to a gift. Hugh Raggy § of Portesmuwe gives to the church of Blessed Mary of Quarraria and the monks there a house with a cellar and‖ solar, in the town of Portesmuwe, and moreover he concedes to

---

* Augment. Off. Cart. Antiq., Vol. 21, f. 39.

† Quarr Abbey in the Isle of Wight, near Ryde.

‡ Augment. Off. Cart. Antiq. Vol. 18, No. 266.

§ *Caggy* is written in the margin of the MS., by a modern hand, but the name was evidently 'Raggy' as in the gift witnessed by Benjamin.

‖ Solar, a house or loft over a cellar, an upper chamber. In some parts of England a garret is still called a 'sollar.'

them a certain piece of land of another of his holdings, so that they and their successors shall render thence annually to the Brothers of the ' Domus Dei' of Portesmuwe and their successors 12d. at the Feast of St. Michael. "Witnesses, Sir Matthew, Prior of Southwick, *Brother Nicholas, Prior of the ' Domus Dei,' &c., &c.*"

ROBERT, in 1268.* The name of this Warden and the date are obtained from an agreement made in the 52nd year Hen. III, (1268), between Robert Walerand and Robert, Master of the Hospital of Portsmouth, preserved in the Record Office.†

SIR ROGER DE HARWEDONE, about 1296. The exact date is not known, but he appears to have been collated to the Wardenship of the Hospital by John de Portissara during the latter part of his episcopate. As the Bishop was consecrated in 1282, and died December, 1304, the above date will be not far from accurate. When Bishop Portissara was about to go abroad on matters connected with the well being of the State, he nominated Sir Roger de Harwedone to be one of his Vicars General during his absence. He also presented him to the rectory of Edyndon, Wilts, on the 9th September, 1303, and to the rectory of Downton in the same county, on the 18th November of the following year. This Warden was also one of the Bishop's executors, and subsequently Vicar General to his successor Bishop Henry Wodeloke, and is so named in 1312. In 1314 he became prebendary of Lichfield, and resigning the government of "Domus Dei," was succeeded by his nephew,

SIR WILLIAM DE HARWEDONE,‡ 1314, who was collated to the Wardenship by Bishop Wodeloke, on the 16th June, 1314, and the Dean of Droxford was directed to induct

---

* This was I believe, a 'Robert de Cnoel,' appointed by Bishop John de Gervase.

† Exchequer, Pedes Finium 52. Hen. III. No. 21.

‡ It was during the incumbency of this Warden, viz. in 1325, that the Chantry was founded (see Page 9).

him. In 1328 he was presented to the valuable rectory of Crondal by Bishop John de Stratford, and he continued to hold the Wardenship, together with that rectory, till his decease. His will was proved before Bishop Adam de Orleton at Farnham Castle, on the 22nd March, 1339-40.

EDMUND DE ARUNDELL, his successor, was collated on the 18th March, 1339-40, and the Prior of Southwick was ordered to induct him. He was appointed prebendary of York in 1341. At his death in 1347

JOHN DE EDYNDON, was appointed Warden of the Hospital by his uncle, Bishop William de Edyndon,* on the 12th March, 1347. He was ordained Accolite by Bishop Edyndon in the chapel of his manor at Esher on the 2nd February, 1348-49, as "*Custos Hospitalis Sancti Nicholai de Portesmouthe*"; and Subdeacon, by the same title, at Farnham Castle on the 22th March, 1349. He had after this date many other ecclesiastical appointments, including the Mastership of St. Cross Hospital, near Winchester, the rectory of Cheriton, and the Archdeaconry of Surrey. On the 12th November, 1351, the Bishop allowed him to exchange the Wardenship of St. Nicholas' Hospital for the tythes of the manor of Nuthangre with

THOMAS DE EDYNDON, who was collated on the same day to the Wardenship, and Sir John Payne, Precentor of the Church of St. Marie's, Southampton, was directed to induct him. He was ordained Subdeacon by the title "*Custos Hospitalis Sancti Nicholai de Portesmuthe*" at Esher, on the 20th September, 1354; also Deacon at Farnham Castle as such, on the 20th April, 1359. He further held successively the rectories of Wonston, Alresford, Morstead and Downton. During Bishop Edyndon's last illness, within four days of the Bishop's death, he resigned the

---

* Among the ordinations of William de Edyndon, Bishop of Winchester from 1345 to 1366, occurs the name 'Stephen atte Mule' (or 'de Molendinis' as he is also termed) who received holy orders as a professed brother in the House of St. Nicholas of Portsmouth (*frater professns in Domo Sancti Nicholai de Portesmuthe*); Subdeacon 22 September, 1347; Deacon 7 March 1348-9; and Priest on 28 March, 1349.

Wardenship viz. on the 2nd October, 1366, and the Bishop collated

JOHN DE WORMENHALE to the vacant office on the same day. Great care was taken to record the transaction with all possible minuteness :—" On the second day of October in the year of our Lord 1366, at South Waltham,* the Wardenship of the Hospital of St. Nicholas, Portesmouth, was conferred upon Master John de Wormenhale, Doctor of Laws ; being vacant by the free and spontaneous resignation of Master Thomas de Edyndon, its late Warden, made at South Waltham aforesaid, in the presence of Master Walter de Sevenhampton, Master John Corfe, John Beautree and Robert de Lincoln, witnesses, on the said second day of October of the year abovenamed ; and then at the Lord Bishop of Winchester's donation ; and the same Master John was canonically appointed Warden of the same Hospital, with all the incumbencies and other rights appertaining to the same. And Master Walter de Sevenhampton, Treasurer of Wolvesey, and Robert de Lincoln, Rector of Alverstoke were directed jointly or separately to induct him." The whole proceeding was evidently an endeavour to have all concluded before the Bishop's death. One admires the prudence of having two to induct *jointly or separately*. If one should be sick or on a journey, the chances were against both being so. "Man proposes, God disposes." The Bishop died on the sixth of October, and, the induction not having taken place, the preferment was considered vacant and the right to present fell to Edward III., who generously carried out the wish of the late Prelate. By writ of Privy Seal tested at Westminster, on the 3rd of February, 1366, the King presented John de Wormenhale to the Wardenship, "vacant and in the King's hands by reason of the vacancy of the Bishopric of Winchester ;" and he was instituted to the same on the 10th February, by Master John Beautree, the Official and Guardian of the Spiritualities of the See.

---

* Bishop's Waltham, Hants.

Master John de Wormenhale was ordained Accolite, by
Bishop Edyndon as Rector of the Church of Felpham,
Sussex, on the 18th December, 1361 ; and was appointed
Chancellor of the Diocese by the same prelate on the 11th
July, 1361, and his Official on the 30th, 1365. He was
holding these offices at the time of the Bishop's death,
who bequeathed to him £40 and a silver cup with a cover.
William de Wykeham, in London on the 22nd February,
1366-7, styles him Canon of Salisbury, and appoints him to
be his Vicar and Commissary General, an office he continued to hold until his death, together with the Wardenship
of the Hospital.

RICHARD DE WYKEHAM, his successor, was collated to
the Wardenship on the 5th July, 1376. His incumbency
was of short duration and on his decease, his kinsman

NICHOLAS DE WYKEHAM, Archdeacon of Winchester,
was appointed Warden on the 30th August, 1378, and was
presented to the rectory of Whitney, Co. Oxon., on the
same day. He subsequently had other preferments including the Archdeaconry of Wilts. He was ordained Accolite by William de Wykeham at Esher, on the 17th April,
1379, and Subdeacon by the Archbishop of Canterbury, in
the Church of Arches, on the 4th June following. In the
last year of his life he refused to pay an assessment of
6s. 8d., but afterwards, it appears, matters were arranged*
He died Archdeacon of Wilts and Warden of the Hospital
of St. Nicholas, in February or March, 1406-7.

The name of the successor of Nicholas de Wykeham,
I am unable to give for certain, as there is a gap in the
Episcopal records of the See. Good authority, I under-
stand, exists for believing that it was

JOHN FOREST, whose relative and *executor*,† Thomas
Forest, died as Official Principal of the Diocese in 1463,
making 1406, the year of Nicholas de Wykeham's death, a

---

* Exchequer Clerical Subsidy, 7 Hen. IV. $\frac{55}{72}$

† See Complaint Document Page 126.

very probable time for John Forest to enter upon the
Mastership.

*   *   *   *

THOMAS KYRKEBY, Prebendary of York, was, we
know, Warden in 1447. He was Master in Chancery from
1439 to 1447, and Master of the Rolls from 1447 to
December, 1461, and Treasurer of Exeter Cathedral; also
Prebendary of Allcannings and of Middleton in the conventional church of St. Mary's, Winchester. He died in
December, 1476. His will, dated the 7th October, 1474,
and the codicil to it on the 8th December, 1476, were
proved on the 5th January, 1479. He had resigned the
Wardenship, some years before his death.

SIR WILLIAM ELYOT, chaplain, was collated to it by
Bishop Wayneflete on the 25th February, 1462-3. He was
afterwards Archdeacon of Barnstable and Chancellor of
Salisbury. Having held the Wardenship within a few
days of thirty years, he resigned it on the 9th February,
1492-3.

JOHN RYSE was presented to the vacancy on the same
day by Dr. Thomas Langton, Bishop of Salisbury and
Postulate of the See of Winchester, and was duly instituted to the office of Warden by Cardinal Morton, Archbishop
of Canterbury, on the 11th February, 1492-3. He was a
native of Southampton, and on the 24th March, 1470,
Bishop Wayneflete granted him letters dimissory to receive
all the sacred orders from any Catholic Bishop having
faculties and grace and favour from the Apostolic See.
This John Ryse was still Warden on the 30th April, 1507,
when proceedings were instituted against him by Bishop
Fox. On a recent visitation by the Bishop, the Hospital
had been found in a ruinous and neglected state; the
Warden was therefore cited to appear before the Bishop or
his Commissary in the conventional church of St. Mary
Overy, Southwark, to show cause why all tithes, profits and
emoluments should not be sequestered. Directions were
specially given that the citation should be personally

served upon him, if possible. If not, the edict of citation, or a true copy of it, was to be publicly affixed to the door of the Hospital. These proceedings led to his resignation of the Wardenship. He afterwards became Treasurer, and subsequently Precentor of Exeter Cathedral, and died on the 2th of May, 1531.

WILLIAM STYNT, Bachelor of Laws, was now appointed Warden by Bishop Fox. He was ordained Accolite on the 29th December, 1506, and collated to the rectory of Meon Stoke on the 27th February, 1509-10; ordained Deacon on the 3rd March, 1514; and Priest on the 5th June 1515. He died holding these preferments in March, 1522.

JOHN INCENT, Doctor of Laws, Vicar General to Bishop Fox, Rector of Kimpton and late Rector of All Saints, Southampton, was collated, (the last Warden,) on the 22nd September, 1522. He was ordained Deacon on the 18th February, 1512-13; and Priest on the 12th March following. In 1524 he was presented to the Mastership of St. Cross Hospital near Winchester. He surrendered the Hospital of St. Nicholas of Portsmouth to Henry VIII. on the 2nd June, 1540, and two days afterwards was rewarded with the Deanery of St. Paul's, which he held, together with the Mastership of St. Cross Hospital and the rectory of Kimpton, till his death in 1545.

There is a very curious complaint document, which supplies valuable information about the monies of the ' Domus Dei,' and the unfaithful use thereof by one of the Masters. It also supports the opinion that John Forest was the predecessor of Thomas Kyrkeby as Warden. There is no date to the complaint, but it may be considered a writing of the end of the reign of Henry VI., or early in the days of Edward IV. Of this the reader shall judge for himself. I give a literal copy of it without the contractions:—

Exchequer Treasury of Receipt, Miscell. Books. A_{12}^{3} Chapter House fol. 237. (Inventories of Monasteries, &c.)

Fyrst that the powr pepull has nott ther bred baked and ther drynke brewed in the howsse as yt was wont for to be, and sythens this master that now ys com thether; butt the master has caryed yt, as all the brewyng vessels, to a ferme that longith to the same a myle fro the howsse, by reason wherof the powr pepull be in manner undone. Item, the meyr of the towne owght to see the weght of the bred and the goodnes of the same bred and ale. Go the corne nevr at so hye a price allveys the bred and ale to be of a goodnys; butt the master will not obey to that and so servys the powr pepull at hys pleysure, that ys, wt vere cowrse bred and smaller drynke, wiche ys contrary to all good consyens and to the foundacion wt no charyte.

Also this howsse may dispend by year of temporall land four score pounds, whereof the powr pepull has a pece of them, as syx men and syx women evry weke syx pence apece, and then a priest for hys wages. And evry fortnight they have seven lovys of bred and fyve galons of ale apece.

And the master that now ys maye dyspend 8 or 900 markes by the yer or mor, and kepyth ther no ospitalite, wiche ys a gret dekay to the towne.

Indorsed—God's howse of Portesmouthe.

Addressed—To Mr. Forest delyver this.

If we suppose, as the writing and spelling imply, that this complaint was forwarded about the end of the reign of Henry VI., the Master referred to must have been Thomas Kyrkeby, who resigned his office in the second year of Edward IV. (1462), and very probably it was his dishonest conduct which led to his leaving the Mastership. It will be observed that the paper is addressed to Mr. Forest, i.e. we may fairly believe, Thomas Forest, Bishop Waynflete's Official, the distinguished personage to whom I have already alluded, and one to whose care a formal complaint would as a matter of business be forwarded.

The following are the documents in full, which prove that Benjamin, Nicholas, and Robert, were Masters of the " Domus Dei," not long after its foundation.

I.

Augment. Off., Cart. Antiq, Vol. 21. fol. 39.

" Universis sanctæ matris Ecclesiæ filiis præsens scriptum visuris vel audituris, Willelmus de Clamorgan, filius Phillipi de Clamorgan, salutem in Domino. Noveritis me, divinæ pietatis intuitu, et pro salute animæ meæ et antecessorum et hæredum meorum dedisse, concessise, et hâc præsenti cartâ meâ confirmâsse

Deo et ecclesiæ beatæ Mariæ de Quararia, et monachis ibidem Deo servientibus, undecim solidatas quieti redditus, quas mihi consuevit Fulco do Wymering annuatim persolvere pro tenemento quod tenuit de me in Heleseye, et quicquid juris in dicto redditu et tenemento habui vel habere potui, cum omnibus ad dictum redditum et tenementum pertinentibus, absque omni retinemento. Habendas et percipiendas annuatim prædictis monachis et eorum assignatis in liberam, puram, et perpetuam elemosinam, pro dicto tenemento, a dicto Fulcone et hæredibus suis vel ab eo quicumque illud tenuerit, ad duos terminos anni scilicet, ad Pascham quinque solidos et sex denarios, et ad festum Sancti Michaelis quinque solidos et sex denarios, sine aliquâ occasione. Et ego, Wil-lelmus, et hæredes mei, hunc redditum prædictum cum dicto tenemento et omnibus pertinentiis jam dictis monachis et eorum assignatis, sicut meam liberam puram, et perpetuam elemosinam, contra omnes mortales debemus warantizare defendere, et ab omnibus exactionibus acquietare. Præterea ego, Willelmus, concessi et confirmavi sæpedictis monachis domum, quod Thomas Brico et Alicia matertera mea dederunt eisdem, videlicet, undecim solidatas redditus annui, quas percipere consuevit dictus Thomas Brico annuatim de Fulcone de Wymering, pro tenemento quod idem Fulco tenuit in Heleseye de prænominatis Thoma et Aliciâ uxore ejus. Ut autem hæc mea donacio, concessio, et confirmacio perpe-tuam firmitatem optineant, præsentem cartam sigilli mei impressione roboravi. His testibus: *Benjamin, Capellano, tunc Priore domus Dei de Portesmuwe,* Thoma de Aula, Rogero filio ejus, Ada de Comptone, Roberto de Colevilla, Petro de Cosham, Willelmo de Thantone tunc præposito de Portesmuwe, Stephano Carnifice, Willelmo Ragy, et multis aliis."

TRANSLATION.

"To all the sons of Holy Mother Church who shall see or hear the present writing, William de Clamorgan, son of Philip de Clamorgan, greeting in the Lord. Know ye that, moved by a sense of divine mercy and for the salvation of my soul and the souls of my ancestors and my heirs, I have given, granted, and by this my present charter have confirmed, to God and to the church of Blessed Mary of Quararia, and to the monks there serving God, eleven shillings of quit rent, which Fulco de Wymering has been accustomed to pay to me annually for a tenement which he held of me in Heleseye, and whatever right I had or could have in the said rent and tenement, with all things pertaining to the said rent and tenement, without any retention. To be had and to be received annually by the aforesaid monks and their assigns in free, pure, and perpetual alms, for the said tenement, from the said Fulco and his heirs, or from him whoever shall hold it, at two terms of the year, namely, at Easter five shillings and six pence, and at the feast of Saint Michael five shillings and six pence, without any abatement. And I, William, and my heirs are bound to warrant, defend, and acquit from all exactions this rent aforesaid, with the said tenement and all its appurtenances, to the now said monks and their assigns, as my free, pure, and perpetual alms, against all mortals. Besides, I, William, have granted and confirmed to the often mentioned monks, the donation which Thomas Brico and Alice my mother's sister gave to the same, namely, eleven shillings of annual rent, which the said Thomas Brico was wont to receive annually from Fulco de Wymering, for a tenement which the same Fulco held in Heleseye from the beforenamed Thomas and Alice his wife. But that this my gift, grant, and confirmation may stand firm for ever, I have strengthened the present charter with the impression of my seal. Witnesses: *Benjamin Chaplain, then Prior of the "Domus Dei" of Portesmuwe*, Thomas de Aula, Roger his son, Adam de Comptone, Robert de Colevilla, Peter de Cosham, William de Thantone, then Governor of Portesmuwe, Stephen Carnifex, William Ragy, and many others."

II.

Augment. Office, Cart. Antiq. Vol. 18. No. 266.

Sciant præsentes et futuri quod ego, Hugo Raggy de Portesmuwe, pro salute animæ meæ et animarum antecessorum et successorum meorum, dedi, concessi, et hâc præsenti cartâ meâ confirmavi Deo et ecclesiæ Beatæ Mariæ de Quarraria et monachis ibidem Deo servientibus et in perpetuam elemosinam, domum quamdam cum cellario et solario cum omnibus pertinentiis suis in villâ de Portesmuwe. Quas domos erexi in terrâ quam emi de Thoma Clerico et Aliciâ uxore ejus, filiâ Johannis Truc. Dedi, insuper, et concessi eisdem monachis quandam placeam terræ de alio tenemento meo, quæ placea jacet inter prædictam domum et portam meam, et se extendit in longitudinem a prædictâ portâ quantum dicta domus et cellarium se extendunt, et continet in latitudine duodecim pedes usque ad solarium, et indequantum dictum solarium se extendit, continet quinque pedes et dimidium, sicut divisæ manifeste ostendunt quæ positæ sunt inter me et prædictos monachos. Hanc domum cum cellario et solario et placcâ prædictâ cum omnibus pertinentiis suis, habebunt et tenebunt prædicti monachi et eorum successores, liberè, quietè, benè, pacificè et integrè, in liberam, puram et perpetuam elemosinam: ita quod illi et successores sui reddent inde annuatim fratribus Domus Dei de Portesmuwe et eorum successoribus duodecim denarios ad festum Sancti Michaelis pro omni servicio et exactione sæculari: et ego, prædictus Hugo Raggy, et hæredes mei tenemur prædictis monachis prædictæ ecclesiæ de Quarraria et eorum successoribus

prædictam domum cum cellario et solario et placeâ prædictâ et eorum pertinentiis contra omnes homines et feminas in perpetuum warantizare. Et ut hæc
mea donatio, concessio, et confirmatio firma, rata, et stabilis permaneat inperpetuum, præsentem cartam sigilli mei impressione roboravi. Hiis testibus
domino Mathæo, Priore de Suwyk, *fratre Nicholas, Priore domus Dei*, Stephano
Justiciaro tunc Præposito, Ricardo Coopertorio, Nicholas Raggy, Willelmo
Tregoth, Ada Sunewyne, Hereberto Clerico tunc serviente, Roberto Clerico, et
toto Burgomoto de Portesmuthe.

TRANSLATION.

Let people present and future know that I, Hugh Raggy, of Portsmuwe, for
the salvation of my soul and of the souls of my ancestors and successors, have
given, granted, and by this my present charter have confirmed to God and to the
church of the Blessed Mary of Quarraria, and to the monks there serving God, and
for perpetual alms, a certain house with a cellar and solar, with all its appurtenances in the town of Portesmuwe. Which houses I have built on land which I
bought from Thomas Clerk and Alice his wife, daughter of John Truc. Moreover,
I have given and granted to the same monks a certain place of land of another
my tenement, which place lies between the aforesaid house and my gate, and
extends in length from the aforesaid gate so far as the said house and cellar
extend, and contains in width 12 feet to the solar, and thence so far as the
solar extends it contains five feet and a half, as the boundaries plainly show
which are put between me and the aforesaid monks. This house with the
cellar and chamber and the place aforesaid with all their appurtenances, the
aforesaid monks and their successors shall have and shall hold, freely, quietly,
well, peaceably, and entirely, in free, pure and perpetual alms, with the condition, that they and their successors shall render thence annually, to the brethren of the 'Domus Dei' of Portesmuwe and to their successors, twelve pence at
the feast of St. Michael, for all service and secular exaction : and I, the aforesaid Hugh Raggy, and my heirs are held to warrant, to the aforesaid monks of
the aforesaid church of Quarraria and to their successors, the aforesaid house
with the cellar and solar and the place aforesaid, and their appurtenances,
against all men and women, for ever. And that this my gift, grant, and confirmation, may for ever remain firm, valid, and stable, I have strengthened the
present charter with the impression of my seal. Witnesses : Sir Matthew,
Prior of Suwyk; *brother Nicholas, Prior of Domus Dei ;* Stephen Justice
then Governor; Richard Coopertor; Nicholas Raggy; William Tregoth;

K

Adam Suneyne; Herbert Clerk, then serving, Robert Clerk, and all the court of the Borough of Portesmuthe.

No date.

III.

"Pedes Finium."   52 Hen. III. No. 21.

Hæc est finalis concordia facta in Curiâ Domini Regis apud Westmonas⁻terium in Octabis Sanctæ Trinitatis, anno regni Regis Henrici, filii Regis Johannis, quinquagesimo secundo, coram Martino de Litlebire, Magistro Rogero de Seyton et Johanne de Cobbeham, Justiciariis, et aliis Domini Regis fide-libus tunc ibi præsentibus, inter Robertum Walerand querentem per Jordanum de Wyvill, positum loco suo ad lucrandum vel perdendum, et *Robertum, Magis-trum Hospitalis de Portesmuwe* impedientem, de uno mesuagio et duabus carucatis terræ cum pertinentiis in Parvâ Kyngstone et Magnâ Kyngstone: unde placitum Warantiæ Cartæ summonitum fuit inter eos in eâdem Curiâ; scilicet quod prædictus Magister recognovit prædicta tenementa cum pertinen-tiis esse jus ipsius Roberti ut illa quæ idem Robertus habet de dono ipsius Magistri et fratrum prædicti Hospitalis: Habenda et tenenda eidem Roberto et hæredibus suis de prædicto Magistro et successoribus suis et fratribus prædicti Hospitalis inperpetuum: faciendo inde Capitalibus Dominis feodorum illorum pro prædicto Magistro et successoribus suis et fratribus prædicti Hospitalis omnia servicia quæ ad illa tenementa pertinent.   Et prædictus Magister, et successores sui, et fratres prœdicti Hospitalis warantizabunt eidem Roberto, et hæredibus suis, prædicta tenementa cum pertinentiis per prædicta servicia contra omnes homines inperpetuum.   Et pro hâc recognicione, warantiâ, fine et concordiâ, idem Robertus concessit prædicto Magistro et fratribus prædicti Hospitalis, in escambium prœdictorum tenementorum, medietatem manerii de Lasseham cum pertinentiis, cum advocatione ecclesiæ de Lasseham: habendam et tenendam eidem Magistro et successoribus suis et fratribus ejusdem Hospi-talis de prædicto Roberto et hæredibus suis inperpetuum: faciendo inde capi-talibus Dominis feodorum illorum pro prædicto Roberto et hæredibus suis omnia servicia quæ ad illa tenementa pertinent.   Et prædictus Robertus et hæredes sui warantizabunt eidem Magistro et successoribus suis et fratribus Hospitalis prædictam medietatem ejusdem manerii, et advocationem prædictæ ecclesiæ cum pertinentiis, per prædicta servicia contra omnes homines inperpe-tuum.

TRANSLATION.

This is the Final Concord made in the Court of our Lord the King at

Westminster in the Octave of the Holy Trinity, in the 52nd year of the reign of King Henry, the son of King John, before Martin Litlebire, Master Roger de Seyton and John de Cobbeham, Justices, and other faithful subjects of our Lord the King then and there present: between Robert Walerand, plaintiff, by Jordan de Wyvill appointed in his place to gain or to lose, and *Robert, Master of the Hospital of Portsmouth*, defendant; concerning a messuage and two carucates* of land with the appurtenances in Little Kyngston and Great Kyngston: whereupon a plea of *Warantia Cartæ*† was taken out between them in the same court: namely that the aforesaid Master acknowledged the aforesaid tenements with their appurtenances to be the right of the same Robert, as those which the same Robert has as a gift from the same Master and the brethren of the aforesaid Hospital: To be had and to be held by the said Robert and his heirs from the aforesaid Master and his successors and from the brethren of the aforesaid Hospital for ever: by making thence to the capital lords of those fiefs, for the aforesaid Master and his successors and the brethren of the aforesaid Hospital, all the services which pertain to those tenements. And the aforesaid Master and his successors and the brethren of the aforesaid Hospital will warrant to the same Robert and his heirs the aforesaid tenements with the appurtenances, through the aforesaid services, against all men, for ever. And for this recognition, warrant, fine, and concord, the same Robert granted, to the aforesaid Master and brethren of the aforesaid Hospital in exchange of the aforesaid tenements, the moiety of the manor of Lasseham with the appurtenances, together with the advowson of the church of Lasseham: to be had and held by the same Master and his successors, and by the brethren of the same Hospital from the aforesaid Robert and his heirs, for ever: by making thence to the capital lords of those fiefs for the aforesaid Robert and his heirs all the services which pertain to those tenements. And the aforesaid Robert and his heirs will warrant to the same Master and his successors, and to the brethren of the Hospital, the aforesaid moiety of the same manor, and the advowson of the aforesaid church with the appurtenances, through the aforesaid services, against all men, for ever.

Sutht. Dors.

---

* Carucate—about 100 acres.

† *Warantia Cartæ.* A writ for compelling the defendant to warrant lands, &c.

OLD DOCUMENTS RELATING TO THE DOMUS DEI.

THROUGHOUT the story of the "Domus Dei" it has been my endeavour to support every statement by a trustworthy authority, and I believe that, generally speaking, my efforts have been attended with success. Many of the papers consulted and used need not be given at length, as they possess no further special value, but the following are so important or so interesting, that I deem it a privilege to place them before the public.

NO. I.

Peter de Rupibus, 1204—1238.

In Cox's "Magna Britannia" are these few words about Peter de Rupibus :—

"Peter de Rupibus or La Roche, Knight. He was consecrated at Rome by the mediation of many presents. He was a man of great prudence and advised King John to despise the Pope's excommunication. He was made Lord Chief Justice in 1214, and after King John's death, Protector of the Kingdom during the minority of King Henry III. He went into the Holy Land in 1226, and, returning in 1231, died in Farnham in 1238, after having been Bishop thirty-four years."

This great Bishop not only founded the Hospital of St. Nicholas, but took the greatest possible interest in its well doing. Among the many gifts presented to it I find the following :—a payment is made in 1225, by the order of Bishop Peter de Rupibus, by the Provost or Bailiff of the Bishop's

Manor of Fareham "in liberatâ fratribus de Portesmue, pro vendicione
domorum Nicholai de Kivil datarum fratribus de ordine predicatorum per
dominum Episcopum. C solid." The good Bishop kept his ship at Portsmouth,
and various expenses relating to it are, from time to time, mentioned in the
records of his day.

NO. II.

The following is the oldest document known relating
to the "Domus Dei," and fixes very nearly the date of the
foundation of the Hospital.

Confirmation by King John of grants made to the [Hospital at Portsmouth
built in honour of the Holy Trinity and of the Blessed Virgin Mary, and of
the Holy Cross and of the Blessed Michael and all the Saints of God.

Rotuli Chartarum 16 John M. 6 (A.D. 1214-15).

Johannes Dei gratiâ Rex Angliæ, etc. Sciatis, nos, intuitu Dei et pro salute animæ
nostræ et antecessorum et successorum nostrorum et omnium Cbristi fidelium,
confirmamus hospitali ædificato apud Portesmuthe in honore Sanctæ Trinitatis et
Beatæ Mariæ Virginis et Sanctæ Crucis et Beatæ Michaelis et omnium Sanc-
torum Dei, et fratribus ibidem Deo servientibus, ad sustentationem pauperum
Christi, omnia mesuagia quæ Willelmus, Archidiaconus Tamptone, prædicto
hopitali dedit, et cartâ suâ assignavit, in puram, liberam, et perpetuam elemosinam, scilicet duo mesuagia quæ fuerunt Petri capellani in Portesmuthe, in vico
Sanctæ Mariæ, quæ jacent contigua ex parte australi ejusdem vici a mari versus
orientem, et mesuagium quod fuit Thomæ de Insula in eodem vico, et mesuagium quod fuit Ricardi de Vaus in eodem vico, et mesuagium quod fuit Eyl-
brichti di Kingestone in eodem vico, et mesuagium quod fuit Godefridi mercatoris
in vico Ingles, et mesuagium quod fuit Henrici de Cycestria in eodem vico, et
mesuagium quod fuit Sefughel de Manewode in eodem vico, et mesuagium quod
fuit Stephani de Insula in eodem vico, quæ durant ab australi angulo ejusdem
vici usque ad mare versus occidentem, et quandam terram in Portesmuthe quæ
vocatur Westwode, quam idem hospitale habet de dono burgensium de
Portesmuthe, sicut carta eorum rationabiliter testatur, et quindecim solidatas
redditus percipiendas a Ricardo Britone et hæredibus suis, quas idem hospitale habet de dono Simonis Foristarii, sicut carta ejusdem Simonis testatur.
Quare volumas et firmiter peæcipimus, quod prædictum hospitale et fratres

ibidem Deo servientes habeant et teneant prædicta mesuagia et terram et redditum prædictum, cum omnibus pertinentis suis, bene et in pace, libere et quietè et integrè, cum omnibus libertatibus et liberis consuetudinibus ad supradicta pertinentibus, sicut prædicta est et sicut cartæ prædictorum donatorum rationabiliter testantur, salvo jure nostro in omnibus, ita scilicet quod nichil quod ad nos vel donationem nostram pertineat sub donationibus supradictorum comprehendatur. Testibus: domino P. Wintoniensi Episcopo; W. Comite Arundelliæ; S. Sair de Quincy, Comite Wintoniæ; Willelmo Bruwer; R. filio Walteri; Gaufrido de Mandevill; Willelmo de Albini. Data per manum magistri Ricardi de Marisco, Cancellarii nostri, apud Havering, secundo die Novembris, anno regni nostri sextodecimo.

TRANSLATION.

John, by the grace of God, King of England, etc. Know ye, that we, in holy recognition of God, and for the salvation of our souls, and the souls of our ancestors and successors, and of all Christ's faithful people, confirm to the hospital built at Portesmuthe, in honour of the Holy Trinity, and of the Blessed Virgin Mary, and of the Holy Cross, and of the blessed Michael and all the Saints of God, and to the brethren there serving God, for the maintainance of Christ's poor, all the messuages which William, Archdeacon of Taunton, gave to the aforesaid hospital, and assigned by his charter, in pure, free, and perpetual alms : namely, two messuages which belonged to Peter the chaplain in Portesmuthe, in Saint Mary's street, which lie contiguous on the south side of the same street, from the sea towards the east; and a messuage which belonged to Thomas de Insula in the same street; and a messuage which belonged to Richard de Vaus in the same street; and a messuage which belonged to Eylbricht de Kingestone of the same street; and a messuage which belonged to Godfrey the merchant in Ingeles street; and a messuage which belonged to Richard Waln in the same street; and a messauge which belonged to Henry of Chichester in the same street; and a messuage which belonged to Sefughel de Maneswode in the same street; and a messuage which belonged to Stephen de Insula in the same street; which altogether extend from the south angle of the same street as far as the sea towards the west, and certain land in Portesmuthe which is called Westwode, which the same hospital has from the gift of the burgesses of Portesmuthe, as their charter testifies; and fifteen shillings of rent to be received from Richard Britone and his heirs, which the same hospital has by the gift of Simon Forister, as the same Simon's charter testifies. Wherefore we will and firmly command that the said Hospital and the brethren there serving God may have and hold the aforesaid messuages, and land, and the aforesaid rent, with all their appurtenances, well and in peace, freely and quietly and totally, with all liberties and free customs pertaining to the above said, as is aforesaid, and as the charters of the aforesaid donors reasonably testify, saving our right in all matters, so namely that nothing may be comprehended under the donations of the abovesaid, which may pertain to us, or our donation. Witnesses: P. Bishop of Winchester, W. Earl of Arundel, S. Earl of Winchester, Saier de Quincy, William Bruwer, R. Fitz Walter, Geoffrey du Mandevill, William de Albini. Given by the hand of Master Richard de Marisco, our Chancellor at Havering, the second day of November, in the sixteenth year of our reign.

NO. III.

Patent Roll, 20. Henry III., 1235.

At the period when the "Domus Dei" was founded, cutaneous diseases were very common, and very severe on account of the uncleanly habits of the people. The absence of vegetable food, and the custom of consuming salt meat throughout the winter tended greatly to aggravate this trouble. Bishop de Swinfield at Martinmas 1290, salted fifty-two beeves besides sheep and swine. These Houses of God must therefore have been sources of immense comfort to thousands of sufferers, and especially so to the pilgrims and strangers who landed in England afflicted with leprosy. The following grant tells of relief supplied to a poor leprous priest:—

"The King to whom all these present letters shall come. Know ye that we have granted to the Master and Brethren of the Hospital of St. Nicholas of Portesmuthe, that the house with appurtenances, which belonged to William de la Wike in Portesmue, which we granted to Philip, the leper clerk (Philippo Clerico Leproso) for his support during his life, they shall freely, and without hindrance, receive it from the same Philip, to have and to hold to the said Hospital for ever, provided that the aforesaid Master and Brethren shall minister necessaries to the same Philip from their house during his entire life, or find him the same out of their goods and profits.

Tested by the King at Reading, the 9th January, 1235."

NO. IV.

Fell Records. Writs for Payments, 19, Edward I. (1291.)

Edward &c.—Pay &c. to our beloved and faithful *John le Botiler, 30s., for the 18th and 19th years (1289-90) of our reign, to wit, 15s. for each year, which we granted him yearly to be received, &c., in recompense for three quarters of wheat which were valued yearly at 15s., and which the Master and brethren of God's house of Portsmouth received each year from the manor of Wymering, which, together with the corn aforesaid, was valued at £40 yearly, and which we granted to the same John, according to that extent, in part satisfaction of sixty librates† of land which we granted to be assigned to him for the manor of Ryngwode, which he surrendered and quit-claimed to us, &c. Witness ourself, at Westminster, the 1st December, anno 20th. (1291).

V.

Confirmacio Cantariæ de Portesmuthe pro animabus Johannæ Plokenet et Roberti di Harewedone.

Registro Episcopali Domini Johannis de Stratford Wyntoniensis Episcopi Fol. 14.

Universis sanctis matris eclesie filiis presentes litteras inspecturis. Johannes, permissione divinâ, Wyntoniensis Episcopus,—salutem in domino sempiternam. Noveritis, nos, litteras infrascriptas, non cancellatas, non rasas, nec suspectas, vidisse & inspexisse, sub continenciâ infrascriptâ. Omnibus sancte matris eclesie filiis presentes litteras visuris vel audituris, Willielmus de Harewedone, Custos domus sancti Nicholai de Portesmuthia, ac ejusdem loci Confratres,—salutem in domino. Quoniam largicione piâ domine Johanne, sororis et heredis domini Alani Plokenet defuncti, domine de Kylpeke, quondam uxoris domini Henri de Bohun, temporibus modernis ab eâdem recepimus, multa bona. Considerantes eciam quod dicta domina Johanna nobis dicto Willielmo de Harwedone, Custodi domus predicte, Fratribus & Sororibus ejusdem domus, totum jus suum & clamium quod habuit vel aliquo modo

---

*This John le Botiler was the son and heir of John le Botiler, Knt. He died in 1309, and was buried in Wymering Church. There was a dispute between the Vicar of Wymering, and the Prior and Convent of Southwyke, as to his horse and armour, claimed as a mortuary.

†A *librate of land* (librata terræ) was land worth £1 a year, the number of acres depending on the quality of the land.

habere potuit in manerio de Berughtona in comitatu Suthamptonie, pro se
suisque heredibus, relaxabit, et inperpetuum quietum clamavit. Nos, volentes
eidem juxta possibilitatem nostras vices rependere repensivas, concedimus
eidem pro nobis et successoribus nostris inperpetuum, quod nos & successores
nostri unum Capellanum ydoneum nobis & Custodi de Portesmuthe qui pro
tempore fuerit, per dictam dominam Johannam & heredes suos presentandum,
admittemus in societatem nostram, ac sustentabimus & tractabimus,sicut unum
de Cappellanis domus nostre, dabimusque eidem Cappallano in omnibus singulis
annis, sicut uni de cappellanis domus nostre predicte. Qui quidem cappellanus
divinis officiis in domo nostrâ sicut alii nostri cappellani debebit interesse, et
singulis diebus divina officia pro animabus dicte Domine Johanne, Domini
Roberti de Harwedone, quondam Custodis domus predicte, ac etiam pro animabus domini Willielmi de Harwedone predicti, nunc Cnstodis ejusdem, omni-
umque parentum, amicorum predictorum defunctorum inperpetuum celebrabit.
Et dictus Capellanus, nobis & Custodi qui pro tempore fuerit, in canonicis
mandatis & licitis obediet reverenter. Eodem vero Cappellano cedente vel
decedente vel aliâ ex causâ legittimâ amoto, loco ipsius dicta domina Johanna
& heredes sui nobis & custodi, qui pro tempore fuerit, alium ut promittitur
ydoneum presentabunt. Et dictus Custos & successores sui ad ipsorum presen-
tationem dictum cappellanum unum post alium successivè inperpetuum substi-
tuent & admittent. In cujus rei testimonium Sigillum dicti Custodis fecimus
hiis apponi. Data apud Portesmuthe vicessimo die mensis Januarii, anno
Domini Millesimo, CCCmo XXVto. Et anno regni Regis Edwardi decimo
nono.

Nos vero, Johannes, permissione divinâ Wyntoniensis Episcopus, omnia &
singula in dictis litteris contenta, prout superius exprimuntur quatenus ad nos
attinet, rata, grata habentes pariter & accepta, ipsâ auctoritate nostrâ pontificali
confirmamus. In cujus rei testimonium sigillum nostrum presentibus duximus
apponendum. Data apud Waltham VIII. kalendis Februarii, anno Domini
Millesimo CCCmo, XXVto. et consecracionis nostre Tercio.

TRANSLATION.

Confirmation of the Chantry of Portsmouth for the souls of Johanna Plokenet
and Robert de Harewedone.

To all the sons of Holy Mother Church who shall inspect the present letters, John, by divine permission, Bishop of Winchester,—eternal salvation in
the Lord. Know ye, that we have seen and inspected the under-written deed,
not cancelled, not erased, nor suspected, in the terms following :—To all the

sons of Holy Mother Church who shall see or hear the present deed, William de Harewedone, Warden of the house of St. Nicholas of Portesmuthia, and the brethren of the same place,—greeting in the Lord.   Whereas by the pious liberality of the Lady Johanna, sister and heir of Sir Alan Plokenet, deceased, Lady of Kylpeke, formerly wife of Sir Henry de Bohun, we have received from the same, in recent times many gifts: considering also that the said Lady Johanna, for herself and her heirs, has released and for ever quit-claimed, to us the said William de Harwedene, Warden of the said house, and to the brothers and sisters of the same house, all her right and claim, which she had, or in any manner could have, in the manor of Broughton, in the county of Southampton : We, being desirous, according to our ability, to make a just and suitable return to the same, concede to the same, for us and our successors for ever, that we and our successors, will admit into our society a Chaplain suitable to us and to the Warden of the Hospital of St. Nicholas of Portsmouth for the time being, and will sustain and treat him as one of the chaplains of our house, and will give to such chaplain yearly as to any one of the chaplains of our house aforesaid. And the said chaplain for his part, as our other chaplains, shall be obliged to be present at the divine offices in our house, and shall for ever celebrate daily the divine offices for the souls of the said Lady Johanna, of Sir Robert de Harewedone (formerly Warden of the aforesaid house) and for the souls of Sir William de Harewedone aforesaid, now Warden of the same, and of all parents and friends of the aforesaid deceased. And the said chaplain shall reverently obey us and the warden who may be for the time, in all canonical and lawful commands. And on the same chaplain withdrawing, or dying, or from any other ligitimate cause being removed, the said Lady Johanna and her heirs shall present to us, and to the Warden who may be for the time, another fitting one in his place, as is before set forth : and the said Warden and his successors for ever at their presentation will substitute and admit the said chaplain, one after the other successively. In testimony of which matter we have caused the seal of the said Warden to be affixed to these letters. Dated at Portesmuthe, 20th day of January, A.D., 1325, and the 19th year of the reign of King Edward, the son of King Edward.

Now we,*John, by divine permission, Bishop of Winchester, by our pontifical authority confirm all and singular contained in the said letters, as they are above expressed, so far as to us appertaineth, accounting them alike valid,

---

* John Stratford obtained the See in 1322, and presided over it ten years ; four of them he was Chancellor of England. In 1332 he was removed to Canterbury.

agreeable, and acceptable. In testimony of which matter we have considered that our seal should be affixed to these presents. Dated at Waltham, 8 Kalends Febr., (25th of January) A.D., 1325, and the 3d of our Translation.

THE MURDER OF ADAM MOLEYNS.

At a critical period of the reign of Henry IV. we find that a distinguished Bishop of Chichester, Adam Moleyns was cruelly murdered, and that the murder took place close to the "Domus Dei" of Portsmouth. The questions at once arise, who was Adam Moleyns and what was the cause of his murder. That he was a man of good family is certain. Gedler in his 'Universal Lexicon' mentions him as one of the Molineux family, but, strangely enough, by a clerical error he entitles him Adam, Bishop of *Chester* instead of Chichester. In a list of the Bishops of Chichester, in the same work, Adam Moleyns is found in his proper place. Dean Hook, whom to know is to love and revere, gives in a note of Vol. V. Page 160, "Lives of the Archbishops of Canterbury," nearly all that is known of this ill-fated man :—

"ADAM MOLEYNS OR MOLINEUX. The time and place of his birth are unknown, we only know that he was a Doctor in the Civil Law ; that he was Archdeacon of Taunton in 1440 ; held a Stall at York in 1441; that in the March of that year he became Dean of St. Burians, and in the October Dean of Salisbury. Having been formerly clerk or secretary to the Privy Council,* he was in 1444 made Keeper of the Privy Seal. He was consecrated to the See of Chichester at Lambeth, on the 6th of January, 1446, and held the living of Harietsham in Kent *in Commendam.* He was a benefactor to the See, bestowing on

---

* Adamus Molins, legnm Doctor, Sarisburiensis Decanus, necnon et S. Birini in Cornubiâ, et Regiorum Consiliariorum quandoque Amanuensis, consecratus est mense Novembri 1445, et privati Sigilli Custos mox constitutus. Occisus est Portesmuthae à nautis quibusdam, ad id sceleris perpetrandum per Richardum Ducem Eboracensem summissis ac subornatis, Junü nono 1449. Dedit ille ad ornatum summi altaris in Ecclesiâ suâ vela quaedam ex holoserico pretiosissima, coloris quem vulgò dicimus Crimosin, qui antiquitus (ut credo) purpureus fuit. (Godwin de Praesulibus Angliae. Hen. VI, 24)

the Cathedral some rich vestments, and procuring for the
lands of the Bishop an exemption from the jurisdiction of
the Court of Admiralty. He acted as an assessor of the
Archbishop of Canterbury to try Elinor Cobham, Duchess
of Gloucester, for witchcraft. In 1443 he accompanied
the Earl of Suffolk into France, to treat of the marriage of
Henry VI. with Margaret of Anjou. He naturally shared
in the unpopularity of the Suffolk party,* increased by this
royal marriage. He was one of the Commissioners at
Tours to negotiate a truce with France, which was pro-
longed to the year 1449. He was disgusted with the state
of public affairs and determined to quit the country and live
abroad. He resigned his See, it is generally supposed, for
this purpose. He certainly received a pension of 500 marks.
When preparing for his voyage at Portsmouth, he was basely
murdered in a boat by some seamen.† It was reported that
this murder was committed at the instigation of Richard,
Duke of York. This was probably a mere scandal but it
follows, that, if such were the case, Moleyns was leaving
England, not, as it was said, that he might retire from public life, but to effect some political intrigue. The Duke of
York was not a man likely to doom anyone unnecessarily
to death, though in the party violence of the day, little
regard was paid to the sacredness of human life."

The good Dean, with his wonted charity, is gentle to
all, but, while with him we admire the Bishop's brilliant
talents and his steady devotion to a miserably weak Sovereign, we cannot but believe that from first to last he was

---

* 'Adamus Molendinus, nobilis parentum stemmate, ingenio nobilior,
virtutum vero calculo nobilissimus, bonus, ut fama prædicat, literas incredibili
quodam candore fovebat. Quare operæ pretium erit, *Hermanni Schedelii*,
historiographi, de eo judicium subjicere :—"Inter quos et amicus noster *Adam
de Molineux*, secreti regis signaculi et custos et literarum cultor, amisso capite,
truncatus jacuit." Hæc ille. Causa ejus mortis civile bellum, hinc *Henricianis*
hinc *Eadveardinis* de imperio contendentibus.' (Leland Comm de Script. Brit.
page 454).
"Nobiles viri quamplures necati, nec sacerdotio præditis parsus est
(Dux Eboracensis). Inter quos et amicus noster Adam Molynes, secreti regis
signaculi custos et literarum cultor, amisso capite truncátus jacuit." (Schedel
Liber Cronicarum, Nurenberg, 1493, fo. 288.)
† It is evident from the 'Process' that Moleyns was not murdered in a boat.

a zealous, and at times, an unscrupulous politician; and so during "the convulsive and bleeding agony of the feudal power," made for himself a very dangerous position. As Bishop of Chichester, he was the King's Confessor; as Keeper of the Privy Seal, he was a prominent state servant; and circumstances had in many other ways rendered him an object of hatred to the York party. But his chief crime was, that with the "crafty avaricious and despotic Suffolk," he had headed the Queen's party. The alliance ended, we know, in the murder of both. Suffolk, when the cry was loud and against those who had given up France, basely accused the prelate of advising the surrender of the French province. The cowardly sacrifice, of one who had been a faithful ally, saved the ambitious noble only for a little moment. Moleyns was murdered on the 9th of January, 1449, and in the May following Suffolk, on the high seas, was seized as a traitor, beheaded with a rusty sword, and his body cast contemptuously on the sands of Dover.

But, in the story of the "Domus Dei," the murder of Bishop Moleyns is chiefly interesting as connected with the 'Process,' held more than 50 years after, for the absolution of the inhabitants of Portsmouth from the sentence of excommunication. Other Bishops have been murdered in England, but no old document remains setting forth proceedings similar to those noted in the Register preserved in Winchester Cathedral. Walter de Stapledon, Bishop of Exeter, was unhorsed at the north gate of St. Paul's, taken to Cheapside, and there stript and beheaded on the 15th of October, 1326. Archbishop Sudbury was murdered by the insurgent populace on the 14th of June, 1381. And William Ayscough, Bishop of Salisbury, was dragged out of the Church of Edington, in Wilts, and murdered, on the 29th of June, 1450. But no Process remains to tell how the Church dealt with those who perpetrated these dark crimes.

The following paper is therefore, I believe, unique of

its kind, and I publish it with confidence, because I feel sure it will be read by many with great pleasure.

NO. VI.

Processus habitus apud Portysmouthe.

E. Registro Domini Domini Ricardi Fox, Wintoniensis Episcopi, Tom. 2. Fol. 88—90.

RICARDUS, permissione divinâ, Wintoniensis Episcopus, dilectis nobis in Christo, Abbati Monasterii de Tychefeld, ordinis premonstratensis, et Priori prioratus de Suthwyk ordinis Sancti Augustini, nostre Wintoniensis diocesis, ac Magistro Johanni Dowman, legum doctori, nostro in spiritualibus vicario generali,—salutem, graciam et benedictionem. CUM bone memorie dominus Adam Molens, legum doctor, Cicestrensis Episcopus, per inhabitantes de Portysmouthe mortem subierit temporalem, cujus pretextu ipsi inhabitantes et tota eorum sequela majoris excommunicationis sentenciam et Dei omnipotentis indignationem incurrebant, et terra eorum multas passa est ruinas et jacturas; inhabitantes ejusdem ville moderni, volentes ab hujusmodi vinculo liberari et penitenciam condignam et legitimam in hâc parte subire, et de Dei omnipotentis mesericordiâ plenius confisi, nobis, quatinus de remedio eis in hâc parte providere oportuno dignaremur, instanter et humiliter supplicarunt.

Nos, igitur, Ricardus, Episcopus antedictus, saluti animarum eorundem inhabitancium providere cupientes, cum ecclesia nemini redeunti claudit gremium : ad inquirendum juxta juris exigenciam de hujusmodi delicto, et inhabitantes predictos à sentenciâ hujusmodi absolvendum et penitenciam salutarem et condignam eis imponendam et injungendam; ceteraque omnia alia et singula facienda, exercenda, et expedienda, que in premissis et circa ea necessaria fuerint seu quomodolibet oportuna, vobis conjunctim et divisim vices nostras tenore presencium committimus, et plenam in Domino concedimus potestatem; vosque commissarios nostros ad suprascripta conjunctim et divisim ordinamus, constituimus et deputamus per presentes. In cujus rei testimonium sigillum nostrum presentibus apponi fecimus. Datum nostro sub sigillo, primo die mensis Aprilis, Anno Domini, Millesimo Quingentesimo Octavo. Et nostre translationis anno Septimo.

Sexto die, mensis Aprilis hâc septimâ ante meridiem ejusdem diei, anno domini millessimo quingentesimo octavo, indictione undecimâ, pontificatus sanctissimi in Christo patris et domini nostri domini Julii, divinâ providenciâ eo nomine pape Secundi anno Quinto, parrochiani ville de Portysmouthe, Wintoniensis diocesis, utriusque sexus, in multitudine copiosâ una cum domino Roberto

Adam, vicario de Portysmouthe prædictâ, superpelicio induto, ad pulsationem campano in ecclesiâ parrochiali de Portysmouthe antedictâ factam, ad eandem ecclesiam parrochialem venerunt. Et quia Janue ipsius ecclesie, ob causas Commissarios infrascriptas moventes, clause fuerant, nunciatum fuit eis ut ad ecclesiam nuncupatam Domum Dei de Portysmouthe accederent. Quibus ad et in dictam ecclesiam congregatis, verbo Dei per Religiosum virum, Fratrem Hugonem, ordinis observanciarum, ville Southamptonie dicte diocesis proponito, causâque eorum congregationis declaratâ, venerabiles viri, Magistri Johannes Dowman, legum doctor, Reverendi in Christo patris et domini domini Ricardi permissione divinâ, Wintoniensis Episcopi vicarius in spiritualibus generalis, domini Thomas Oke, Abbas Monasterii de Tychefeld, dicte Wintoniensis diocesis, ordinis premonstratensis, et Thomas Kent Prioratus de Suthewyk, ejusdem diocesis, ordinis Sancti Augustini Prior, ipsius Reverendi patris Commissarii in hâc parte sufficienter et legitimè deputati, stolis induti, commissione dicti Reverendi patris eisdem Commissariis factâ eis presentâ et publicè perlectâ, onereque Commissionis hujusmodi in eos acceptato et per ipsos juxta tenorem ejusdem procedendum fore decreto, cum virgis in eorum manibus, dictos vicarium et parrochianos, propter facinoris enormitatem per inhabitantes dicte ville in bone memorie dominum Adam Cicestrensem Episcopum extra dictam ecclesiam nuncupatam domum Dei inhumaniter et manibus sacrilegis, nono die mensis Januarii, Anno domini Mellessimo　　　*

*　　　　*　　　　　per inhabitantes hujusmodi abstractum, et in villâ de Portysmouthe predictâ morti crudeli suppositum, commissi et perpetrati ad prefatam ecclesiam nuncupatam domum Dei, tanquam inhabiles et inidoneos ad essendum in ecclesiâ Dei, fugerunt et excluserunt. Qui, sic exclusi, ad locum delicti in quâ idem Dominus Adam, Cicestrensis Episcopus, mortem subiit, festinanter iverunt. Quibus ad locum delicti existentibus prelibatus Frater Hugo consuluit ut ipsi, considerato delicto, pedibus nudis et tibiis, qui pati potuerint, ad valvas occidentales ecclesie parrochialis de Portysmouthe transirent se, ibidem more penitentum in precibus prostraturi, ac penitentiam et absolutionem eis impendi et ingressum ecclesie eis indulgeri petituri. Et incontinente ipsi domini Commissarii una cum Fratribus Roberto Goffe de Suthwyke predictâ, Suppriore, Thoma Elton ejusdem loci canonico, Thoma Blankpayne de Tychefeld priore, Thoma Godewyn, Willielmo Lambe, Thoma Godfrey ejusdem loci canonicis, in ordine sacerdotali constitutis; dominis Willielmo Osmunderlawe de Wydley rectore, Stephano Soyward de Portesey, Edwardo Yong de Portchestur, vicariis; Johanne Creke dicte ecclesie nuncupate domus Dei et Thoma Belle de Alverstoke capellanis; Thoma Mershe de Suthwyk et Thoma Monmouthe de Tychefelde noviciis, et ceteris predictis, ad

ecclesiam parrochialem predictam iverunt. Et postquam dictam ecclesiam intra-
verant prelibatus dominus Robertus Adam, de Portysmouthe vicarius, et parrochiani hujusmodi, pedibus et tibiis pro majori parte eorundem parrochianorum
nudis, precibus insistentibus una cum dicto Fratre Hugone ad dictas valvas
occidentales accesserunt et se humiliter ibidem prostraverunt. Et, ostiis ipsius
ecclesie de mandato ipsorum Commissariorum ut prefertur undique clausis,
dictis vicario et parrochianis extra ostium occidentale dicte ecclesie parrochialis, in cimiterio ejusdem, more penitentum prostratis, prelibatus Frater
Hugo et dictus vicarius, nomine suo et singulorum suorum parrochianorum, ad
dictum ostium occidentale pulsarunt, et sibi ac parrochianis hujusmodi dictum
ostium aperiri et ingressum sive aditum ecclesie ac penitenciam et absolutionem
lamentabiliter pecierunt. Quibus, pulsatione et petitione sic factis, iidem domini
commissarii intus rogaverunt quisnam ibidem esset. Qui quidem Frater Hugo
et vicarius, nomine suo et parrochianorum suorum singulorum, responderunt,
peccatores adesse et veniam a Deo pro injectione manuum violentarum in dominum Adam Cicestrensem Episcopum per inhabitantes ipsius ville de Portysmouthe, dictonono die mensis Januarii, factâ, petere et penitenciam subire
paratos. Qui quidem commissarii eisdem Fratri Hugoni ac vicario et parrochianis responderunt, quod dubitarunt an potuerunt juxta petitionem factam
concedere, eo quod sanguis ipsius episcopi mortui vindictam contra taliter
delinquentes clamitavit ante dominum testantibus quatuor elementis, Aiere videlicet, Aquâ, Igne et Terra.—Primo Aiere, eo quod pestilenciis et aliis infirmitatibus
plures inhabitancium ibidem pro majori parte fuerunt mortui, et terra eorum
non fuit fertilis sed reddita sterilis. Secundo, Aqua, eo quod mercatores, ob
dictum facinus et propter infamiam inhabitancium hujusmodi, cum eorum
navibus ad portum ibidem applicare noluerunt, et ex eo quod terre eorum in
diversis partibus aquis absorpte et devastate fuerunt, et inhabitantes ibidem
quam plurima alia damna et incommoda per aquam sustinuerunt. Tercio,
Igne, eo quod edificia illius ville et aliarum convicinarum pluries fuerunt igne
consumpta. Quarta, Terrâ, eo quod eorum terre non produxerunt fructus ut
prius fecerunt et ex eo quod gramen, in loco ubi dictus Episcopus passus fuit
cum terrâ ex utrâque parte, marescit et non virescit, et sic habitationes eorum
deserte fuerunt, adeo quod vix aliquos, qui eas inhabitare voluerunt, invenire
potuerunt, et sic eorum edificia ruine dedita fuerunt, et inhabitantes ibidem per-
petuâ notati infamiâ. Et ob illas et plures alias causas non fuerunt, nec esse
potuerunt habiles, nec poterant addmitti ad intrandum ecclesiam. Qui, adhuc
prostrati, humiliter et lamentabiliter pecierunt ingressum ecclesie affirmando quod
ob causas et rationes per dictum fratrem Hugonem exponitas, penitentibus et

penitenciam agere et ad ecclesiam redire volentibns ecclesia non claudit gremium, et assuerunt se vello peragere penitenciam quamcunque eis injungendam. Quibus responsionibus sic factis, dicti domini commissarii dixerunt, quod voluerunt descendere ad locum delicti, et, si invenerint eos penitentes et paratos opere ad complendum id quod verbo asseruerunt, tunc ipsi commissarii officium eorum ipsis impartirentur, et sic ipsi, vicarius et parrochiani, ad locum delicti more penitentum redierunt. Quibus precedentibus, et ipsis dominis commissariis cum sacerdotibus predictis superpelliciis et stolis indutis, aperto eis ostro occidentali predicto, paulò post sequentibus, iidem domini commissarii, cum advenerint dictum locum delicti, et eos in precibus humiliter prostratos et penetenciam ac absolutionem lamentabiliter petentes invenerint, ut ipsi parrochiani possent majorem graciam habere ad penetenciam recipiendam et commissarii ad injungendum, et eos absolvendum, voluerunt quod, ibidem prostrati, orationem dominicam ter quinquies et cimbolum apostolorum trinâ vice dicerent, dummodo iidem commissarii cum hujusmodi sacerdotibus, et aliis litteratis quamplurimis septem psalmos penitenciales genuflexo ibidem dicerent. Et incontinente dictis septem psalmis per prefatos dominos commissarios inceptis, cum perventum fuerit ad psalmum '*Miserere mei Deus*,' iidem domini commissarii dictos vicarium et parrochianos* [virgis disciplinaverunt, ipsis disciplinantibus dicentibus versus '*Miserere mei Deus secundum magnam mesericordiam tuam*,' et ipsis disciplinatis, per se vel alios, versus, '*Et secundum multitudinem miserationum tuarum dele iniquitatem meam*, respondentibus.] Quibus sic disciplinatis ac dictis septem psalmis finitis, domini commissarii predicti injunxerunt parrochianis quod in eodem loco delicti erigerent crucem. Et quamcitò commodè potuerint ibidem construerent capellam, in quâ pro animabus dicti domini Ade Episcopi defuncti et omnium fidelium defunctorum Christifideles ad altissimum preces fundere possent. Et quod in die parasceves tunc proximo sequentis, et sic eorum in dictâ parochiâ futuri successores parrochiani, singulis annis in die parasceves nudis pedibus et tibiis adirent dictum locum, pro dicti episcopi et omnium fidelium defunctorum animabus ad Deum oraturi et oblationes ibidem juxta vires facultatum suarum facturi. Et quod, infra triennium extunc proximo sequens singuli parrochiani hujusmodi, seu saltem certi eorundem parrochianorum secundum discretionem inhabitancium, ibidem peregre proficiscerentur ad locum in

---

* The Scribe has evidently made several mistakes when copying, as the wording of the MS. is quite unintelligible. It is as follows :—" virgis disciplinaverunt ipsis disciplinaverunt ipsis disciplinantes dicente versus '*Miserere mei Deus secundum magnam misericordiam tuam*' et ipsis disciplinatis, per se vel alios, versus '*Et secundum multitudinem miserationum tuarum dele iniquitatem meam*' respondente." The alterations made above express, I believe, what was intended by the drawer up of the Process.

quo idem Adam Episcopus defunctus tumulatur, ibidem veniam nomine omnium inhabitancium et pro ipsis petituri, et pro ipsius Episcopi defuncti et omnium fidelium defunctorum animabus oraturi et oblationes facturi. Necnon quod ipsi parrochiani moderni, et eorum in parrochiâ predictâ successores parrochiani futuri, seu saltem de quolibet domicilio eorundem ad minus unus in eodem loco delicti, nono die mensis Januarii, quo idem Episcopus subiit mortem, cum candelis cereis in eorum manibus ardentibus, pro animabus dicti defuncti et omnium fidelium defunctorum singulis annis orationes ad Deum funderent et anniversarium servarent et quod in exequiis et missâ 'de Requiem' personaliter interessent. Et ulterius, iidem domini Commissarii injunxerunt dictis vicario et parrochianis quod redirent ad dictum ostium occidentale ecclesie parrochialis de Portysmouthe, ibidem se humiliter prostraturi, ac disciplinam iterum et penitenciam aliam ac absolutionem recepturi. Et incontinente iidem parrochiani more penitentum, dictis vicario et ceteris presbiteris ac clericis, cum cruce erectâ, thuribulariis et cereforariis eos precedentibus, letaniam decantantibus, Commissariis predictis cum virgis in eorum manibus eos sequentibus, ad dictum ostium occidentale redierunt. QUOS quidem vicarium et parrochianos sic prostratos, iidem Commissarii, precibus et orationibus certis per eos prius dictis, disciplinaverunt, et ipsos a sentenciâ excommunicationis, quam incurrerant, et primo generaliter, et deinde ipsos pro majori parte in specie, absolverunt. Et insuper ipsi Commissarii injunxerunt dictis vicario et parrochianis, quatinus ipsi cum candelis accensis in eorum manibus intrarent ecclesiam, et misse 'de Requiem' pro animâ ipsius Episcopi defuncti et animabus omnium fidelium defunctorum et 'de Sancto Spiritu' decantande, interressent et oblationes ad easdem Missas juxta eorum posse (?) facerent, que oblationes provenientes servarentur ad edificationem dicte capelle. Etiam iidem Commissarii injunxerunt eisdem vicario et parrochianis, quod peragerent quamcunque penitenciam per prefatum Reverendum dominum, Ricardum Wintoniensem Episcopum, ipsis imposterum injungendam. Et dum misse, prima videlicet 'de Requiem,' per Abbatem, et secunda 'de Sancto Spiritu,' per Priorem predictum, ad summum Altare decantate fuerant, major pars parrochianorum tempore offertorii utriusque misse oblationes fecit. Et ultra illas duas missas, diverse alie misse private, quarum certe fuerunt de quinque vulneribus et certe de nomine Jhesu ad alia altaria in Navi ipsius ecclesie parrochialis celebrate fuerunt, parrochianis predictis singulis missis interessentibus. Quibus missis omnibus et singulis sic celebratis, iidem commissarii, una cum presbiteris et clericis predictis, Letaniam videlicet "Salve festa dies" decantantes, parrochianis eos sequentibus, villam de Portysmouthe predictâ in solemni processione circuierunt. Et cum pervenerant ad locum delicti, ibidem sisterunt gradum, et psalmo 'de profundis' cum oratione pro anima ipsius Episcopi defuncti et animabus omnium fidelium defunctorum, per eosdem Commissarios ac presbiteros et clericos ibidem dicto, ipsi Commissarii ac presbiteri et clerici residuum Letanie hujusmodi decantantes, parrochianis eos sequentibus, ad dictam ecclesiam parrochialem processionaliter redierunt. Et processione finitâ dictus Magister, Johannes Dowman, intimavit eisdem parrochianis et ceteris ibidem presentibus, quod dictus Reverendus pater, omnibus dictum locum visitantibus, et ibidem stationes facientibus psalmum ' de profundis,' aut orationem dominicam quinquies cum salutacione angelicâ quinquies et simbalo Apostolorum, ibidem pro animabus dicti defuncti et omnium fidelium defunctorum dicentibus, tociens quotiens quadraginta dies indulgencio concessit. Et deinde, post meridiem ejusdem sexti diei Aprilis, iidem Commissarii ac presbiteri et clerici solemnes exequias, pro animâ dicti Episcopi defuncti et animabus omnium fidelium defunctorum, in eâdem ecclesiâ parrochialis de Portysmouthe decantaverunt, majori parte parrochianorum predictorum ibidem interressente.

TRANSLATION.

Process held at Portsmouth.

Richard, by divine permission, Bishop of Winchester, to our beloved in Christ the Abbot of the Monastery of Tychefeld, of the Premonstratensian Order, and the Prior of the Priory of Suthwyk, of the Order of St. Augustine, of our diocese of Winchester, and Master John Dowman, Doctor of Laws, our Vicar General in spiritualities Greeting, Grace, and Benediction. Whereas the Lord Adam, of good memory, Doctor of Laws, Bishop of Chichester, suffered temporal death through the inhabitants of Portysmouthe, on account of which the inhabitants and all their followers incurred the sentence of the greater excommunication and the anger of Almighty God, and their land has suffered many ruins and losses: the present inhabitants of the same town, desiring to be freed from such a bond, and on this behalf to submit to a fitting and legitimate penance, and trusting more fully in the mercy of Almighty God, earnestly and humbly supplicated us, that we would deign to provide a fitting remedy for them on this behalf. We therefore, Richard, the Bishop aforesaid, desiring to provide for the salvation of the souls of the same inhabitants, since the church closes her bosom to no one returning to her, by the tenor of these presents commit to you conjointly and singly our offices, and grant you full power in the Lord to enquire according to the demands of justice concerning such crime, and to absolve the aforesaid inhabitants from such sentence, and to impose and

L2

enjoin on them a salutary and fitting penance, and to do, exercise, and effect
all and singular other matters which, in the premises and respecting them, may
be necessary or in any manner opportune; and we ordain, constitute, and depute
you, conjointly and separately, by these presents, our Commissaries for the purposes above written. In testimony of which matter we have caused our seal
to be affixed to these presents. Given, under our seal, on the first day of the
month of April, in the year of our Lord one thousand five hundred and eight,
and in the seventh year of our translation.

On the sixth day of the month of April, at seven o'clock in the forenoon
of that day, in the year of Our Lord, 1508, the 11th Indiction, the 5th year of
the pontificate of the most holy father in Christ and Lord, our Lord Julius, by
Divine Providence Pope, the second of that name, the parishioners of the town
of Portysmouthe, in the diocese of Winchester, in a great multitude of each sex,
together with Sir Robert Adam,* vicar of Portysmouthe aforesaid, vested in
a surplice, at the tolling of a bell in the parish church of Portysmouthe aforesaid, came to the same parish church. And because, on account of the causes
undermentioned moving the Commissaries, the doors of the church had been
closed, it was announced to them that they should go to the church called the
'Domus Dei' of Portysmouthe. To whom assembled at and in the said church,
the word of God being set forth by the Religious man, brother Hugh, of the
order of Observantists of Southampton in the said diocese, and the cause of
their congregation being declared, the venerable men, Master John Dowman,
Doctor of Laws, Vicar General in spiritualities of the Reverend Father in
Christ and Lord, the Lord Richard, by divine permission Bishop of Winchester,
Sir Thomas Oke, Abbot of the monastery of Tychefelde in the said diocese of
Winchester, of the Premonstratensian order, and Sir Thomas Kent, Prior of
the Priory of Suthewyk in the same diocese, of the order of St. Augustine,
Commissaries of the same Reverend Father sufficiently and lawfully appointed
on this behalf, vested in stoles, the commission of the said Reverend Father
made to the said Commissaries being presented to them and publicly read
through, and they, having taken on them the burden of such commission, and
resolved that they would proceed according to the tenor of the same, with rods
in their hands drove out and excluded, as disqualified and unfit to be in the
church of God, the said vicar and parishioners, on account of the enormity of
the crime committed and perpetrated, at the said church called the Domus Dei,

---

* Sir Roger Adam was instituted to the Vicarage of Portsmouth 5th May, 1507,
and to that of Portsea on the 29th November, 1509, whereupon he resigned that of
Portsmouth.

by the inhabitants of the said town against the Lord Adam, of good memory, Bishop of Chichester; who was inhumanly and with sacrilegious hands dragged by the inhabitants out of the said church, and in the town of Portsmouth aforesaid subjected to a cruel death, on the 9th of January, in the year of our Lord One Thousand　＊　＊　＊　＊　Who, thus excluded, went in haste to the place of the crime in which the same Lord Adam, Bishop of Chichester suffered death. To whom, being at the place of the crime, the above mentioned brother Hugh counselled, that, having considered the crime, they who could suffer to do so should pass with naked feet and legs to the western doors of the parish church of Portysmouthe, there in the manner of penitents to prostrate themselves in prayers, and to seek penance and absolution to be bestowed on them, and admission to the church to be granted them. And thereupon, the same lords Commissaries, together with brothers Robert Goffe of Suthewyk aforesaid Subprior, Thomas Elton of the same place, Canon, Thomas Blankpayne of Tychefelde Prior, Thomas Godewyn, William Lambe, Thomas Godfrey of the same, Canons, arranged in sacerdotal order; Sir William Osmunderlawe of Widley, Rector, Sir Stephen Seyward of Portesey, Sir Edward Yong of Portchestur, Vicars, Sir John Creke of the said church called the Domus Dei and Sir Thomas Belle of Alverstoke, Chaplains, Thomas Mershe of Suthewyk and Thomas Monmouthe of Tychefelde, novices, and the others before named, went to the aforesaid parish church. And, after they had entered the said church, the above mentioned Sir Robert Adam of Portysmouthe the Vicar, and the parishioners thereof, the feet and legs of the same parishioners for the most part being naked, instant in prayer, went, together with the said brother Hugh, towards the said western doors, and there humbly prostrated themselves. And the doors of the church, by the command of the Commissaries, as is before stated, being closed on all sides, the said Vicar and parishioners on the outside of the western door of the said parish church, in the cemetery of the same, being prostrate in the manner of penitents, the before mentioned brother Hugh and the said Vicar, in his own name and in that of everyone of his parishioners, knocked at the said western door and lamentably prayed for the said door to be opened, and for entrance or admission to the church, and penance and absolution for himself and such parishioners. Which knocking and petition being so made, the same lords Commissaries enquired from within who might be there. They for their part, brother Hugh and the Vicar, in the name of himself and of everyone of his parishioners, replied that sinners were present, and that they sought forgiveness from God for the laying of violent hands on the Lord Adam, Bishop of Chichester, by the inhabitants of the town of Portysmouthe, perpetrated on the said ninth day of the month of January, and that they were prepared to undergo penance. Which indeed Commissaries replied to the same brother Hugh and to the Vicar and parishioners, that they doubted whether they could grant according to the petition made, because the blood of the dead Bishop cried for vengeance before the Lord against those sinning in such a manner: the four elements being witnesses, namely—Air, Water, Fire, and Earth. First, Air, because by pestilences and other weaknesses more of the inhabitants there for the greater part were dead, and their land was not fertile but rendered sterile. Secondly, Water, because merchants, on account of the said crime and by reason of the infamy of such inhabitants, have been unwilling to call at the port there with their ships: and, besides that, their lands in the various places had been inundated and devastated by the water, and the inhabitants there had sustained very many other damages and losses through water. Thirdly, Fire, because the buildings of that town and of other neighbouring places had been often consumed by fire. Fourthly Earth, because their lands have not brought forth fruits as they had formerly done, and, moreover, that the grass in the place where the said Bishop suffered, with the land on each side, is withered and does not flourish; and thus their habitations were deserted, insomuch that they could scarcely find any persons who wished to inhabit them, and so their buildings have fallen to ruin, and the inhabitants there have been marked with perpetual infamy. And, on account of these and many other causes, they were not fit, neither could have been so, neither could they be admitted to enter the church. Who, still prostrate, humbly and lamentably besought admission to the church, affirming that on account of the causes and reasons set forth by the said brother Hugh, the church would not close her bosom to those who were penitent, and were desirous to perform penance and to return to the church, and they asserted that they were willing to perform whatever penance should be enjoined on them. Which answers being so made, the said Lords Commissaries said that they were willing to descend to the place of the crime, and, if they should find them penitent and prepared to accomplish in deed that which they declared in word, then they the Commissaries would impart to them their office: and so they, the vicar and parishioners, in the manner of penitents, returned to the place of the crime. Who going before, and the Lords Commissaries with the aforesaid priests vested in surplices and stoles, the aforesaid western door being opened to them, following a little behind them, the same Lords Commissaries, when they had come to the said place of the crime, and had found them humbly prostrate in prayers and lamentably seeking penance and absolution, in order that the parishioners might be able to have greater grace to receive penance. and the Commissaries to enjoin it and to absolve them, they desired that there prostrate they should say the Lord's Prayer fifteen times and the Apostles' Creed thrice ; while the same Commissaries with such priests and other literates, as many as possible, should there say the seven penitential psalms with genuflexion. And thereupon the said seven psalms being begun by the said Lords Commissaries, when they came to the psalm "Miserere mei Deus," (have mercy upon me, O God,) the same Lords Commissaries disciplined the said vicar and parishioners with rods, they, the disciplinants saying the verse "Miserere mei Deus secundum magnam mesericordiam tuam," (have mercy upon me, O God, after thy great goodness) and the disciplined answering by themselves or others the verse "Et secundum multitudinem meserationum tuarum dele iniquitatem meam," (and according to the multitude of thy mercies do away mine offences.) Who being so disciplined, and the said seven psalms being ended, the Lords Commissaries aforesaid enjoined on the parishioners that they should erect a cross in the same place of the crime ; and, as soon as they conveniently could, they should construct a *chapel there, in which the faithful in Christ might be able to pour out their prayers to the Most High for the souls of the said Lord Adam, the Bishop deceased, and of all the faithful deceased ; and that on Good Friday then next following, and so their successors, the future parishioners in the said parish, on Good Friday in every year, with their feet and legs bare, should go to the said place to pray for the souls of the said Bishop and of all the faithful deceased, and to make offerings there according to their means ; and that, within the three years then next following, every such parishioner, or at least certain of the same parishioners, according to the discretion of the inhabitants there, should proceed abroad to the place in which the same Adam, the deceased Bishop, is buried, there to seek forgiveness in the name of all the inhabitants, and to pray for the souls of the same deceased Bishop and of all the faithful departed and to make oblations : and also that they the present parishioners and their successors, the future parishioners in the said parish, or in any case one at least from each of their families, in the same place of the crime, on the ninth day of the month of January, on which the same Bishop suffered death, with burning wax candles in their hands, every year should

---

* On the Map of Portsmouth drawn in the reign of Henry VIII. before 1540, also on that of the reign of Elizabeth, there is a little building occupying a place between the Church and the present Memorial Cross. In the Elizabeth plan there is written over the little building the word ' Chappel.' What object could there be in putting a chapel so close to the ' Domus Dei ?' It was, I feel certain that alluded to in the Process, and erected over the very spot where Bishop Moleyns was murdered.

pour out their prayers to God for the souls of the said deceased, and of all the faithful deceased, and should keep the anniversary, and should be personally present at the funeral services and at the Mass "de Requiem." And further the same Lords Commissaries enjoined on the said vicar and parishioners, that they should return to the said western door of the parish church of Portysmouthe, there humbly to prostrate themselves and again receive discipline and another penance and absolution. And thereupon the same parishioners, in the manner of penitents, returned to the said western door, being preceded by the said vicar and other priests, and singing the Litany, with the cross erect, and incense bearers and candle bearers, and followed by the aforesaid Commissaries with rods in their hands. And then, the same Commissaries, certain prayers and addresses having been previously said by them, disciplined the vicar and parishioners so prostrated, and absolved them from the sentence of excommunication which they had incurred, at first generally, and afterwards for the most part separately. And, moreover, the Commissaries enjoined on the said vicar and parishioners that they, with lighted candles in their hands, should enter the church, and should be present at the singing of the Mass "de Requiem" for the soul of the same Bishop deceased, and the souls of all the faithful deceased, and the Mass "de Sancto Spiritu;" and should make offerings at the same Masses according to their means, which offerings should be saved towards the building of the said chapel. The same Commissaries also enjoined on the same vicar and parishioners, that they should perform whatever penance should be afterwards enjoined them by the aforesaid Lord Richard, Bishop of Winchester. And while the first Mass, namely "de Requiem," by the Abbot, and the second "de Sancto Spiritu," by the Prior aforesaid, were sung at the high altar, a great part of the parishioners made oblations in the time of the offertory of each Mass. And besides those two Masses, various other private Masses were celebrated at other altars in the nave of the same parish church, certain of which were of the "Five Wounds," and certain of the "Name of Jesus," the said parishioners being present at each Mass. All and singular the which Masses having been celebrated, the same Commissaries, together with the presbyters and clerks aforesaid, went in solemn procession around the town of Portysmouthe aforesaid, singing the Litany, that is to say "Salve festa dies," the parishioners following them. And when they had come to the place of the crime they halted there, and the psalm "De profundis," with a prayer for the soul of the deceased Bishop, and the souls of all the faithful deceased having been there said by the same Commissaries and presbyters and clerks, the Commissaries and presbyters and clerks returned in procession to the said parish

church, singing the remainder of such Litany, followed by the parishioners:
and, at the end of the procession, the said Master John Dowman intimated to
the same parishioners and to others present, that the said Reverend Father
granted forty days' indulgence to all persons visiting the said place and making
stations there, so often as they should say there the "De Profundis" and the
Lord's Prayer five times, with the salutation of the angels five times, and the
Apostles' Creed. And then, in the afternoon of the same sixth day of April,
the same Commissaries, and Presbyters, and Clerks sang solemn funeral services
in the same parish of Portysmouthe, for the soul of the said deceased Bishop,
and for the souls of all the faithful deceased, the greater part of the aforesaid
parishioners being there present.

THE DEED OF SURRENDER.

Monastic life in the Church of Christ is nearly as old as
Christianity itself. No sooner did persecution set in than
Christians fled to desert and solitary places for safety, and,
when persecution ceased, the anchorite maintained from choice
the retirement, to which originally he had been driven by
heathen cruelty. But the solitude and isolation of the
early devotee were soon found to be insufficient to satisfy
the necessities of the religious life. Public worship, the
participation of the sacraments, and mutual help soon
called for the union of common life with solitude. The
anchorite became of necessity a cenobite; and so rapid
then was the progress of Monasticism in the East, that
Pachomius, the first disciple of the great St. Anthony,
found himself Superior of 7000 cenobites. True, not seldom, pride, and ostentation, and hypocritical simulations
of rigour, and bitter controversy, and other abuses resulted
from the admiration of such extensive self-devotion, but it
is equally certain, that the example set by the early monks
tended greatly to forward Christianity in the East.

In the West, Monachism was little known until the fourth century, when it was introduced into Rome and northern Italy by St. Athanasius, into Africa by St. Augustine, and afterwards into Gaul by St. Martin de Tours. It had then quite an eastern form, but it was soon found necessary to apply considerable relaxation, and at last to make a thorough change. This was the work of the holy St. Benedict, who not only cast aside the lingering relics of paganism, but introduced stricter discipline and order and so repressed the irregular and licentious life of the wandering monks. His object was not merely to save the soul of each individual recluse, but to render monastic life in every way useful. His monasteries therefore became schools of learning and training houses of clergy, and to him we are indebted, not only for treasures of sacred lore, but also for the preservation of many of the gems of classical literature. This was the first great work of Monachism in the West, wrought out mainly through the influence of a giant reformer, who, strange to say, is described by St. Gregory the Great as '*scienter nesciens et sapienter indoctus*'—learnedly ignorant and wisely unlearned.

The next marked religious movement in connection with Monasticism took place in the 12th Century, under Francis of Assisi, the founder of the Franciscan Order. In common with the older orders of monastic life, he held closely to the three vows of chastity, poverty, and obedience, but of these he maintained that poverty was spiritually by far the most powerful. He therefore allowed no property either for his order or any member of it. The very clothes the Franciscan wore, the girdle of his loins, the book of Divine Office were not his own, they belonged to God and His Church. The progress of this order was marvellous. In less than half a century it reckoned no fewer than 33 provinces, possessing 8000 convents with 200,000 members. The spiritual egotism of early monachism now gave place to a far more comprehensive range of spiritual duty. Indeed the temporal necessities of the

suffering and afflicted, lying exposed to the heartlessness of
a cold world, became one great object of cloister care. And
this it was which caused the establishment of hospitals for
the sick, real ' Houses of God,' in connection with monastic
establishments. It is quite true that such hospitals had
been attached to the Church, as inseparable from her work,
from the very beginning of unpersecuted Christianity, certainly from the time of St. Basil; but their number was
greatly increased soon after the foundation of the Franciscans, the dominant principle of that order calling the
attention of the faithful to the bodily as well as the spiritual wants of the sick. As long as life and vigour and
purity continued with the followers of St. Francis and his
rivals, so long did holy men found ' Houses of God,' and no
longer. Hence we find in our own country no ' Domus Dei'
dates earlier than the beginning of the 12th century, the
very time when the zeal and enthusiasm of St. Francis of
Assisi began to be felt throughout Europe; and, we may
fairly conclude, that it was under the influence of that
great reformer of monachism, Bishop Peter de Rupibus was
led to found the ' Domus Dei' of Portsmouth for the comfort of Christ's poor. To St. Benedict the world is indebted
for the preservation of books, which Macaulay justly says
were the " germs from whence a second and more glorious civilization " burst forth; but to St. Francis it owes
that closer attention to the wants of the suffering poor,
which was excited by his marvellous renunciation of every
thing earthly for the sake of Christ and his Church.

Thus monastic life had its work to do, and for centuries
did it with holy zeal. The influence it exercised for good
during the middle ages is beyond all calculation. But too
soon alas! evils crept in—divisions took place, jealousies
were stirred up, purity was often forgotten, and so the confidence of the general public was gradually lost. "The
multiplication of monastic orders was owing to the steady
flow of the tide of corruption ; *' in negotiis religionis facilius

---

* Pet. Clun. Ep. I. 23.

possunt nova fundari quam vetera reparari.' When
the Benedictines evaded the severity of their rule by
qualifying glosses, the Cluniac order arose; but beginning
in the tenth century with a strict rule they sunk into lux-
ury in the twelfth; the Cistercians started to shame them
but soon lost all moral vigour; next the Franciscan men-
dicants appeared, but degenerated more completely in the
first quarter of a century, after their introduction into
England, than other orders had in three or four centuries."
"The glory of Monasticism was the fidelity with which it
discharged its earlier mission; the self sacrifice with which
it taught men to rise superior to the trials and calamities of
life; the unfeigned piety with which the monk resigned
every earthly advantage that he might win a heavenly
reward. But it survived its reputation, and there is more
hope of recovering to life the carcase around which the
eagles have gathered, than of a renovated monkdom. The
ribaldry of Boccaccio and Rabelais, and the more measured
terms of Piers Plowman and Chaucer were mainly instru-
mental in bringing about the downfall of Monasticism; but
this was after it had already been shorn of its splendour,
and when scarcely a ray remained to it of its true glory."*

In England the stunning blow to Monastic institutions
was given by Henry VIII. just at the time when corruption
had reached its height, not only in the cloister but in the
palace. Christendom had been shaken to its foundations by
the unfaithfulness of Christians; the very priesthcod, regular and secular, was clothed in selfishness; and, as all history
has proved, where the priests are luxurious and idle the
laity are of necessity immoral. An unscrupulous monarch
was the instrument of vengeance to act upon an effete
monachism. Fifty seven surrenders were made to him
in 1539, of which thirty seven were monasteries, and
twenty nunneries. When all had thus resigned, commissioners were appointed by the court of augmentations to

* Blunt's Doctrinal and Historical Theology. pp. 487, 493.

receive the revenue and goods belonging to these houses,
to establish the pensions that were to be given to those
that had been in them ; and to pull down the churches, or
such other parts of the fabric as they thought superfluous,
and to sell the materials. This having been done others
began to get hospitals to be surrendered to the king.
Burnet tells us that when Dr. Ridley " inveighed against
the superstition towards images, and there was a general
disposition over all the nation to pull them down," Portsmouth was the first to set an example of iconoclastic zeal.
It is satisfactory to know that the master of her "Domus Dei"
was not moved by an equal zeal to be the first to surrender
to the King possessions which had been solemnly dedicated
to God. That unholy task fell to the lot of the unscrupulous Thirleby, who sold the Mastership of St. Thomas's
Hospital, Southwark, for a mitre, and then in the most
reckless way accommodated himself to every change that
followed ; convenience rather than principle being his
watchword. But within a year other Masters became unho-
lily generous, all seeming to make the best bargain they could
with the Crown. On the 2nd June, 1540, John Incent,
Master of the Hospital of St. Nicholas, signed the following obsequious deed of surrender on behalf of himself and
the brethren and sisters. and two days afterwards was rewarded with the deanery of St. Paul's.

No. VII.

Omnibus Christi fidelibus, ad quos præsens scriptum pervenerit, Johannes
Incent, Legum Doctor, Magister Domus sive Hospitalis Sancti Nicolai de
Portysmouthe, Wintoniensis diocesis, et ejusdem loci confratres et sorores, salutem in Domino sempiternam. Nòveritis, nos, præfatos magistrum, confratres
et sorores, unanimi consensu et assensu nostris, animis deliberatis, certâ scientiâ
et mero motu nostris, ex quibusdam causis justis et rationalibus, nos, animas
et conscientias nostras specialiter moventibus, ultro et sponte dedisse et conces-
sisse, ac per præsentes dare, et concedere, reddere et confirmare illustrissimo
principi et domino nostro, Henrico octavo, Dei gratiâ Angliæ et Franciæ regi,
fidei defensori, domino Hiberniæ, et in terrâ supremo capiti Anglicanæ ecclesiæ,

totam dictam domum sive Hospitale Sancti Nicolai de Portesmouthe predictâ, necnon omnia et singula maneria, dominia, messuagia, gardina, curtilagia, tofta, terras et tenementa, prata, pascua, pasturas, boscos, redditus, reversiones, servitia, molendina, passagia, feoda militum, wardas, maritagia, nativos, villanos, cum eorum sequelis, communias, libertates, franchesias, jurisdictiones, officia, curias, letas, hundreda, visus franci plegii, ferias, mercata, parcos, warenna, vivaria, aquas, piscarias, vias, *chiminos, vacuos fundos, advocationes, nominationes, præsentationes et donationes ecclesiarum, vicariarum, capellarum, cantariarum, hospitalium, et aliorum ecclesiasticorum beneficiorum quorumcunque, rectorias, vicarias, cantarias, pensiones, portiones, annuitates, decimas, oblationes, ac omnia et singula emolumenta, proficua, possessiones, hereditamenta, et jura nostra quæcunque, tam infra Comitatum Southamptoniæ quam infra Comitatum Wiltesiæ, vel alibi infra regnum Angliæ, Walliæ ac Marchiarum eorundem, eidem Domui sive Hospitali Sancti Nicolai de Portesmouthe prædictâ quoque modo pertinentia, spectantia, appendentia, sive incumbentia, ac omnimodas chartas, evidentias, scripta et munimenta nostra eisdem domui sive hospitali, maneriis, terris et tenementis, ac cæteris præmissis cum pertinentiis, seu alicui inde parcellæ, quoquo modo spectantia sive concernentia, habenda, tenenda, et gaudendenda dictam domum sive hospitale, scitum, fundum, circuitum, et præcinctum de Portesmouthe prædictâ, necnon omnia et singula dominia, maneria, terras, tenementa, rectorias, pensiones, et cætera præmissa, cum omnibus et singulis suis pertinentiis, præfato invictissimo principi et domino nostro regi, heredibus et assignatis suis imperpetuum, cui in hâc parte ad omnem juris effectum qui exinde sequi poterit aut potest, nos et dictam Domum sive Hospitale Sancti Nicolai de Portesmouthe prædictâ, ac omnia jura nobis qualitercumque acquisita, ut decet, subjicimus et submittimus, dantes et concedentes, prout per præsentes damus et concedimus, eidem regiæ majestati heredibus et assignatis suis, omnem et omnimodam plenam et liberam facultatem, auctoritatem, et potestatem, nos et dictam domum de Portesmouthe prædictâ, unacum omnibus et singulis maneriis, terris, tenementis, redditibus, reversionibus, servitiis, et singulis præmissis, cum suis juribus et pertinentiis quibuscumque disponendum, ac pro suâ liberâ regiâ voluntate et libito ad quoscunque usus majestati suæ placentes, alienandum, donandum, convertendum, et transferendum, hujusmodi dispositiones, alienationes, donationes, conversiones, et translationes per dictam majestatem suam quovismodo fiendas; extunc ratificantes ratasque et gratas ac perpetuo firmas nos habituros promittimus per præsentes.

---

* Tolls for passing through a forest with loaded carts or horses.

Et nos præfati Magister, confratres, sorores, et successores nostri, dictam domum, præcinctum, scitum, mansionem, et ecclesiam Sancti Nicolai de Portesmouthe prædictâ, ac omnia et singula maneria, dominia, messuagia, gardina, cartilagia, tofta, prata, pascua, pasturas, boscos, subboscos, terras, tenementa, ac omnia et singula cætera præmissa, cum suis pertinentiis universis, domino nostro regi et assignatis suis, contra omnes gentes warrantizabimus impepetuum. In cujus rei testimonium, nos, præfati magister, confratres, et sorores, huic scripto sigillum nostrum commune præsentibus, apponi fecimus. Datum secundo die Junii, anno Domini millessimo quingentessimo quadragesimo, et regni illustrissimi domini nostri regis Henrici Octavi tricesimo secundo.

Per me Joannem Incent.

Capta et recognita coram me Willelmo Petre die et anno prædictis.

Per me Willm. Petre.

TRANSLATION.

To all the faithful in Christ to whom the present writing shall come, from John Incent, Doctor of Laws Master of the House or Hospital of St. Nicholas of Portsmouth in the diocese of Winchester, and the brothers and sisters of the same place, eternal salvation in the Lord. Know that we, the aforesaid master, brothers and sisters, with our unanimous consent and assent, having deliberated in our minds, of our certain knowledge and mere motion, from divers just and reasonable causes, ourselves, our minds and consciences specially moving, have willingly and freely given and granted, and by these presents do give and grant, render and confirm to our illustrious prince and lord, Henry the Eighth, by the grace of God, King of England and France, defender of the faith, lord of Ireland, and on earth supreme head of the English Church, all the said House or Hospital of St. Nicholas of Portsmouth aforesaid, and all the site, ground, circuit, and precinct of the same House of St. Nicholas of Portsmouth aforesaid, and also all and the singular manors, domains, messuages, gardens, court-yards, tofts, lands, and tenements, meadows, grazings, pasturages, woods, rents, reversions, services, mills, ferry-tolls, knights' fees, wards, maritages, bond-men, villains, with their appurtenances, commons, liberties, franchises, jurisdictions, offices, courts, courts-leet, hundreds, views of frank-pledge, fairs, markets, parks, warrens, fish-ponds, waters, fishing-rights, roads, ways, vacant grounds, advowsons, nominations, presentations and donations of churches, vicarages, chapelries, chantries, hospitals, and of other ecclesiastical benefices whatsoever, rectories, vicarages, chantries, pensions, portions, annuities tenths, oblations, and all and singular our emoluments, profits, possessions, heriditaments, and rights, whatsoever, as well within the county of Southampton as within the county of Wilts, or elsewhere in the Kingdom of England, Wales, and the Marches of the same, to the said House or Hospital of St. Nicholas of Portsmouth aforesaid, in any manner, pertaining, belonging, appending or applying, and our various charters, evidences, writings and muniments of every kind, to the same house or hospital, manors, lands and tenements, and to the other premises with their appurtenances, or to any parcel thereof belonging or concerning: To have, to hold, and to enjoy the said House or Hospital, the site, ground, circuit, and precinct, of Portsmouth aforesaid, and also all and singular the domains, manors, lands, tenements, rectories, pensions, and the other premises, with all and singular their appurtenances, to the aforesaid most invincible prince and lord our King, his heirs and assigns for ever: to whom, in this behalf, to every effect of right which thence might or can follow, we, as becomes us, yield and submit onrselves and the said House or Hospital of St. Nicholas of Portsmouth aforesaid, and all the rights howsoever acquired by us,—giving and granting, as by these presents we give and grant to the same Royal Majesty, his heirs and assigns, all and every manner of full and free faculty, authority, and power, to dispose of ourselves and the said House of Portsmouth aforesaid, together with all and singular the manors, lands, tenements, rents, reversions, services, and the singular premises, with their rights and appurtenances whatsoever, and according to his own free royal will and pleasure, to alienate, grant, convert, and transfer to whatsoever uses may please His Majesty, ratifying the dispositions, alienations, donations, conversions and translations of this sort, by His said Majesty in any manner thenceforth to be made, and we promise by these presents to hold the same good, acceptable, and firm for ever. And we the aforesaid master, brothers, sisters, and our successors, will for ever warrant against all people, to our Lord the King and his assigns, the said house, precinct, site, mansion and church of St. Nicholas of Portsmouth aforesaid, and all and singular manors, domains, messuages, gardens, court-yards, tofts, meadows, grazings, pasturages, woods, under-woods, lands, tenements, and all and singular the other premises, with the whole of their appurtenances. In testimony whereof, we the aforesaid master, brothers and sisters, have caused our common seal to be affixed to this writing. Dated 2nd June, A.D., 1540, and 32 Henry VIII.

By me John Incent.

Taken and recorded before me, William Petre, on the day and year aferesaid.

By me Willm. Petre.

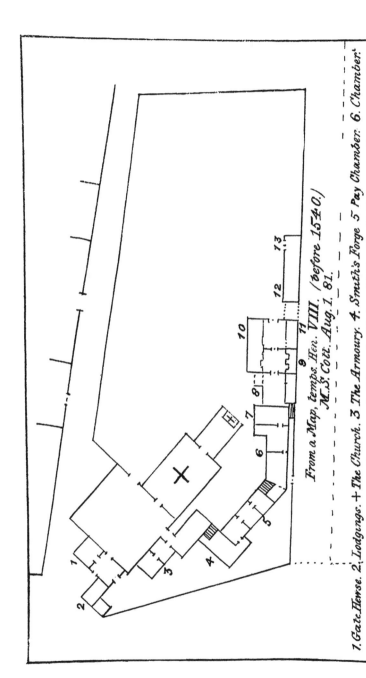

No. 16

From a Map, temps. Hen. VIII. (before 1540.)
M.S. Cott. Aug. 1. 81.

1. Gate House. 2. Lodgings. + The Church. 3. The Armoury. 4. Smith's Forge. 5. Pay Chamber. 6. Chamber.
7. Great Chamber & Captayne's Chamber. 8. Hall. 9. Kechy. 10. Larder. 11. Nursery. 12. Bakehowse. 13. Stable.

CALCOTT, LITH PORTSEA.

REVENUE OF THE "DOMUS DEI."

The 'Act for the dissolution of Abbeys,' secured to the crown the possession of one-fifth of the lands of the kingdom, and, by means of the Court of Augmentations, the greatest possible care was taken to realize to the utmost every penny coming from the property of the suppressed houses. But it must not be supposed that this general confiscation met with approval from the public. At the outset all admitted that the number of religious houses was far too great, and so the first suppression was deemed a wise proceeding; but, when an act was passed vesting all monastic possessions in the king, the country became dissatisfied, and as Burnet strongly puts it, "this suppression of abbeys was universally censured." Even Henry was afraid to take to himself those vast estates without feigning that he intended to use them for the glory of God. With his own hand he wrote the following preamble to the draft of an "Act for the King to make Bishops." Well would it have been for his memory had his deeds accorded with his professions as thus expressed! "Forasmuch as it is not unknown the slothful and ungodly life which hath been used amongst all those sort which have borne the name of religious folk; and to the intent, that, from henceforth, many of them might be turned to better use, as hereafter shall follow, whereby God's Word might be the better set forth; children brought up in learning; clerks nourished in the universities; old servants decayed to have livings; alms houses for poor people to be sustained in; readers of Greek, Hebrew, and Latin to have good stipend; daily

M

alms to be ministered; mending of highways; exhibition
for ministers of the Church; it is thought unto the King's
Highness most expedient and necessary, that more bishop-
rics and colleges shall be established."* The godless
monarch promised largely, but lied as unblushingly. He
soon forgot his wonderful schemes for the moral and religious advancement of his people. God's money was used
freely by him to keep up an extravagant household; for
"the upholding of dice-playing, masking and banquetting";
nay for the support of every kind of loose indulgence.
And thus the royal heart became more and more hardened.
So much so, that, when he appealed to parliament to join
with him in another sacrilegious raid upon heaven's treasures, he openly avowed that the money gathered in by
the abolition of charities, many of them very rich, should
be spent in carrying on wars against France and Scotland;
"and for the maintenance of your most royal estate, honour, dignity, and estimation, which all your most loving
subjects, of natural duty, be bound to conserve and increase by all such ways and means as they can devise."
It is sometimes said, that, with all the King's selfishness, he
was certainly most liberal in his pensions to those who had
been inmates of the suppressed houses. Never was a
statement more false. The monks of Tewkesbury Abbey,
for example, thirty-four in number, received out of a revenue of £1595 15s. 6d., six of them a pension of £8 or £9
a year, the remainder £6 13s. 4d.; while in the smaller
monasteries the poor sufferers obtained sums varying from
£4 to 53s. 4d. But, if the monks were little cared for, such
was not the case with the revenues of monastic property.
Receivers were cautiously selected to take down every far-
thing, showing no favour; and to send in a carefully
drawn up account to the Chancellor of the Court of Augmentations. The following is the return made of estates
which belonged to the 'Domus Dei' of Portsmouth, and it

* 31 Henry VIII., c. 9.

proves that Roger Tycheborne was a very intelligent and pains-taking servant of the Crown.

NO. VIII.

Late Hospital of St. Nicholas in Portsmouth, commonly called Godishouse.

Exchequer; Augmentation Office. Ministers' Accounts. Southampton, 31-32 Henry VIII. No. 139.

Manor of Broughton.

Account of Roger Tychebourne, gentleman, Special Receiver of all the possessions, as well Spiritual as Temporal, pertaining to the said late Hospital, namely from the 27th March, 31 Henry VIII,—on which day the said late Hospital, with all the possessions, rights and appurtenances of the same house, was surrendered into the hands of the same King, by John Incent, clerk, doctor of laws, late Master of the same Hospital, and the brothers and sisters of the said house, and freely and willingly by their writing was given and granted to the same King, his heirs and successors,—until the Feast of St. Michael, Archangel, thence next following, in the 32nd year of the same King's reign, that is to say for half-a-year.

Arrears. None, because this is the first account of the same Computer.

Rents of Assise of Free Tenants.

But renders account of 7s. 6d. of rent of assise of certain lands and meadows there called Typtofte, in the occupation of Thomas, Earl of Rutland, payable yearly on the term of St. Michael the Archangel only, as appears by a certain Rental thence made and renewed, produced and examined at the time of making the Account. And of 13s. 4d. of rent of assise of certain lands and meadows called Brode Marshe, in the occupation of Lord Dacres, payable yearly on the same term. And of 2s. of rent of assise of six acres of land at Paddiche, formerly in the occupation of John Cuttler, now in the occupation of Francis Dawtre, knight, payable yearly on the same term. And of 11s. of rent of assise of certain lands and meadows called Whittons, in the occupation of William Brent, payable yearly on the same term. And of 5s. of rent of assise of certain lands and meadows formerly in the occupation of William Rengbrue, now in the occupation of John Broyne, Esquire, payable yearly on the same term. And of 13s. 4d. of rent of assise of certain lands and meadows in the occupation of Edward Harris, gentleman, payable yearly on the same term. And of 7s. of rent of assise of certain lands and meadows called Galruge, in the occupation of Thomas Hynckpen, Esquire, payable yearly on the same term. And of 8s. of rent of assise of certain lands and meadows called Alwarde, in the occupation of John Eyer, payable yearly on the same term. And of 5s. of rent of assise of certain lands and meadows called Worsetters in the occupation of Robert Blake, payable yearly on the same term. And of 6s. of rent of assise of certain lands and meadows formerly in the occupation of John Schort, now in the occupation of George Scheperd, payable yearly on the same term. And of 2s. 6d. of rent of assise of two messuages in the occupation of John Kebell, son and heir of George Kebell, payable yearly on the same term. Of any profit arising from the price of one pound of pepper of rent of assise of a piece of ground in the same place, in the occupation of John Kebell, gentleman, he renders no account, because it was delivered to the Auditor as pertaining to his office. But he renders account of 14d. of rent of assise of two closes at the end of the village of Broughton aforesaid, in the occupation of the aforesaid John Kebell, payable yearly on the same term. And of 3s. of rent of assise of certain lands and meadows called Grenis, in the occupation of John Mersche, payable yearly on the same term. And of 11s. 2d. of rent of assise of a tenement and certain lands in the occupation of the aforesaid John Mersche, payable yearly on the same term. And of 8s. of rent of assise of a cottage in Mascalle in the occupation of John Regat, payable yearly on the same term. And of 6d. of rent of assise of certain lands formerly in the occupation of Henry Clarke, now in the occupation of the heirs of John Masey, payable yearly on the same term. And of 12d. of rent of assise of a cottage called the Priest's House, in the occupation of the Rector of the church of Broughton aforesaid, payable annually on the same term. And of 8s. of rent of assise of a meadow called Spirewell, otherwise Chawlewell, late in the occupation of the Prior and Convent of Motissont, now in the occupation of John Sandis, Lord Sandis, payable yearly on the same term.   113s. 6d. Exd.

Customary Rents of Tenants there.

And of 37s. 8d. of customary rent of a messuage, two virgates and a half of land, and of a barn and thirty acres of land with the appurtenances, in Broughton aforesaid: also of a cottage there near Tymber's Crosse, in the occupation of Robert Ockebourne, by copy of Court Roll, to be held to himself, Matilda his wife, and Edward their son, for the term of the life of the one of them living the longest, payable in equal portions on the usual terms there. And of 16s. of customary rent of the same pasture called Blackmore, near East Tynderley, in the occupation of the same Robert Ockbourne and of Edward his son, for the term of the life of either of them living the longest, payable yearly on the same terms. And of 6s. of customary rent of two closes called Planestonis, in the occupation of Robert Harris and of Alice his wife, for the term of their life payable yearly on the same terms. And of 16s. 8d. of customary rent of a tenement and one virgate of land, with the appurtenances, in the occupation of Henry Goddard for the term of his life, payable yearly on the same terms. And of 10s. 10d. of customary rent of a messuage, and one virgate of land with their appurtenances, in the occupation of Margery Abbot, widow, payable yearly on the same terms. And of 12s. of customary rent of a messuage and one virgate of land, in Broughton aforesaid, and of certain lands and pastures in Tyderley called Chepencrofte, in the occupation of Henry Acton for the term of his life, payable yearly on the same terms. And of 8s. of customary rent of a messuage and one virgate of land, with their appurtenances, in the occupation of Richard Acton, Johanna his wife, and John their son, for the term of the life of either of them living the longest, annually at the same terms. And of 5s. of customary rent of three closes of meadow at Forde, namely, Blakemore, Habtathe, and Eastleese, with their appurtenances, in the occupation of John Lote for the term of his life, payable yearly on the same terms. And of 15s. of customary rent of a messuage, one virgate of land and two closes called Bowers and Bonnye, in the occupation of Elizabeth Smith for the term of her life, of Robert Mesche and Richard Philipp, sons of the same Elizabeth, payable yearly at the same terms. And of 5s. 8d. of customary rent of a messuage and half a virgate of land with the appurtenances in the occupation of Robert Coper, junior, for the term of his life, payable yearly at the same terms. And of 40s. of customary rent of a messuage with two virgates of land pertaining to the same messuage, in the occupation of John Sabb for the term of the life of himself and of Henry his eldest son, payable yearly at the same terms. And of 10s. of customary rent of one virgate of land with a close and a meadow called Pitlands, near Brodelane, in occupation of John Schayland, for the term of his life, payable yearly at the same terms. And of 8s. of customary rent of a close and a virgate of land in the occupation of Margery Coper, widow, payable yearly at the same terms. And of 7s. of customary rent of the closes called the Frithe, situated in the parish of Motissount, late in the occupation of Richard Purdell, and formerly of Richard Basset, now in the occupation of William Purdell, son of the aforesaid Richard

Purdell, for the term of his life, payable at the same terms.   Sum £9 17s. 10d.

Rents of Tenants at the Lord's will.

And of 20s. of rent of a meadow called Ockeley, now in the occupation of Katherine Wellis, widow, at the lord's will, payable in equal portions at the Feasts of St. Michael the Archangel, and of the Annunciation of Blessed Mary the Virgin.   And of 3s. 4d. of rent of a cottage called Smythe's Forge, in the occupation of John Molde at the lord's will, payable yearly on the same terms. And of 16s. of rent of one virgate of land in the occupation of Richard Loppe at the lord's will, payable yearly on the same terms.   And of 12s. 7d. of rent of two closes called Sutheleese and Vatercombe, in the occupation of Robert Ockborne at the lord's will, payable yearly on the same terms.   And of 2s. of rent of a close called Gosemore in the occupation of Augustine Whithed, at the lord's will, payable yearly on the same terms.   And of 26s. 8d. of rent of certain lands and pastures called Overton Lesse in the occupation of John Weldon at the lord's will, payable yearly on the same terms.   And of 5s. of rent of a pasture called Wintersdowne in the occupation of all tenants there at the lord's will, payable yearly at the term of St. Michael Archangel only. Sum, £4 5s. 7d.

Farm of the Manor.

And of £6 of the farm of the site of the manor of Broughton aforesaid, with all the arable lands, meadows, grazings, pastures, underwood, and other their appurtenances, (except wards, marritages, reliefs,* eschaets, fines, liberties, franchises, pannages†, and all perquisites of courts, views of frank-pledge, and two principal chambers with stable for horses, reserved to the said late Master and his successors), so together let to Robert Ockborne by indenture dated December 1st, 14 Henry VIII. for the term of forty years, rendering thence annually to the aforesaid John Incent, his successors and assigns, £6, at the feasts of the Annunciation of Blessed Mary the Virgin, and of St. Michael the Archangel, by equal portions.   And the said Robert agrees that he himself and his assigns, at their own proper charges and expenses, shall find for the aforesaid John Incent and his steward, with all their attendants for the time being, as well straw, hay, and horses' provisions, as food and drink; also all other necessaries so often and whenever it shall happen that any Court shall be held there: and the said Robert and his assigns shall collect all the rent of the tenants of the manor aforesaid, with all stray beasts, amercements, fines, and perquisites of Courts, and shall render a proper account and payment thereof

---

* Reliefs—fines paid by the heir at a tenant's death.
+ Pannages—waste of hedges, &c.

annually to the aforesaid John Incent and his successors, twice a year at the court to be held there, during the term aforesaid. And the same Robert shall well and sufficiently repair, sustain, and maintain all and every kind of repairs pertaining or belonging to the same manor, and so, in the end of his term, all these, thus well and sufficiently made and repaired, shall quit in the same state as he had received them, or in a better state. And the same Robert and his assigns shall have and receive in the woods and underwoods pertaining to the site of the manor aforesaid, sufficient timber for the repairs of the house and hedges, and for fires, ploughs, and carts, by the delivery and assignment of the aforesaid John Incent and his successors, or of their deputies on this behalf, during the term aforesaid, as is more fully contained in the said indentures, namely, for the said two terms falling within the time of this Account, in this the nineteenth year of his tenancy. And of 46s. 8d. of the farm of all those pastures there called Frenchemore, Fulsey, Fyshweres, and Frenchemore Comles, within the parish of West Cudderly aforesaid, so together let to John Tyler and his assigns by indenture, dated May 3rd, 25 Henry VIII, for the term of 24 years, rendering thence annually 46s. 8d. in equal portions on the Feasts of the Annunciation of Blessed Mary the Virgin, and of St. Michael the Archangel. And the aforesaid John Tyler, that he, his executors and assigns, occupying the aforesaid pastures, shall make suits of Court twice a year in the Manor of Broughton aforesaid : and further he agrees, that he and his assigns shall repair, sustain, and maintain all the hedges and ditches of the said pastures at their own proper costs and expences, during the term aforesaid, and so, in the end of the aforesaid term, the said pastures, well and sufficiently repaired, shall surrender. And the aforesaid John Tyler agrees, neither he himself nor his assigns shall cut or carry wood or underwood there growing, without special license of the said Master or his successors, during the aforesaid term, as is more fully contained in the same Indentures : viz., for the said two terms falling within the time of this computation, in the seventh year of his Term. Sum, £8 6s. 8d.

Perquisites of Courts.

And he renders account of 20s. of perquisites of Courts held within the time of this Computation ; namely of certain rents payable annually, by the tenants of the aforesaid manor, at two views of frank-pledge held there every year, viz., from rents of this kind for two views of frank-pledge happening there within the time of this Computaiion. Of any profit arising from amercements and other casualties appertaining to the said Court, he renders no account, because no Courts have been held there this year by the the oath of the said Computer. Sum, 20s.

Rents of Assise in Froddington.

But he renders account of 4s. of rents of Assise of certain lands lately pertaining to the late Abbot of Tychefyld, in the occupation of Thomas Wriothesley, knight, payable yearly on the term of St. Michael the Archangel, as appears by a certain rental thereof made and renewed, produced and examined at the time of making this Computation.   Sum, 4s.

Rents customary of Tenants there.

And of 13s. 4d. of customary rent of a messuage and certain lands and pastures, with appurtenances called Feldershe lande, lying on the west side of the street called Feldershe lane, late in the occupation of Milo Garnett, with common of pasture of Portisdowne belonging to the aforesaid lands and pastures, now in the occupation of John Darbye by copy of Court, payable yearly, at the Feasts of the Annunciation of Blessed Mary the Virgin, and of St. Michael the Archangel, in equal portions. And of 5s. of customary rent of two cottages and four acres of land formerly in the occupation of Robert Warner and of another acre of land, lying in Suthfeld (Southfield) in two hills in the same field, lately purchased by John Incent, Master of the same Hospital, now in the occupation of Thomas Atwood, by copy of Court, payable yearly at the same terms. And of 34s. 10d. of customary rent of a messuage and garden adjoining, and of two virgates of land formerly in the occupation of Richard West, and of a messuage and a virgate of land lately in the occupation of William Dewke, now in the occupation of John Pynne, by copy of Court, payable yearly at the same times. And of 21s. 4d. of customary rent of two cottages, with their appurtenances, lately in the occupation of Richard Stubber, and of a virgate of land with its appurtenances called Wade, and of a garden formerly in the occupation of Robert Gylam, now in the occupation of Thomas Turner, by copy of Court, payable yearly at the same terms. And of 6s. 8d. of customary rent of a cottage containing five acres of land lately in the occupation of John Milbye, now in the occupation of Thomas Turner, by copy of court, payable yearly at the same terms. And of 27s. 4d. of customary rent of a messuage and three virgates of land with the appurtenances in Frodington aforesaid, and of a croft lately in the occupation of John Palmer, now in the occupation of Thomas Palmer by copy of Court-roll, payable yearly at the same terms. And of 13s. 4d. of customary rent of two cottages and a croft adjoining, and of certain lands, containing by estimate ten acres of land, late in the occupation of Richard Bull, now in the occupation of John Hereley by copy of Court, payable yearly at the same terms. And of 39s. 6d. of customary

rent of two cottages with their appurtenances formerly in the occupation of
Richard Merer, and of a cottage with its appurtenances late in the occupation
of John Meldye, and a virgate of land with its appurtenances formerly in the
occupation of John Germyn, and a cottage with its appurtenances late in the
occupation of Stephen Closche, now in the occupation of William Peryn by
copy of Court, payable yearly at the same terms. And of 23s. 8½d., of customary rent of a messuage with its appurtenances formerly in the occupation of
William Pynnyng, and of divers land called Hoggisland, and two cottages with
their appurtenances lately in the occupation of John Lede, now in the occupation of John Tudson by copy of Court, payable yearly at the same terms. And
of 11s. 10d. of customary rent of a tenement and a virgate of land with a garden
adjoining and their appurtenances, late in the occupation of Richard Mandall,
now in the occupation of William Fawcooner, by copy of Court, payable yearly at
the same terms. And of 23s. 8½d. of customary rent of a messuage and a virgate of land called Fychette, and of a toft of a messuage and a virgate of land
called Dabyes, with their appurtenances, in the occupation of John Chatton,
Esquire, payable yearly at the same terms. And of 10s. 9d. of customary rent
of a messuage and a virgate of land with the appurtenances, late in the occupation of Anne Hogfyld, now in the occupation of John Harewood, otherwise
Hogfylde, by copy of Court, payable yearly at the same terms. And of 7s. of
customary rent of a tenement and seven acres of land, late in the occupation of
Thomas Crowe, formerly in the occupation of John Willisman, by copy of court
payable yearly at the same terms. And of 9s. of customary rent of a cottage and
and two acres of land and a croft, and five acres of land with a garden in Bock-
land, in the occupation of Edmund Stubberet, by copy of Court, payable yearly
at the same terms. And of 9s. of customary rent of a close called Ruschep-
lantimore, lying near Northdowne, in the occupation of James Benstede, by copy
of Court, payable yearly at the same terms.   Sum, £12 17s. 8½d.

Farm.

And of £18 8s. of the farm of the site of the manor of Frodyngton aforesaid with all the demesne lands, arable and pasture, pertaining to the same site
of the manor, in as ample mode and form as a certain Henry Bickeley lately
held the same site, lands, and pastures, excepting the rents of the tenants there,
the perquisites of the courts, the heriot fines, and all other rents pertaining to
the same, together with the Hall, parlour, chamber, stable, and dovecot, wholly
reserved to the said Master and to his successors, with free entrance and egress
to and from the premises, so together let to James Benested by Indenture dated
July 25th, 31 Henry VIII., for the term of 41 years, paying rent thereof yearly

£18 sterling, at the Feasts of the Nativity of our Lord, the Annunciation of Blessed Mary the Virgin, the Nativity of St. John the Baptist, and of St. Michael the Archangel, in equal portions, and rendering yearly three quarters and a half of oats and a cart load of straw, when he should be required to do so by the said Master and his successors during the term aforesaid. And the aforesaid James Benested covenants that he will well and sufficiently repair, sustain and maintain, during the aforesaid term at his own proper charges and expenses, all the necessaries pertaining or belonging to the same manors, houses and barns, with the hedges and walls, (excepting only large timber and roofings of houses, with stones, at the costs and charges of the aforesaid John Incent and his successors during the term aforesaid.) And further the same James and his assigns shall have and receive, in whatever woods and underwoods belong to the site of the aforesaid manor, sufficient housebote,* ploughbote, cartbote, hedgebote and foldbote, by the delivery and assignment of the aforesaid John Incent and his successors during the aforesaid term, as is more fully contained in the said indentures : namely, as well for the said rent of £18 above, payable yearly at the aforesaid terms, reserved, as from and for the price of the three quarters and a half of oats, 7s., and the said cart load of straw, 12d., owing for the entire year, ending at the feast of St. Michael the Archangel falling within the time of this Account, as above, in this the first year of his term. Of any profit arising from the farm of the Hall, parlour, chamber or dovecot aforesaid, above reserved, he renders no account in this year, because no one has wished to rent them during the aforesaid time.   Sum, £18 8s. 0d.

Yearly Times for License to appoint Under Tenants.

And of 12d. from John Tudson, for the annual fine for license to have under-tenants, payable yearly in equal portions at the terms of the Annunciation of Blessed Mary the Virgin, and of St. Michael the Archangel, as appears by the Rental thereof made, produced and examined at the time of making this Account. And of 12d. from Edward Stubber, for a similar fine and license to have under tenants, payable yearly in equal portions at the same terms, as appears by the same Rental.

Perquisites of Courts.

Of any profit arising from the perquisites of Courts held there this year, he renders no account, because no Courts were held there during the whole time of this Account, by the oath of the Computer.

---

* These terms signify all wood required for domestic purposes, and for making and repairing ploughs, carts, hedges and folds.

Rents of Assise of Free Tenants in Burwell.

But he renders account of 4s. of rents of assise of certain lands and pastures there called Ruschemore in the occupation of Anthony Ponde, esquire, payable yearly at the term of St. Michael the Archangel, only, as appears by a certain Rental thereof, made and renewed, produced and examined at the time of making this Account. And of 4s. ½d., of the rent of assise of certain lands in the occupation of John Cossyn, payable yearly at the same term. And of 22½d of the rent of assise of certain lands in the occupation of Agnes Flette, widow, payable yearly at the same term. And of 2d. from the same widow Agnes from and for the relief of suits of Court, payable yearly at the same term. And of 10s. of rent of assise of certain lands in the occupation of Richard Bensted, payable yearly at the same term.   Sum 20s. 1d.

Rents of Assise of Free Tenants in Kingston.

And of 6d. of rent of assise of a messuage and garden adjoining the same, in the occupation of Robert Gay, payable yearly at the term of St. Michael the Archangel only, as appears by a certain Rental thereof made and renewed, produced and examined with regard to this Account. And of 10d. from the rent of assise of certain lands called Cosschins landes, in the occupation of William Hesberd, payable yearly at the same term. And of 15d. from the rent of assise of certain lands and pasturages called Robbert, in the occupation of Thomas Carpenter, payable yearly at the same term. And of 12d. from the rent of assise of a tenement in the occupation of John Balcheffe, payable yearly at the same term. And of 4d. from the rent of assise of certain lands and pasturages called Little Hoggercroft, in the occupation of Robert White, Esquire, payable yearly at the same term. And of 2½d. from the rent of assise of a messuage and certain lands in the occupation of Thomas Turner, payable yearly at the same term. And of 8d. from the rent of assise of certain lands and pasturages called Doggecrofte, in the occupation of the aforesaid Thomas Carpenter, payable yearly at the same time.   Sum, 4s. 9½d.

Farm.

And of 58s. from the farm of two tenements there, with 21 acres of land, lying in Dockefeld, and of 8 acres and a half of land lying in Marfeld and Metefeld, 13 acres of land lying in Biston Feld, with a certain late pool called the 'grete lacke,' containing by estimation ten acres of land, and a little close called Goddishouseclosse, so together let to Thomas Carpenter, by Indentures dated October 2nd, 27 Hen. VIII., for the term of 31 years, rendering thence yearly 58s. at the Feasts of the Annunciation of Blessed Mary the Virgin, and of

St. Michael the Archangel, in equal portions. And the aforesaid Thomas Carpenter and his assigns, at their own proper charges and expenses, will well and
sufficiently repair, sustain, and maintain all the aforesaid tenements, lands, and
closes, with the hedges, and will vacate them at the end of their term thus well
and sufficiently repaired, as is more fully contained in the said Indentures;
namely for the said two terms falling within the time of this Account, in this
fifth year of his term. And of 22s. 6d. from the farm of 28 acres of arable
land lying in the liberty of Portsmouth aforesaid, let to John Butler, by Indenture dated April 16, 26 Henry VIII., for the term of 15 years, rendering thence
yearly 22s. 6d., in equal portions at the Feasts of the Annunciation of Blessed
Mary the Virgin, and of St. Michael the Archangel. And the same John and
his assigns shall well and sufficiently repair, sustain, and maintain all the
hedges and ditches of every kind pertaining to the same lands, and at the end
of his Term shall vacate them thus well and sufficiently repaired. And further
the said John and his executors shall have yearly, during the aforesaid term, the
last crop of the meadow called Goddishouse, made from the 15th day after the
Feast of St. Michael the Archangel annually until the Feast of Blessed Mary
the Virgin; and similarly the said John shall have and carry off all the manure
in Goddishouse aforesaid, during the said Term, as is more fully contained in
the same Indentures: namely, for the said two terms falling within the time of
this Account, in the 7th year of his Term.   Sum, £4 0s. 6d.

Perquisites of Courts.

Of any profits arising from the perquisites of Courts held there this year,
he renders no account, because no Courts have been held there during the
whole time of this Account, by the oath of the Computer.   Sum, Nil.

Portesmouth.

But he renders account of 10s. from the rent of a tenement there with a
garden, adjoining in the occupation of James Michel at the lord's will, payable
in equal portions at the Feasts of the Annunciation of Blessed Mary the Virgin, and St. Michael the Archangel. And of 8s. from the rent of a tenement
in the occupation of Leonard Colman at the lord's will, payable yearly at the
same terms. And of 2s. from the rent of certain lands at Kinghall Grene,
called Morecrofte, in the occupation of Thomas Yonge, at the will of the lord,
payable yearly at the same terms. And of 10s. from the rent of a tenement in
High Street near the church, called the Steyers, with a garden towards the
same church, in the occupation of William Goslinge at the lord's will, payable
yearly at the same terms. And of 4d. from the rent of a certain parcel of land

in the occupation of Robert Lynden, at the lord's will, payable yearly at the same terms. And of 8s. from the rent of a tenement called Angulare Tenement, in the occupation of Alice Schamber, widow, at the lord's will, payable yearly at the same terms. And of 8d. from the rent of a garden lately in the occupation of Master Palsched, now in the occupation of John Chatterton, Esquire, at the lord's will, payable yearly in the same terms. And of 18d. from the rent of a certain piece of land in Goddishouse grene, near the Angulare Tenement, upon which was formerly a tenement called Oxalles, in the occupation of a tenant at the lord's will, payable yearly at the same terms.   Sum 40s. 6d.

And of 53s. 4d. from the farm of a windmill there, with all the tolls of grains and its other appurtenances, pertaining or belonging to the same mill, so together let to John Golde, by indenture dated October 10, 24 Henry VIII. for the term of 10 years, rendering thence yearly 53s. 4d. in equal portions, at the feasts of the Annunciation of Blessed Mary the Virgin, and of St. Michael the Archangel. And the said John and his assigns, at their own proper charges and expenses, will repair, sustain, and maintain all the reparations of every kind of the said mill, as well in wood, and iron, and brass work, as in all other necessaries whatsoever pertaining to the same time, during the term aforesaid ; and so at the end of his term will vacate it well and sufficiently repaired, as is more fully contained in the said Indentures : namely, for the said two terms falling within the time of this Account, in the eighth year of his Term.   Of any sums of money received by the same Computer this year, from and for the site of the late Hospital aforesaid, with the gardens, lands, and soil, existing within the precincts of the same late house, containing among themselves one acre and a half of land ;—or from a small parcel of land, on the south side of the said late house, called Godishouse Churchyard, containing 4 perches in length and as many in breadth ;—or from an acre of meadow adjoining the said house, lately in the hands and proper occupation of the Master of the said late Hospital, during the time of the aforesaid Computer, he renders no Account :— because the said site, lands, and other premises, during the same time were not let, but were occupied by the late Master, Brothers, and Sisters of the aforesaid late Hospital.   Sum, 53s. 4d.

Isle of Wight.

But he renders account of 6s. 8d. from the customary rents of a messuage and 20 acres of land, there in the occupation of Thomas Lacy by copy of Court, payable yearly in equal portions, at the feasts of the Annunciation of Blessed

Mary the Virgin and of St. Michael the Archangel. And of 5s. of customary rent of certain lands called [?   ] in the occupation of John Forest, by copy of Court, payable yearly at the same terms. And of 16s. of customary rent of a messuage in Broke, and twenty eight acres of arable land, and of two buttes of meadow in the occupation of John Dewgard, by copy of Court, payable yearly at the same terms. And of 10s. of customary rent of a messuage and 14 acres of arable land, and 4 buttes of meadow, in the occupation of Thomas Leper, by copy of Court, payable yearly at the same terms. And of 23s. 4d. of customary rent of a messuage with a courtyard and five crofts of arable land, containing between them 40 acres of land, and 30 acres of land late in the occupation of William [?] by copy of Court, now in the occupation of [?], payable yearly at the same terms.   Sum, 77s. 8d.

Manor of Stedeham.

Of any sums of money received, by the said Receiver to the use of the King's Majesty, from the issues or profits of the aforesaid manor, during the whole time of this Computation, he renders no account, because the said manor of Stedeham, with all and singular its right, and the whole of the appurtenances, is annexed and bound to the honor of Petworth of the same lord the King, and the issues and profits of the same manor are rendered to the said lord the King by Geoffrey Chamber, Receiver of the same lord the King, of his honor aforesaid.   Sum, Nil.

Sum total received £74. 12s. 2d.

Exoneration of Rents.—From which.

The same Computer, in exoneration or allowance made in the said computation of and for the moiety of £76 16s. 9½d. from part of the issues, rents, revenues, and profits of the possessions pertaining to the said late Hospital, owing at the Feast of the Annunciation of Blessed Mary the Virgin in the 30th year of the King aforesaid, falling within the time of this Computation, because the said late Master of the same late Hospital, received and had all the issues, rents, revenues, and profits aforesaid, owing to the late Hospital at the said Feast of the Annunciation of Blessed Mary the Virgin, happening before the dissolution of the said late hospital, for the use, and sustentation, and for the expenses of same Hospital, the brothers and sisters there, from the recognizance of the same Master: and so in such exoneration this year £33 8s. 4¾d.   Sum, £33 8s 4¾d.

Defect of Rents.

And in defect of rent of a tenement with a garden adjacent, in Portesmouth, late in the occupation of James Michill, at 10s. a year, remaining in the hands of the lord the King, for want of a tenant during the whole time of this Computation, by the oath of the said Computer, 5s. And in defect of rent of another tenement, there late in the occupation of Leonard Colman, at 8s. a year, remaining in the hands of the said lord the King, for want of a tenant during the same time, 4s. And in defect of rent of a toft or piece of land in Godishousegrene near the Anguler Tenement, called Yoxhalle, late in the occupation of [?] at 18d. a year, remaining in the hands of the same lord the King from the same cause, during the said time, 9d.   Sum, 9s. 9d.

Fees and Stipends.

And in fee or stipend of the said Computer, as special Receiver of all the possessions aforesaid, at 53s. 4d. a year: namely, in allowance of such fee or stipend for the half-year ending at the feast of St. Michael the Archangel, in the said 32nd year of the King aforesaid, 26s. 8d. And in fee of John Wyntreshull, Esquire, steward of all the domains, manors, lands, and tenements belonging to the said late Hospital, by the writing of John Incent, doctor of laws, Master of the late Hospital aforesaid, and the brothers and sisters of the same place, dated under their common seal on the 12th day of August, 26 Henry VIII. aforesaid, thereof made to himself during his life, with a certain annuity or annual rent of 40s. for the exercise and occupation of the aforesaid office, to be received annually at the feasts of the Annunciation of Blessed Mary the Virgin, and of St. Michael the Archangel, by the hands of the Receivers, Bailiffs, Farmers, and other officers of the domains, manors, lands and tenements aforesaid, to be paid every year during the life of the same John Wintreshull, with clause of distraint in the manor of Broughton for the non-payment of the annuity aforesaid, as is more fully contained in the said writing, namely, in the allowance of such fee for the half-year ending at the feast of St. Michael the Archangel, in the said 32nd year of the King aforesaid, 20s. And in fee of Henry Acton, Woodward of all the woods of the manor of Broughton, at 3s. 4d. a year; namely in allowance of such fee for the aforesaid time, 20d. And in stipend of [?] Reaper of Broughton aforesaid, at 3s. 4d. a year; namely in allowance of such fee for the time aforesaid, 20d. And in stipend of John Woode, clerk, chaplain of the said Hospital, engaged to celebrate divine service and to administer the sacraments within the chapel or church there, at £6 13s. 4d. a year; namely in allowance of such stipend for the half-year ending at the Feast of St. Michael the Archangel in the said year, the 32nd of the King aforesaid, 66s. 8d.   Sum, 116s. 8d.

Payments to the Poor, with their diets.

And in monies paid by John Incent, clerk, doctor of laws, to twelve brothers and sisters of the said hospital, for their diet, from the 27th day of March, 31 Hen. VIII. to the 11th day of September, 32nd year of the same King, namely during the period of 24 weeks, at the rate of 7d. per week for each of such brothers and sisters, as more fully appears in a certain bill thereof made by the said John Incent, rendered at the time of making this Computation £8 8s. And in similar monies paid by the said late Master to the same brothers and sisters for their stipends, namely to each of them for every quarter of a year 3s. 4d. ; that is to say, in such allowance for the quarter of a year ending at the Feast of the Nativity of St. John the Baptist, in the said 32nd year of the aforesaid King, 40s. And in similar monies paid by the said Computer to the aforesaid brothers and sisters for their diet, from the said 11th day of September, in the said 32nd year of the King aforesaid exclusive, to the Feast of St.Michael the Archangel thence next following inclusive, namely for 18 days, at the rate of 1d. a day for each of them, 18s. And in similar monies, paid by the same Computer to the same brothers and sisters for their stipends, due for the quarter of a year ending at the said Feast of St. Michael the Archangel, in the said 32nd year of the King aforesaid, at the rate of 3s. 4d. for each of them, 40s. Sum, £13 6s.

Cost of necessaries.

And in monies paid by the same Computer for wax candles, bought for the altar of the church or chapel of the Hospital aforesaid, during the time of the Computation aforesaid, 12d. And in costs and charges of the aforesaid Roger Tycheborne so superintending the domains and manors aforesaid, and renewing the rentals of the same domains and manors, and paying the aforesaid stipends and diets of the poor, as aforesaid, for the space of three weeks, together with 13s. 4d. for the writing of the said rentals from the valuation of the officers of the lord the King, 51s. 11d. And in stipend of the Auditor's clerk writing this Computation, 6s. 8d. Sum, 59s. 7d.

Deliveries of monies.

And in monies delivered by the said Computer to Richard Poulet, Esquire, Receiver of the lord the King of the Augmentations of the revenues of the Crown of the same lord the King, in the county of Southampton, from the issues of his office for this year, from the recognition or bill of the same Receiver before the Auditor, £14 8s. 3¼d. Sum, £14 8s. 3¼d.

Sum of all the allowances and deliveries aforesaid £70 8s. 8d.

And due £4 3s. 6d.

Henry Bickeley, late Mayor of Portesmouth, from and for such sums of money received by him from James Bensted, the farmer of Frodyngton, for a certain rent issuing from lands and tenements, lying within the liberty of Portesmouth, parcel of the possessions of the said late Hospital, towards the payment of the fee farm of the same town, as more fully appears by a bill of the same Henry, dated 14 October, for the year ending at the Feast of St. Michael the Archangel, in the said 32nd year of the King aforesaid, signed and renewed in the same year by his own hand.   54s. 2d.

Thomas Lord Sandes, from and for the rent of assise of certain of his lands called Spirewell, otherwise Chalwel, in Broughton, in the right of the late Priory of Mottessonte, being this year in arrears, and not paid.   8s.

John Kebull of Tuderley, gentleman, from and for such sums of money received by him from the farm of certain lands called Overton leases, parcel of the manor of Broughton aforesaid, due for the half-year ending at the Feast of St. Michael the Archangel, in the said 32nd year of the King aforesaid.   13s. 4d.

Anthony Ponde, Esquire, from and for the rent of assise of certain lands and pastures called Rashmere in Hamuldon aforesaid, being this year in arrears and not paid.   4s.

Thomas Wriothisley, Knight, from and for the rent of assise of his lands in Froddington, in the right of the late monastery of Tichefelde, this year being in arrear, and not paid.   4s.

Valor Ecclesiasticus, Henry VIII.

Hospital of St. Nicholas of Portysmouth.

John Incent, now Master.

Is worth, in the form of the lands together with other rents, as well spiritual as temporal, as appears by a certain account book, signed by the hands of the Commissioners of the lord the King.   £79 13s. 7½d.

Reprisals (or Deductions.)

In charitable gifts, fees, and other repayments, as appears by the said account book.   £45 14s. 2d.

| And remains worth | £33 19s. 5½d. |
| Tenths thereof | 67s. 11½d. |

N

THE OLD HOSPITALS OF HAMPSHIRE AND

THE RELIGIOUS HOUSES AND ORDERS

MENTIONED IN THE "STORY OF THE 'DOMUS DEI' OF PORTSMOUTH."

The following notes, chiefly from 'Cox's Magna Britannia,' will be found interesting to any who may not be well acquainted with the suppressed ecclesiastical establishments of Hampshire. The monasteries and orders noticed have been already, brought before the reader by name :—

St. Crosse's, near Winchester, an Hospital, founded by Henry Beaufort, Cardinal and Bishop of Winchester, half-brother of King Henry IV., who, by licence from King Henry VI. Reg. 21., granted to the Master and Brethren of the Hospital of the Holy Crosse, near Winchester, divers manors and lands, &c. to the yearly value of £500, for the maintainance of two chaplains, five and thirty poor men, and three women, to be governed by the said Master. The Cardinal dying before his foundation was completed, King Henry VI. Reg. 33. incorporated them under a Rector of their own, by the name of 'The New Alms House of Noble Poverty', established near Winchester by Henry, Cardinal of England, and Bishop of Winchester, son of John, late Duke of Lancaster, of noble memory,

with grant of a common seal, and power to purchase, &c.
The Hospital or College of St. John de fothering bridge
was given to it, of which House the ancient custom was,
by the first foundation, to dine a hundred poor every day,
if so many came.

SOUTHAMPTON, an Hospital called 'Domus Dei,' founded
and endowed by Philippa, Queen of King Edward III.,
with divers possessions, for the maintenance of a Custos and several poor men and women, besides some
scholars. Gervase de Hampton, Margaret de Redvariis,
and many others, gave diverse lands, &c. to this Hospital,
all whose gifts were recited and confirmed by King Edward
III. The patronage of this Hospital was in that King,
who gave it to the Provost and scholars of Queen's-Hall
in Oxford, and to their successors for ever. He also granted
to the Custos, scholars, brothers, and sisters of that hospital,
and their successors, the alien priory of Sherburn in the
county of Southampton, with all its lands, &c., with this
privilege, to be freed from all taxes and tollages for ever.
Richard, Duke of York, the father, and Richard, Earl of
Cambridge, the grandfather of that King, are in the said
grant alleged to be buried in this Hospital.

BASINGSTOKE, an Hospital, founded by King Henry III.
ad sustentationem Ministrorum Altaris Christi, i.e., for
the maintenance of the Ministers that serve at the altar
of Christ.

QUARRER or QUARRERA, an Abbey of Cistercian
Monks, built and endowed. by Baldwin de Rivers, Earl of
Devon. Richard, Earl of Exeter, son of Baldwin, confirmed to God, the Holy Virgin, and Gaufridus, Abbot of
Savigny, (to which Abbey it was made a cell) this house
and divers lands and revenues given by his father, adding
others to pray for the souls of his father and mother.
Henry Fitz-Empresse, who writ himself Son of the Duke
of Normandy, and Earl of Anjou, Engelgerius de Bohun,
and William de Vernon, Earl of Devon, were benefactors
to this house.

SUTHWYK or SOUTHWICK, a Monastery of Canons Regular of St. Augustine, founded and endowed with divers lands by King Henry I., who granted them not only a freedom from taxes and all other exactions, but all sorts of liberties ; as not to be impleaded for any matter, but in the presence of himself, or his heirs, &c. The manor and parsonage of Southampton, valued at £60 15s. 1d., besides the salary of £6 13s. 4d. paid out of it yearly to the curate, belonged to it, and was, after the dissolution, exchanged with the Lord Chancellor, Sir Thomas Wriothesley, by King Henry VIII. Reg. 38. for other lands.

TYCHEFELD or TITCHFIELD, an Abbey of Monks, called Præmonstratentes, founded by Peter de Rupibus, Bishop of Winchester, upon the manor of Tychefeld, by the grant of King Henry III., to whom it belonged. He endowed it with several lands and revenues, and the King granted to the Monks very great liberties in the said manor and their lands; as to be free from tolls, suit of forest-courts, lawing of dogs, &c. Eva de Clinton, Reginald de Alba-mara, Baldwin de Ripariis, Lord of the Isle of Wight, Gilbert de Mansel, and Peter de Sukemund were great bene-factors to this Abbey. This last gave certain lands in Ingeyenne, to hold of the chief Lord by half a knight's-fee, and of himself and his heirs by a pair of spurs, or 3d. to be paid at the Feast of St. Michael. All these gifts were confirmed to this house by King Edward II. Reg. II. The Abbot of Hales-Owen in Shropshire, founded by the same Bishop, was the Visitor of this abbey, and John Powl, Abbot, visited in 1420, and took an inventory of all their goods and stock, which is set down in the Monas-ticon.

CANONS REGULAR OF ST. AUGUSTINE. It is unknown how far St. Augustine ever framed any formal guidance of monastic life, but a rule based on his writings was adopted by as many as thirty monastic fraternities ; of which one was that of the ' Canons Regular of St. Augustine,' estab-lished about the middle of the 11th century. Their discipline was not so severe as that of the monk properly so called, but more so than that of the secular or parochial clergy. They wore a long cassock, with a white rochet over it, all covered by a black cloak, whence they were often called Black Canons. In England, where they were established early in the 12th century, they had about 170 houses.

CISTERCIANS. An order which takes its name from Citeaux, (Cistercium) near Dijon, and was founded by the Benedictine abbot, Robert de Molême, in 1098. Within little more than a century after their foundation the Cistercians possessed nearly 2000 abbeys in various parts of Europe. They were exceedingly strict, poverty was their watchword, all splendour in their churches was avoided, not even a cross could boast of silver or gold. They never had a cure of souls, and were known by wearing a white robe with a black scapulary. The number of Cistercian abbeys in England at the time of the general surrender was 75, besides 26 nunneries. Riches and indolence brought this powerful order into decay. Even before the Reformation many of their convents had died out.

PREMONSTRATENSIANS. An order which was established at one time very generally throughout Germany. It was founded, in the early part of the 12th century, by St. Norbert, a native of Xanten. Struck by the looseness and carelessness of the Clergy, secular as well as regular, he resolved to attempt a reform. The spot chosen by him for his cloister was, he fancied, revealed to him, and called *Pré Montré*, or in Latin, *Pratum Monstratum* 'the meadow pointed out,' from which the name of the order was taken. It was substantially that of the Canons Regular of St. Augustine, and aimed, by reformed rules, to return to the primitive fervour of the monastic institute, and above all things to give holy instruction to the people. Music was deemed a beautiful and helping handmaid of religion. This order spread rapidly in France, the Low Countries, and Germany, while it was very coldly received in Italy and Spain. As usual, time brought with it relaxation of discipline ; a reform was attempted which only created division. The order gradually fell into unpopularity, except in Germany, and has now almost entirely disappeared. In Austria, here and there, is found a thinly peopled but wealthy house of Nobertines, but it is an order evidently fast approaching its end.

OBSERVANTISTS. In the time of Leo X. the Franciscan Order was much disturbed by a controversy of some standing as to the original rule and practice laid down by St. Francis. The quarrel ended in division. The less rigid party, under the name 'Conventuals,' obtained a distinct General, and authority for a mitigated attention to their rules. Their churches and convents admit greater richness of architecture and decoration ; and they are at liberty to acquire and retain, in the name of the order, the property of these and similar possessions. The stricter community, known as 'Observantists' or Franciscans *Strictioris Observantiæ (Observantes)*, renounced all property, adhering to the rigid law of poverty as laid down by St. Francis At the close of the last century they are said to have numbered above 70,000, distributed over 3000 convents, and they still are a very numerous and wide spread body, as well in Europe as in America, and in the missionary districts of the East.

THE "DOMUS DEI" AND THE FORTIFI-CATIONS OF PORTSMOUTH.

HE "Domus Dei" has, from the day of its surrender to the present moment, been connected with the defence and government of Portsmouth. As early as the first year of Edward VI. (1547) we find the "Churche at Goddeshouse," "the Loft in the Armory," and "the Armory" used as storehouses for "munycions sent by the Lord Grete Mr. from the Towre." In the time of Elizabeth, the Master's House, the Hall, and Kitchen were converted into a fitting dwelling for the Queen's 'Captayne' or Governor of Portsmouth, and were occupied as the Government House until the early part of this century. Further, there is every reason to believe that, from the time when Portsmouth became a fortified town with a garrison, the troops have always worshipped in the Church of the "Domus Dei." Fortifying Portsmouth is therefore closely connected with the preservation of the buildings of the old Hospital, and on that account deserves some notice in the Story of the "Domus Dei."

Although Portsmouth was, when a small fishing village, created a Borough by Richard I.,* it made little or no

---

* The lion-hearted King embarked from Portchester for Palestine and landed there on his return. Hence, it is said, we find the star and crescent on the Borough Shield.

progress for the next three centuries. In 1345, when
Edward III. was raising a fleet for the invasion of France,
while the Isle of Wight provided 13 ships and 220 men,
Southampton 21 ships and 576 men, and Lymington 9
ships and 158 men, Portsmouth could only send 5 ships
and 96 men. And, just twenty two years later, although
on the 15th day of November, in the 16th year of that
King's reign (1343), the crown had, out of compassion &c.
("compacientes statui hominum nostrorum villæ de Portesmouth qui, per diversa incendia, roberias, et destructiones
aliegenarum hostium nostrorum diversis vicibus ibidem de
guerrâ applicantium, multipliciter sunt depressi, ac volentes
eo prætextu cum hominibus prædictis agere generosè &c.")
granted certain privileges to enable the inhabitants to wall*
and fortify the town, ("in muragio et fortifacione villæ,")
so utterly unprotected was Portsmouth, that the Nor-
mans entered the harbour with a great force, and set
fire to the whole town.† This raid appears to have called
forth no effort to raise even a small fortification, for it was
only in the time of Edward VI. that the "toures in the

---

* "Rex omnibus ad quos, etc, salutem. Supplicarunt nobis homines villæ
de Portsmouth, ut, cum quintodecimo die Novembris, anno regni nostri Angliæ
sextodecimo, in auxilium villæ prædictæ claudendæ, paviendæ, et emendandæ,
concesserimus eisdem hominibus, quod, a predicto quintodecimo die usque ad
finem octo annorum tunc proximè sequentium plenarie completorum, de rebus
venalibus ad dictam villam venientibus certas consuetudines caperent, prout
in litteris nostris patentibus eisdem hominibus inde confectis plenius conti-
netur." The scheme turned out a failure. Within three years the inhabitants
found that heavily taxing outsiders was in reality heavily taxing themselves,
and besought the King to relieve them by cancelling the letters patent, and so
doing away with the troublesome tolls. The town had suffered severely and
the enclosing been but little furthered—"homines et mercatores, tam alieni-
genæ quam indiginæ, ad villam prædictam accedere non curarunt, sicque iidem
homines predictæ villæ de Portesmuth, proficuum aliquod de hujusmodi conces-
sione hucusque non perciperint seu percipere possent, præterquam quadraginta
solidos, quos circa reparacionem et emendationem clausuræ dictæ villæ appo-
suerunt; velimus eisdem hominibus concedere, quod ipsi dictas litteras nostras
nobis, ex causâ prædictâ, restituere posse cancellandas, ita quod de collectione
custumarum prædictarum decetero exonerari possent." Forty shillings, equal
to about £20 of the present time, did, we may be sure, very little towards protecting Portsmouth. Patent Roll, 18 Edward III. pt. 2. m. 37.

† "Normani intraverunt cum magnâ potentiâ et miserunt in flammam
ignis totam villam." Henry de Knyghton.

haven mouth were begun." Richard III. during his short
reign turned his attention carefully to Portsmouth. He
" set forward " the towers begun by Edward IV, and, curiously enough, the first State Paper, telling of the appointment of a Governor of Portsmouth, dates very soon after
his accession to the throne. In the Harleian MS. 433. f. 25,
the King concedes to "William Vuedale (Uvedale) Esquire,*
the Keepership of the castle and town of Portchestre, Portesmouthe, and of the country there about; also the super-
vision and government of the town of Portsmouth and of
the royal place there, as long as it shall be pleasing to the
King;" and in Har. MS. 433. f. 35. b. is given to "William Mirfeld Thoffice of keeping of the Castelle of Portchestre and of the fforeste and warren ther; and also the
supervisore and guuernour of the Towne of Portsmouthe,
and of the place ther, with other ut patet in billâ for terme
of lyff. "Portsmouth was now just developing into importance. Its vast and well placed harbour was evidently
deemed an object well worthy of government care. And
this is supported by the facts, that in 1500 Henry VII.
made Portsmouth a royal dockyard, and " Henry VIII., at his
first warres into France, erected on the southe part of the
toune IV. great brewing howses, with the implements, to
serve his shippes at such tyme as they should go to se in
tyme of warre." He also " ended the tourres in the haun
mouthe, at the procuration of Fox, Bishop of Winchester."†
Still, with all this attention, Portsmouth could in no way
be called a fortified town, for, on the further testimony of
Leland, we are invited to believe that the defences erected
by Henry VIII. were but of the feeblest kind :—
    "The towne of Portsmouthe is mured from the est
tour a forough lengthe, with a mudde waulle armed with
tymbre, whereon be great peaces of yron and brassen ordi-
nauns ; and this peace of waulle, having a ditch without

---

* He lies buried in Southwick Chuich.

† Leland Itin. Vol. III. p. 32.

it, runneth so far flat south south-east, and is the place
moste apte to defend the toun there open on the hauen.
Ther runneth a ditch almost flat est for a space, and within
it is a waulle of mudde like to the other, and so theus goeth
rounde aboute the toun to the circuite of a mile. Ther
is a gate of tymber at the north-est ende of the toun, and
by it is cast up an hille of erthe diched, wherein be gunnes
to defend entre into the toun by land. Ther is much vacant gronnd wytin the toun walle. Ther is one fair streate
in the toune from west to north est. The toun is bare
and little occupied in tyme of peace."*

In 1552 Edward VI., writing to his friend Barnaby Fitz
Patrick, fully confirms Leland's description :—

"From this we wente to Portismouth toune, and there
viewed not only the toune itself and the hauen, but also
divers bulwarkes ; in viewing of which we find the bulwarkes chargeable, massie, and ramparted, but il facioned,
il flanked, and set in unmete places ; the toune weake in
comparison of that it ought to be ; the hauen notable
greate, and standing by nature easie to be fortified. And,
for the more strength thereof, we have devised two strong
castellis on either side of the hauen, at the mouth thereof ;
for at the mouth of the hauen is not past ten score over, and
for a mile and a heaf hable to bear the greatest ship in
Christendom."

But possibly some may think that Leland and the boy
king† were poor judges of defences. If so, the following
interesting letter, addressed by the Governor of Portsmouth
to the Privy Council, will satisfy any reasonable mind :—

---

* Leland Itin. vol. III. p. 81.

† Cardan, the Italian physician, who saw Edward VI. professionally in 1552, said
that he was ' a marvellous boy '—"*monstrificus puellus*"—and Sir James Mackintosh,
(History, Vol. ii. p. 249) states that the Journal he wrote " bears marks of an un-
tainted taste and of a considerate mind."

NO. IX.

State Papers, Domestic, Edward VI., Vol. I. No. 19.

The Captayne of Portismouth to the Counsell xvii February, 1546-7.

To the ryght honorable and my syngulcr good lords, the lords of the King's majisties most honorable preve counsell. Geve this with all possyble dylygence.

It may please your honorable lordships, to be advertysyd, that, thys nyght at viij of the clocke within night, I did receve the kings majisties comyssyon for the leveing of iic. men within the sheres of Surrey, Wylyts, and Berkesher. And, imedyately upon the receypt thereof, I have dyspached my brother wt ii. of my household Sarvants into the same Sheres, so that, I trust, the men shalbe at Portsmouthe by the day apoynted in your lordships' letters, which is the xxviii of thys present. I do not dout but that your lordships dothe ryght well consydre the estate of thys Towne, and how it lyeth open, so that at a lowe water men may cum into yt although they were xxx in rank. And also, the gates to the water syde ar so weke, that iiii. or fyve good felowes with a peec of Tymber may lay them on the ground, and the walls, with thys frost that hathe byn now of late, doeth mowther away and begynnyth in dyvers places to fall into the dyke ; besides that the felds adjoyning to the dytchys brynke growe full of bushys and fursys, vere mete to be made playne for the suerty of the Towne, which I doubt to doo wout commandment from your lordships, which yf I may have shalbe shortly don. And, for settyng on c. of the iic. to worke as laborers, I lacke both tolys and caryage with Tymber plancks, and many other things wherewith I could occupy them yf I had yt, yet neverthelesse they shalbe doing.

Of Mr. Captayne of the Wyght I have not yet hard any thyng towching the iic, whiche I shuld receve of hym, and therefore I have geven my brother (whom I have sent for the leveying of the men) xx£ in hys purse to be geven to them in prest tyll the King's Matie. money shall cum, trusting that your good lordships wyll with spede geve ordre how they shalbe payd from tyme to tyme.

Here lackyth also Gonners for the grete ordenaunce, who are in nomber in thys Towne but xv. And here is about thys Towne xvij. pecys of brasse and xlviij. pecys of Iron, as thys boke can declare, which I send to your lordships herein enclosyd.

The Ships with the kyng's matis. vyctuells ar not yet gon, but ar putt backe agayne with the contrary wynde.

This after nowne ther cam ii ships Spanyards into the Rode here, who sayd that they durst not passe the Sees homward for fere of six tall ships,

Scotts or Frenchmen; they were in doubt whiche they wer, that wer on the Southe part of the wyght within a kennyng of the land.*

And thus, haveyng no doubt but that I wyll render unto your lordships a good accompt of the Kings majestis Towne here, or ells to lay my bonys therin, I shall always pray Almighty God to send your lordships th'encrease of moche honor. From Portismouth this xvj of February at xi of the clock, at mydnight.

Your lordships bowden
Edward Vaughan.

The anxiety of the Captain of Portsmouth to repair the works as the walls were "fast mowthering away," and his simple story, that "four or five good felowes with a pece of tymber may lay the gates to the water side on the ground," make it perfectly certain that the poor guns of those days, however numerous, were of litte worth when mounted on platforms ready to fall after a few discharges. On the 30th November, 1585, it is reported to the Lord Grete Master, that, through the weakness of the platform, the gunners dare not fire a salute on the Queen's coronation day. If such was the state of things even in the time of Elizabeth, the use of the 'Ordynaunce,' as mounted on the batteries of Portsmouth and "within Goddeshouse" on the 16th February, 1546-7, may be easily imagined.

NO. X.

State Papers Domestic. Edward vi. Vol 1, No. 20.

Ordynaunce belonging to the Towne of Portismouthe, February 16th, 1546-7.

In the Bastylian betwixt Mr. Rydleyes Tower and the Towne,
upon the great platform of the Towne Wall.

First oone Culveryn of Brasse, wt a forlocke.

---

* Within a month after the accession of Edward, it became quite certain that a struggle with Scotland was close at hand. On the 27th of February, 1547, Sir Andrew Dudley was instructed to cruise off the Scottish coast, and within a fortnight he had captured the Scottish vessel 'Lion.' The ships spoken of as "lately victualled," and the active proceedings on the part of the "Captayne of Portesmouthe" are clearly movements made on account of the war about to take place with Scotland, and therefore possibly with France. (Ellis, "Second Series" Vol. ii p. 17.)

Item oone Doble Culveryn of Brasse of Arcanes makyng
It. oone Frenche Canon of Brasse.
It. oone Scottisshe Doble Culveryn of Brasse.
It. oone Saker of Brasse with a Rose and a garter aboute it.
It. oone Saker of cast Iron of Levett's making.
It. iiii Bumbards of Iron, with their Chambers.

In the grene Bulwark towards the Wynd Myll hyll.

Item a Canon of Brasse of Peter Bawde's making.
It. a Culveryn of Brasse of the same man's makyng with a forlocke.
It. a Frenche Demy Canon of Brasse.
It. a Frenche Saker of Brasse.
It. a Demy Slyng of Iron with ii chambers.
It. too Flanckers of Iron with their iiii chambers.
It. oone porte piece of Iron with ii Chambers.

In the new Mownt at the end of the iiij bruhouses.

Item three Fowlers of Iron, with eche of theym oone Chamber.

In Davy Savor's Bulwerk.

Item ii Sakers of cast Iron of Levett's makyng.
It. oone hole Slyng of Iron with ii Chambers.
It. ii Flanckers of Cast Iron with their Chambers.

In the new Bastylian at the gate.

Item oone Saker of cast Iron of Levett's makyng.
It. oone Fowler of Iron with a Chamber.

Upon the Mownte at the gate.

Item oone Saker of Brasse with the Rose and the garter aboute it.
It. too Fawconnes of Brasse.
It. a Demy Culveryn of cast Iron of Levett's makyng.
It. oone quarter Slyng of Iron with ii Chambers.
It. Fyve Flanckers of Iron with their Chambers.

At the Wall's ende by the Towne gate.

Item oone Saker of Brass broken, with the Rose and the garter aboute it.
It. oone Flancker of Iron, with a Chamber.

In the new Bastylian towards Kyngston.

Item iii Flanckers of Iron with their Chambers.

In the Bulwerk towards Kyngston.

Item oone Saker of Brasse with the Rose and the garter upon it.
It. oone Fawcon of Brasse with the Rose upon it.
It. oone quarter Slyng of Iron with ii Chambers.
It. iii Flanckers of Iron with their Chambers.

Upon the Wall to the Docke Warde.

Item oone Saker of cast Iron of Levett's makyng.
It. oone Saker of cast Iron of Flaunder's makyng.

In the Bulwerk at the Myil bridge goyng to the Docke Wardes.

Item oone Doble Culveryn of Brasse of Peter Bawde's making.
It. ii Sakers of cast Iron of Levett's makyng.
It. oone Slyng of Iron.
It. iii Flanckers of Iron with theyr Chambers.

Upon the grene before goddeshouse gate.

Item too Sakers of cast Iron, the oone of Levett's makyng, and the other
of Flaunder's makyng.
It. too Serpentynes of Iron with their Chambers.
It. oone port piece of Iron without any Chambers.

Within goddeshouse.

Item oone Fawconet of Brasse.
The Number of Brasse pieces of Ordynaunce as well great as small xxii.
The Number of Iron pieces of Ordynaunce of all sorts xlviii.
The hole Number of pieces of Ordynaunce as well of Brasse as of iron
lxv.
Ordenaunce from Portesmouth xvi February, 1546-7

Such was the weak state of Portsmouth during the
reign of Edward VI.   Under the rule of Mary, neglect
made it still weaker.   Religious excitement, deadly persecution, and busy conspirator-hunting prevented in her time
anything like attention to national defences.   The whole
country for a season lost heart.   But the fall of Calais, on
the 7th January, 1558, seems to have brought it to a deep
sense of its degraded condition.   On the 20th January,
the Parliament assembled and granted a subsidy to carry
on the war against the French King and the Scots, " who

daily do practise by all dishonourable ways and means, with the aid and power of all their confederates and allies, to annoy their majesties and this their realm, and other the dominions of the same; and, by all likelihood, if time and place do permit, do mind to make some invasion into sundry parts of this realm, as well upon the sea coast as elsewhere."* Money having been voted, something had to be done; if not by the honest and patriotic, the selfish and unprincipled were, we may be quite sure, ready to feign active measures and share the spoil. On the 30th March, Thomas Harvey, Knight Marshal, received instructions about taking muster of the forces at Portsmouth, and on the last day of October, £500 were remitted for payment of the Garrison. Nothing more was done. Happily for Portsmouth, and still more so for the country at large, before the end of the year the Queen died. There was no issue by the Spanish alliance, and so, by God's mercy, the world had an opportunity of seeing " a noble and puissant nation rousing herself like a strong man after sleep and shaking his invincible locks."† Yes! with Elizabeth came a wondrous change for the better. England was herself again. A writer intimately acquainted with every State Paper of that Queen's reign justly remarks, "The wisdom and energy of Elizabeth's government are conspicuous in the care taken to put the defences of the realm in a complete state of efficiency." " In her reign, defences were promoted by the systematic organization of the militia, by the holding of frequent musters periodically, at intervals of about three years, and by surveys of all the creeks and landing places, and by attention to the breed of horses in gentlemen's parks throughout the kingdom. All this was carried on by commissions addressed to the

---

* 4 and 5 Philip and Mary, c. 11.

† Milton''s "Areopagitica."

nobility and gentry in every county."*   As navies, especially in Spain, were becoming formidable, we naturally find
great attention given to Portsmouth and its vast and well
placed harbour.   The State Papers connected with fortifying Portsmouth during the reign of Elizabeth would fill
a volume with highly interesting details.   The following
pressing appeal to the Privy Council from the Governor
of Portsmouth, and the order from the Queen to the Earls
of Arundell and Sussex will show how soon, after Elizabeth's accession to the throne, energetic steps were taken
for strengthening the fortifications of the country.†   The
wording of Captain Turnour's petition is quaint, but it
tells of a good man and true.

NO. XI.

State Papers, Domestic, Eliz. Vol. 2, No. 12.

To the right honorable the lords and other of the Queen's majesties' privy
Counsell.

My good Lords ye experience by execution and sight of mayne mischiefs,
which are insident to ye warres and daile ministred by princis, hath taught me,
a simple man, to judge ye better of myne own estate, and of ye place wherein I
serve, to ye which I owe my life.   And albeit in respect of my duetie to ye
Quene's highnes, and in perfourmannce of such servic as is loked for at my
hands, I waye not my life any more then I ought.   Yet, I consider what honor
it were to you all to appoint my servic so, as if ye enemey came to seeke us, I
might either be able to repulce him, or at ye lest, if I were his praye, to make

---

* Introduction to " Catalogue of State Papers Domestic Elizabeth."

† Beer for the Navy was not forgotten.   Henry VIII. had erected brew-
houses, (once occupying the site of the present Four-House Barracks) but without
fresh water they were useless.   The Earl of Winchester therefore writes thus,
on January 14th, 1560, to his "loving friend Sir William Cecill, Knight, prin-
cipall Secretarie to the Quene's Majestie:—"
    " The brue house and the freshe water must be had at Portesmouth as in
the great booke is declared " (State Papers Dom. Eliz. Vol. ii, No. 3.)
    The daily allowance of a sailor, in the time of Elizabeth, was :—1lb. of
biscuit, one gallon of beer, 2lbs. of beef four days a week; the other three,
stock fish, butter, and cheese instead of beef.   Pay, 5d. a day at sea; 4½d.
when in harbour.   (State Papers Dom. Eliz. April 13. 1565.)

hym buy me so deare ere he waune me, as he should never hast after to fetche enie more of ye price. And yis help were a fortificacion in Portismouth, which like as it is a quarter built allready, and wold with small charge be finished to such force as yt might for ever be kept with fewer men then her Majistie hath here at yis instant, against ye frenche kyngs worst or eny other enimie. So should it allso be able to receve ye riches of ye Ile, and what more is, take away ye unnecessary chargs consumid here in keping other forts which ys beynge finished, and may well appeare to be vanelie maynteyned. I am ye bolder, my lord, to offer you my opinion, because I knowe your L. carfull to forsee ye safety of us all, and your contrey; and that you consider the greatnes of your ennimie ye frenche kyng, his gredie ambicion, and advancement of his pride and corrage by his late conquests,* by ye wch he hathe brought us to our olde bounds. And what honour it were to hym to take foote hold here of us, who have masterid them in their countrey, and kept them trebutarie your L. can wisely judg. So may it, therefore, seeme good unto you to determine uppon yis fortificacion, and to remove ye trust uppon old presidents, how yis peece hath bene kept in tymes past, because, as our strength is lessenid, our ennimies are increasid. And to conclude, forasmuch as my words may want credit in yis matters, yt may please you to use ye opinion and judgement of Mr. Worsely, who, if he be comanded to perus yis litell plot, I dought not, shall conferme my words concerning ye forte. And thus I humbly ende, and leve to trouble you. From Portismouthe ye 26 Januarie, 1558-9.

The derth and scarcitie of victualls and other necessaries insident to ye soldior is here very great, wch may be grtly redressid if yt may stand with your L. plesurs to consider me with a pay.

Your Lordshipes humbly at commandment,
Edward Turnour.

NO. XII.

State Papers Dom. Eliz. Vol. 14, No. 42, (1560.)
By the Quene.

To our right trustie and welboved cosen and counsailor, the Earle of Arundell, lord Steward of our howse, and lord warden of our forrest, within our Com. of Southt.; And to our right trustie and right welbeloved cosen, Therle of Sussex, Chief Justice and Justice in Oyer of all our forrests, parks, warrens,

---

* Calais, after having been held by the England 210 years, was retaken by the Duke of Guise, January 7th, 1558.

and chases of this side Trent; and, in their absence, to the Lieutenant and Woodward of the same Forrest.

Right trustie and right welbeloved and trustie and welbeloved, wee grete you well. And wheareas wee have committed the surveie of all our castles and forts, within our ysle of wight and the seacoste within our countie of Southtn., to our trustie and right welbeloved the Lord St. John, and the repaire of the same castles and forts by his discrecion, from time to time; for the doing whereof wee have given him letters, under our signe manuell and signet, authorizing him to the doing thereof, and also imprested him money for that purpose, wch Reparacions cannot be made with out necessarie Timber. Wee, therefore, mynding our said castles and forts to be kept in good reparacion, will and commaund you to delyver, from time to time, to our Mr. Carpenter, of our Works of the said castles, and of all other our work within Portismouth and our saide Isle of Wight, all soche timber as the said lord St. John shall wright unto you, for indenting with the saide Mr. Carpenter, from tyme tyme, for all soch tymber as you shall delyver upon the lord John's letters for the saide reparacions. And thes our letters shalbe Warrant sufficient with the letters and indentures of the lord St. John, and Mr. Carpenter mencioning the receipt of the said Timber in that behalfe. Forseing that you suffer the said Mr. Carpenter to make sale of the said loppes and toppes to our most proffet, or make lyme with some part of the same, towards the charges of our said works. Geoven at our honnor of Hampton Courte the viith daie of November, the second yere of our Reigne.

To show further the activity of the government, we have a letter, from an enterprising and self confident engineer, making it clear that plans, for the effectual defence of Portsmouth, were ready for execution so early as 1560, and that an efficient officer was sent down during the year to see them carried out. The Lords of the Privy Council seem to have been in great fear lest the plans should be lost. Mr. Portenary assures their Lordships that, were they known to the whole world, no harm could possibly follow. But he shall speak for himself:—

NO. XIII.

State Papers, Dom. Eliz. Vol. 15, No. 79. (1560)

Most excellent and noble Lords, under that most humble reverence and

obedient service, wch becometh a most humble and obedient servant unto your
excellencies, (whose hand I most humblye kysse) may yt please the same to
heare and consider that which followeth:—

*   *   *   *

Now your excellencies have commanded me, that I shuld go to Portesmouth
to visite the town and situacon thereof, and to take the platt att my discretion.
Whereupon I made a platt wherewith every manne was not satisfied. Wherefore I indevored myself to devise two other platts, that eyther of them is of
such a strength as shalbe imprennable, and also with the least charges that
possible were, which doo content and satisfie your excellencies, as in lykewise
I did at Barwick devise a third platt of an invincible force and of a reasonable
charge. Now, and yt may please your excellencies to putt the case, that all the
platte of Portesmouth were lost and came in whattsoever mannes hands in the
whoale worlde, there could incurre no danger at all, nor any occasion of suspi-
cion. For whosoever mought have them could not thereby ymagin any evill
enterprise toffend yt, but contrary wyse, they wold be glad of them for a patron
and example to fortifye their frontiers thereafter. Because they may be com-
pared to all fortresses which ar of late made in Christiandom, and peradventure
better considered and with a more comodite and force then is in those which
are already made in diverse places. All the new fortresses of fame as Milan,
Placencia, Modana, and Turino in Italye, Chalon in Burgenye, and Antwerp,
no stranger is forbidden the rampares, and all their platts are in every manes
hand. And, in lykemaner, when anye of the said platts shalbe put in execution and buylded at Portesmouth, or at any other place, thorowly as they ar
devised, all reason will geve that no force shuld be hable to prevaile again yt or
put yt in any danger. Provided that yt be furnished but indifferently. Therefore there could not chance so greatt a danger for the losse of souch lyke platts
as some have thought, and made yt so heynous, when the thing shalbe thorowly considered. True yt ys that to losse them, shuld be a great displeasure,
but not that any danger shuld therefore folow.

*   *   *   *

Now, your excellencies doo comand me to goo to Portesmouth, to put in
execution the platt your excellencies are resolved upon, I am prompte and ready
t'obey your whoale comandment to do that service, to use souch diligence and to
take souch pain and travayle as souch a work doth require, and as yt doth be-
com her Majisties faithful servant.

To which end, yf yt mought please your excellencies I woold most humblye
beseech the same to ordeyn, that I should goo thether with souch a comission

as may be thought meet to her Majisties faithful servant yn that vocation, to
be hable thereby to ordeyne a'nd comand for the service of souch a work, to
th'end I may assuredly put the sayd work to his perfect effect, and her Majistie
to be whoally and thorowly served.

Two years after Portenary's letter we find mention
made of the Governor's House. Whether the Captayne
of Portsmouth had yet taken up his quarters in the Master's House of the 'Domus Dei,' I cannot say for certain.
It is highly probable that he had, as a few years later, when
the buildings of the Hospital were all thoroughly repaired,
the Captayne's House is mentioned as a well known part
of the establishment. Kyllwey's report and petition present
an amusing story of travel and prices 300 years ago.

NO. XIV.

State Papers Dom. Eliz. Vol. 24, No. 57.

To the right honorable Sir William Cyrill, knight, secretorie to the Quene's
Majestie these be given.

At my repayre hether uppon Sondaye, as I wrote to your honor I wolde
doo, I founde Sir Adryan Ponings so imbeusied and so nere uppo goinge, as I
colde have noo tyme with him to consider off anye thinge, namelye in what con-
dicion he wolde leave the howse, and, synce his departure, I doo understande
bye my ladye his wyffe, that he hath geven order for the rigginge of the howse,
as nothinge is to remayne butt bare walles. So as I am compelled to bringe
stuffe fro my howse, as well for the kychen as otherwise, and understandinge
that my lorde of Warwicks repayre hether is so nere at hande, and the dystance
of my howse allmoste fortie myles off, besides the troble of iij ferris bye the
waye, as I feare I shall not be hable to gett hyt hether to sarve that turne, the
provission for his diet lykewise is all to seek, as I have great feare I shall not
entertayne hym as I wolde ; and fyndinge thes quarters not onlye barre for
provyssion but also extreme deare, and here noo helpe at all butt for the pennye
and I not storyd of money, ham constraynid therefore to crave furtherance at
your hands for the obtaynge of the Quene's Majesties warrant for one monethes
waggis in prest. More your honor shall understande, that here is delivered,
synce Mr. Poning's departure, bye the hands of this bearer, clarke of the armorye,

fiftie eyght drye fatts off corseletts, harquebutts cccxxv, and flaskets cccxxiij, and of towchboxes cccxxxiij, of morris pykes eleven hundered iiij skore xiiij, for Imployment; of which I truste your honor will cause comyssion to be directid, as of the premesis, to returne sutche dyreccion as bye the lords of the cownsell shalbe thought mete. Thus I leave farder trobelinge your honor commending the same to the marcyfull preservacion of the allmightie. From portesmouthe, the xxixth of September, 1562.

Your honors to comande
Wm. Kyllwey.

How far the appeal for a month's pay was successful is not stated, but this we know that, two days before the application was made, the Queen had given authority for the issue of the usual pay and table money :—

NO.. XV

State Papers, Dom. Eliz. Vol. 24, No. 53.

By the Quene.

Right trustie and right welbeloved cosin, we grete you well. Whereas, at the request of your sonne the Lord Chidiock Poulett, we have· for this tyme excused hym from the charge of our Towne of Portesmouth, and have appointed Sir Willm. Kyllwey, Knight, to tak the charge therof in thabsence of Sir Adrian Ponyngs. We will and require yow to make allowance and payment unto the same Sir Willm. Kyllwey, upon the warrant dormant remaynyng with yow, for the wage and entertainement of the Captayne there, in such sort as the said Adrian Poynys was by the same allowed. To begynne at such day as you shall hereafter understand, untill the retourne thither of the said Sir Adrian Ponyngs. And these our lettres shalbe your warrant in this behalf. Geven under our signet at Hampton Court, xxvij Septembris, 1562.

The fortifications had now been well commenced, and here it is that we, for the first time, meet with an account of the repair of a part of the old "Domus Dei." The floor of the Church having become decayed, £40 were expended to renew it :—

State Papers Dom. Eliz. Vol. 34, No. 31. (24 July, 1564.)

A note of the charges for felling, hewyng, breking into loades, and sawinge of the timber for the flouring of the church in Gods house.

Item, the fellinge, squaring, and the breking into loads, also sawing into bordes, and sawing into somer posts and joysts, the charges is   xl£.

Good progress was made in the defences, we may suppose, during the next four years, for, in July 1568, Richard Popinjay reports, that he has spent all the money supplied him, and urges the necessity of carrying on the works with vigour. He forwards with his report a detailed estimate of "the wantes or lackes for the fyrnishynge of the Platforme, wher the greate Ordnaunce lyeth at Portsmouthe."* Acting upon the opinion of the surveyor, evidently an officer possessing the confidence of the authorities, more money (£219 10s. 7d.) is expended on the platform, and in finishing "the watchhowse according to the platte;" and then three commissioners are specially appointed to examine thoroughly "the Towne fortresses, and bull workes of Portesmouthe, and the Ordynanc munytion, armor, and shott, remaynynge in the same, and the defects thereof, &c." The letter of the Commissioners and their "vewe and surveye" are valuable papers, simply as records of the strength or rather weakness of Portsmouth on June 9th, 1571; but they are especially so, as connected with the story of the "Domus Dei," inasmuch as they tell us how "godes howse yarde," "godes howse churche," and "godes howse hawl" were used just 300 years ago, what articles were stored in them, and what was their condition.

* State Papers Dom. Eliz. Vol. 47, No. 51.

NO. XVII.

State Papers Dom. Eliz. Vol. 78, No. 12.   18th May, 1571.

To the ryght honorable our verye goode lord, the lordes and others of the Quenes Majesties most honorable prying Cownsayle.

Ryght honorable, accordynge to the Quenes Majisties Letter, dated the xxiiijth of Apryll last, to us dyrected, we together wythe Sir henry Radeclyf, have taken vewe and surveye of the Towne, fortreses, and bull workes of Portesmowthe, and of the Ordynanc, munytyon, armor, and shott nowe remaynynge within the same, and the defectes thereof, and mustered the inhabitants of the Towne and Isle of Portesmowth, of whyche owr doynge we have sent here withe unto your honors partycular bookes, subscrybed withe owr handes and the hand of the sayed Sir Henry, nowe Captayne of the sayed Towne and Isle. In the end of whiche booke ys contayned tho defectes and wantes we fynde in the premisses accordynge to owre symple knoledge and understandynge, referryng the consyderacon therof unto your honors, and so most humbly we take owr leave of your honors, praying unto th'almighty God for the longe preservatyon and continuanc of the same. Wryten at Portesmouthe, the xviiijth of May, 1571.

Your honors most humble to commawnde,

H. Wallop,

Wm. Kyngesmyll,

John Basyng.

(Indorsed)

Sir H. Wallop and the rest of ye Comissioners for ye survey of Portesmouth to ye LLs of ye Counsell.

NO. XVIII.

State Papers Dom. Eliz. Vol. 78, No. 12-2.

The Survey of Munition in Portesmouthe, 9th June, 1571.

A book declarynge the veue or Surveye of the munytyon, ordynance, armour, and weapon remaynynge in the Quenes Majisties Towne and Fortresses in Portesmouthe, after the dethe of Sir Adryan Poynynges, knight, late Captayne of the sayed Towne and Fortresses, made and delyvered by Sir Henry

Wallopp, Sir Wyllym kyngesmyll, knight, and John Basyng, Esquire, by virtue of the Quenes Majisties letters, bearyng date the xxiiijth daye of Apryll, A.D. 1572, unto us in that behalfe dyrected into the handes of Sir Henry Radecliffe, knight, remaynynge nowe her highnes Captayne of the Isle and foresayed towne and fortresses of Portesmouthe, the xvjth daye of Maye, in the xiijth yeare of the Raygne of owr most gratyws and Soverayne ladye, Quene Elizabeth, etc., as hereafter more playnly maye appeare.

In godes howse yarde.

SHOTT.	Inp. Cannon Shott	..	145
	It. Canon Shott	..	360
	It. Culveryng Shott	..	34
	It. Culveryng Shott	..	270
	It. Stone Shott of all heygte	..	340
ORDYNANCE	Item, one fawcon of brasse with sponge and lalle mownted		1
	It. fawcon of cast iron with sponge and ladle mownted		3

In godes howse churche.

MUNITYON	Inp. Colyvers	..	99
	It. mowldes for Colyvers	..	50
	It. yf harquebuses serviseible	..	98
	It. of harquebuses unserviseible	..	8
	It of flaskes and tuchboxes of Walnuttrs		100
	It. of flasks unserviseible	..	356
	It. of tutchboxes unserviseible	..	160
	It. of bowes	..	183
	It. of pykes	..	1000
	It. of black bylles	..	1000
	It. Sheves of Arrowes	..	1000
	It. two barryelles of bowstrynga containing xx grose		2
	It. wheles for sakers	..	4
	It. of fawcon wheles-payers	..	1
	It. of Culverynge wheles-payers	..	3
	It. one stock for a canon	..	1
	It. Culvorynge Stockes	..	3
	It. Mynyon Stockes	..	2
	It. Stockes for portpcces and slynges	..	10

	It. of Stockes redy sawed	..	15
	It. of plankes redy sawed for Stockes	..	60
	It. Canon ladles	..	2
	It. plat for ladles, powndes	..	40
	It. Sawlt peter, powndes	..	24
	It. of great Rowles of Matche waghts	..	300
	It. of owld decayed matche not servysable, wayghte		100
	It. of Spanysh and Inglishe Iron, tones one and half		
	It. more of Inglyshe barres of Iron	..	8
	It. drye hydes	..	4
	It. of Morryons	..	41
POWDER	It. of Corne powder grounde, barrelles..		5
	It. more of Corne powder grounde, barrelles		14
	It. of Serpentyne powder, half barrelles		27
	It. more of Serpentyne powder, pontyons		2
	It. more of Serpentyne powder, weights		100
	It. of Corne powder decayed, powndes ..		100
ORDYNANC	It. harquebuses of creoke	..	2
SHOTT	It. Mynyon Shott	..	13

In godes howse hawl.

MUNYTYON	Inp. harquesbusses	..	29
	It. pykes	..	40
	It. black bylles	..	38

Henry Radeclyff. H. Wallop. Wm. Kyngesmyll. John Basyng.

A note of the defects and wants within the Towne and fortresses of Portes-mowthe, and the Iland nowe committed to the charge of Sir Henry Radcliffe, knighte.

    1.   First, the newe platform, the vanner thereof is so decayed by the beatinge and rage of the Sea, as, if it be not presentlye amended, yt wilbe the decaye of the whole walle to the water syde. And also one arche over the northe gate of the same is fallen downe.

    2.   Itm. the Towne walles Ramparts are genally decayed, and divers highe weys used over the same, and no gates hable to be shutte. And the bul-warkes of earthe gretely decayed and ruyned and ordinance lefte in the same.

3. Itm. therbe a nombre of harquebuzes within the said towne of the Quenes Majisties store, wherof the greter parte bee Callyvers in their places.

4. Itm. there is a Smith's forge* joyninge to the Armorie that is altogether unfinished, whereby there can nothinge bee amended belonginge to the Armory, ordynaunce, and munition.

5. Itm. ther is but one Armorer for the kepinge of the Armour and shotte, which is not sufficient for suche a proporcion.

6. Itm. the Armory* that now is is to litle, and so decayed as the Rayne beateth in thoroghe the walle, at evry storme, waich want may be supplied by makinge Goddes howse churche an Armorye and store howse, wherfor it will aptlie serve, with some convenient change, and is a thinge in our opinions, very nedefull to be donne.

7. Itm. the planckes of the platforme of the round towre is so decayed as it is not hable to beare th' ordinaunce.

8. Itm. Wee fynd th Inhabitants of the Towne and Iland very few in nombre, and yet many of them not serviceable, nor well armed, nor furnished for service, as by the particular booke of musters therof to your honor it will apeare more at large.

Henry Radeclyff.   A. Wallop.   Wm. Kingesmyll.   John Basyng.

The honest and accurate survey, made by the Commissioners, proved no mere formal proceeding, but was acted upon at once. It had evidently been called for with the determination, on the part of the authorities, to carry on the works at Portsmouth with the greatest vigour. Of this we find ample proof in the State Papers relating to the fortifications of Portsmouth from 1571 to 1586. In 1573, Frymlege forwards an estimate for making a bridge at the entrance of the Town with gates and drawbridge; and in 1574, William Popinjay, the Government Surveyor, submits his plan for a new quay. In 1577, we find this same Wm. Popinjay engaged in "repairing the breaches there between the two towers." As the instructions conveyed to him and his under officers, through the Governor of Portsmouth, are very stringent, and imply that those

* The Smith's forge and the Armory formed part of the old Hospital.

engaged in public works during "the good old times" spent the money entrusted to them with little regard to economy and efficiency, the orders, dated August 18th, 1577, will, I doubt not, be found interesting and much to the point.

NO. XIX.

State Papers. Dom. Eliz. Vol. 115, No. 5.
August 18th, 1577.

A. L. to Sir Henry Radecliffe concerning the Workes at Portesmouthe.

After our hartie commendacons. There is delivered by her majistie's order unto Richard Popinjay, Surveior of Portesmonth, for the repairing of the breaches there betwene the two towers, so muche money as, uppon a viewe and estimate made by you and others, was thought woulde suffer for the doing thereof; and for that we are desirouse that both the money should be imployed and husbanded into her Majistie's best comoditie, and also the worke to be more carefullie and substancially don and ended, in due and convenient tyme, considring that, in like cases, the under officers are more comonlie addicted to their owne gaine then to the well ordering of her majestie's money, and perfourming their duties as were requisite, it is by us ordered, that the said Surveyor shall firste make you acquainted withe the plotte to be taken for his proceeding in the worke, which he shall afterwardes in noe respect alter without your privitie acd consente; and for the disbursing of the money the sume remaining in his handes shall not be layed oute and payed, but with your knowledge and your hande to be sett to suche paiments as are to be made in that behalfe; which we are the willinger to trouble you withal, for that you signifie unto us that there wilbe, withe good order, some parte of the 500£ saved to be imployed some other waie for her Majisties furder service, and for the better saving of charges from tyme to tyme, and avoiding of confusion in the doing of the workes by retaining more persons in the same then shall necdefullye suffise; suche as the said Surveyor shall from tyme to tyme discharge either for their unhabilitie, or that there shalbe no furder use of their travell, we pray you that pasports, signed wth your hande, or in your absence by your depute and the Surveyor, be without delaye provided & delivered unto them for their departure the whence, that they be not constrained to linger there after ther shalbe noe use of their service. And, when there is a quantitie of timber required for the mending of the said breaches, whereof as you know there is no greate plentie in these parts, we

thincke it convenient, & so praye you to have regarde, that no more be waste-
fullie spent that waie then shall of necessitie serve for that purpose, & thereof
remitting the care & oversight both of that & the rest with you, not doubting of
your care therein, according to the truste reposed in you, We bidd you hartelie
farewell. From the courte of Otelands the xviijth of Auguste 1577.

To these instructions I may add others equally strict,
indeed more so, given about the same date to the same
Surveyor. They relate especially to keeping all the plans
of the fortifications secret, and to the due employment of
able-bodied, qualified workmen. The care taken to see
that " uppon the Sondaye or Sabothe Daye every Clerk be
at the Church with his men, called by his book before
seven of the clock in the morninge," tells well of olden
times.

NO. XX.

Burghley Papers. Bibl. Lansdowne. Vol. 116, No. 23. f. 65.
Articles and Instructions to be kepte and observed by Richard Poppynjaye
Surveyor of Portismouth.

1   ffirste, that the plot nowe agreed & concluded uppon be kepte very
close & secret, & that no Counter thereof be geven, made or delivered, nor the
Plot it self to be shewed or sene of any withoute Warrante from us : & that
the work be followed accordinge to the said plot.

2   Item, that the Pyoners & souldiers be in their worck, at the dys-
position & appoyntment of the said Surveyor, together with the store of
Shovells, Spades, Scavells, Baskets, Handbarrowes, Wheelbarrowes & such
lyke, to be delivered to the men as needeth.

3   Item, that there be to every hundred men but one Clerck, Captaine, leader or overseer, and that every suche Clerck be suche one as hathe
byen a Trayned Souldyer, and hathe experiens of the trayninge and leading of
men and none other.

4   Item, that every Clerck geve dyligent care to kepe his Men at
Worck in due and Convenient tymes appoynted by the Surveyor.

Item, that order be taken by the Surveyor for their Convenient victu-
allinge and lodging reasonably.

Item, that vppon the Sondaye or Sabothe Daye every Clerck be at the Churche, with his men called by his book, before Seven of the Clock in the Morninge, to here not onely the Service but also the Sermon, which bothe to be ended at nyne of the Clock, and that none doe departe the Churche till all be ended, without greate and vrgent Cause, vppon paine to be punished and to lose his Dayes wages.

7   Item, that all those Labourers be for any faulte or dysorder not criminall, at the Punishment and Correction of the Surveyor, all the Workinge Daies, and on the Muster or trayninge Daie at the Dyscretion of the Muster master, and leaders or Capitaines.

8   Item, that yf any of those doe fall syck and be not serviceable, that none suche be holden and retained in wages above two Dayes, but, vppon Notice to the Surveyor of his sicknes, his reconning and accompt be made up and his rest, after Order taken with the victualler, payde him, and to have his Pasporte from the Surveyor and to be Dyschardged, that the Queenes money be not vainly Consumed and spent to no vse.

9   Item, that the Surveyor, according to the Credyte and trust Comitted unto him, take care that all those that shalbe appoynted for this Service, be Lustie stronge, and able to performe their Duties, or other wise to dyscharge any vnmeete, and to receve others in their places, that the worck and service be not hindered.

10   Item, that the Surveyor do prescribe Orders to the Victuallers, Drapers, shoemakers, and others, concerning the Credyte and Order of the men generally and particularly Comitted to his Chardge.

11   Item, that the Surveyor doe foresee that there be placed no superfluus Clercks or other officers, but as affore for every 100 men one Clerck, for the keping and delivering Orderly the store, two Clercks for himself for the Orderly keping, checking, and ingrossing of the Monethely payebookes, one Clerck for the threasorer or Paymaster, and a Marshall for punishinge of suche as shalbe founde to loyter, quarrell, pyke, or other wyse.

12   Item, that the Surveyor be present at every pay to be made, and that he Dyligently see that true and whole payment be made to the worckmen, officers, victuallers, and others; that there be no exclamation or Dysorder therin, and that, vppon suche payment ended, the said Surveyor and Mr. Carpenter do setto their hands and subscrive.

13   Item, that the Surveyor doe appointe one honest and sufficient man for the callinge together the said workemen to worck, and tymes to leave worck, by the sounde of a bell, or other wyse.

14   Item, that, vppon the Dayes of Muster or trayning, therbe ij Drummes appointed for the Muster or trayning Daies onely, and to be set down in the bookes for every of those Daies, per man xijd.*

But what, it may be asked, became of the "Domus Dei," the Armory of which, in 1571, was in so dilapidated a state? It was evidently left to get worse and worse, until at last its condition became so serious, that an immediate repair of all the buildings was deemed necessary. This we learn from the estimate by Thomas Frymleye "of the charge of the repaire of Godes howse in Portesmouthe, 1581." The paper, which we now give, with its full particulars of the outlay required, has already been noticed, and found of the highest importance. The details are very clearly set forth, and the estimate takes in every building of the old Hospital.

NO. XX.

British Museum, Lansdowne MSS. 31. No. 72, (1581.)

The estimacion of the reparacons of Goddes Hous in Portesmouth.

Inprimis, the Gate hous with the lodgings without, ij thousand of Slatte xjs, the slatter xv, the sodder and Plummer iiijs.   xxxs.

Itm. the north Ile of the Church iij score and xv foote longe, the Rafter x foote and a halfe, the Church xxv foot wide, one tonn of lead there, sodder and plummer tenne pound, Tymber iiij load, Sawyer and Carpenter £vi.   £xvj.

Itm. the Armory sixe and fifty foot longe, the Rafter vviij foote, foure thousand tyle xxxijs, the tyler xxxs.   £iij. ijs.

Itm. the Smithes forge xxxij foote longe, the Rafters xviij foot, thousand slatte sixtene shillings and sixe pence, the slatter sixteene shillings.   xxxijs. vjd.

Itm. the Pay Chamber at the end of the forge one thousand of Slatte vs. vjd., the slatter vj. vjd.   xijd.

---

* At the end, in another handwriting, is as follows :—"my L. of sussexe, when he is present at portesmouthe, most not be thus exempted from rule, althoe my L. wold be warned that the plotte of the fortificacion may be kept secrete and not shoede abroade.

Itm. the Chamber from the Pay Chamber to the Captaynes Chamber, sixe score foot longe, the Rafter xvij foote, tenne thousand of slatte, fifty fyve shillings, the slatter foure pounde. £vj. xvs.

Itm. the Roofe over the Captaynes Chamber and the great Chamber fifty sixe foot longe, the Rafter xx foot, four thousand slatte xxijs, the slatter xxs. xlijs.

Itm. the roofe over the dyning chamber xxx foote longe, the Rafter xiv foote, two thousand of slatte xjs, the slatter xiijs. xxiiijs.

Itm. the Pigeon hous, thre thousand of Slatte sixteene shillings and sixe pence, the slatter xxjs., thre studdyes repayring xvs. lijs. vjd.

Itm. the Hall roofe beinge fifty foote longe, the rafter xxiiij foote, tenn thousand slatte fyve and fifty shillings, the slatter £vi. £vij. xvs.

Itm. the Kechin and the larder one hundred foote longe, the rafter xix foot, ten thousand slate five and fifty shillings, the slatter £v £vij. xvs.

Itm. the roofe over the Back gate xviij foot longe, the rafter xvj foot, two thousand slate xjs. the slater xs. xxis.

Itm. the roofe over the Bakehous and the stable iij score and viij foot longe, the rafter xviij foote, tenne thousand of slatte fyve and fifty shillings, the slatter £v. £vij. xvs.

Itm. the roofe over the Nurcery sixe and fifty foote longe, the rafter xiiij foote, two thousand tyle xvjs. the tyler twelve shillings. xxviijs.

Itm. Cresses one hundred, lath sixe thousand, lath nails xxx thousand. £v. vjs.

Itm. Tymber for all Gods hous xxx load, the sawyer and Carpenter £xxviij. £xxviij.

Itm. the Bridge at Portesmouth, Tymber fyve load, the sawyer and carpenter £iiij. xs. £iiij. xs.

Sum Totall is iiij score £xix (£99.)

Itm. lead one Tonne.

Remember the Wall by the churche at Godds hous, and all the Towne wall, with the Rampiers and Bullwarcks.

Thomas Frymleye.

We may suppose that Frymleye's report of the expenditure required for the general improvement of the 'Domus Dei' was not deemed satisfactory, as the alterations proposed by him were not carried out; but in the following year another estimate was prepared by Popinjay. Instead

of £99, it was resolved to expend £500 6s. 8d., and so to
put in perfect condition the Church and all the buildings
connected therewith. Especial attention was to be paid to
the Captayne's house, in order that it might be a fitting
residence for the Governor of the most important military
station in her Majesty's dominions.

How long a time was taken for the execution of the
estimate I cannot say, but it was probably part of a very
large undertaking to thoroughly complete important works
at Portsmouth, and the whole occupied, we may suppose,
several years. I say this because, on February 2th, 1584,[*]
we are informed that £425 were being "paid monthly for
works to be hurried on at Portsmouth;" on June 6th,
1585,[*] the curtain from "the Grene Bull-warke to the
Newe Bull-warke at the bruehowse" had been completed;
and, on March 10th, 1587,[*] orders were given to send from
the Tower, with all possible speed, the Ordnance and Munitions necessary for the fortifications of Portsmouth. All
was now in condition to defend the noblest harbour in the
world. Portsmouth had been so strengthened by Elizabeth
that it could defy the power of Spain[†] or of any other
country, for its Governor[‡] had been provided a House

---

[*] State Papers Dom. Eliz.

[†] The Spanish Armada arrived in the channel, July 11th, 1581, and was
defeated the next day by Drake and Howard. From the 21st to the 28th
Howard maintained a rising fight. About one third of the Spanish armament
returned to Spain. The hurry in sending guns, &c., to Portsmouth is thus
fully explained

[‡] The Governor of Portsmouth has always occupied, and does still occupy
as a Military man, a very prominent position in the country. In the year 1581,
that position was seriously endangered by an Act of Parliament. In order that
the Governor or 'Captayne' of Portsmouth might continue to hold the power,
which had, from the earliest times, been accorded to him, the Earl of Sussex
moved the following Proviso:—

Provide that this acte nor any thing therein contayned shall not extend to
alter, prejudice, or hurt the authority of the Captaine of Portismouth that now
is, for and concerning the charge and goverment of the said towne and Isle of
Portismouth, but that the said Captaine may use and enjoy the same in as
large and ample manner as he did, or might have donne, before the making of
this acte, any thing therein contained to the contrary in any wise not with
standing.

destined in after ages to receive kings and their courts, and the old Church* and Infirmary had been so restored that in these days of Victoria, the latest, and dearest, and best of England's Queens, they are still, after a further and more perfect restoration, a beautiful and honoured House of God, in which brave and loyal soldiers are trained to fight manfully under the banner of the great Captain of their Salvation.

Such is the "Story of the 'Domus Dei' of Portsmouth. The old Hospital was founded in times when holy men deemed it a privilege to provide a home for the sick and suffering, and, during three centuries and a quarter, it proved a source of vast comfort to thousands, who sought therein bodily and spiritual relief. To know the value of a 'Domus Dei' in days long gone by we must bear in mind the miserable homes then possessed by all classes, especially by the poor, and the trying diseases produced therein. Dirt, salt diet, and ignorance of the healing art

---

The causes that move me to require this provisoe be these :—

First, for that the Captaine of this towne hath alwaies had the charge and government of the towne without the superioryty or overrule of any other governor or officer.

Secondly, for that it hath neither Clerke of the Checke, paymaister, nor threasurer that deales with any accoumpt or pay.

Thirdly, for that those men or soldiours that be in pay be all household servants, and ever hath bene since the discharge of the garrison in King Edwardes time.

Fourthly, for that there is a referring vnto ordinaunce and orders heeretofore sett downe or to be sett downe. There never was any direct order sett downe but that the same was allwaies referred to the discretion of the Captaine, who hath and must charge the same as occasion and the time and service shall require.

Fifthly, for that, by this act, the Captaines letters pattentes, gravnted vnder her Maiesties great seale, shall not only be abbridged as well in his pay and charge, but also as it were made voyde and of none effect.

Lastly, the premisses considered I hope this honorable house will have their honorable consideracion, as well of the honor and creditt of the Capten as also of the benefitt and use of his letters pattentes, without abbridging of the same, vnlesse his service or doings deserve the contrary. (Brit. Mus. Bibl. Lansd. No. 31, Art. 71.)

* On 'Twelf Eve' 1590, a terrible storm carried off part of "the roofe of Goddeshowse" and the cost of repairing it was £15. State Papers Dom. Eliz. Feb. 24. 1590.

made life very short, and often very wretched—indeed
nothing but constant out-door occupation saved some parts
of the country from becoming depopulated by disease. We
can therefore well imagine how useful and how beloved
were the twelve brothers and sisters of the "Goddeshowse
of Portesmouthe," whose lives were passed in tending upon
helpless sufferers. Happily through the great progress
of art and science, such christian love has found other
and more efficient means of helping the sick poor. Portsmouth has, from a small fishing village, grown to be the
most distinguished arsenal in the world, with a population
of more than 100,000 souls. It has large military and
civil hospitals, offering, without money and without price,
skilful relief to the suffering, such as in the middle ages
no man ever dreamt of ; and comforts unknown, even in
our own time, to many a nobleman in the wilds of Hun-
gary. For this, and much more, we bless God, and pray
that as a nation we may in gratitude praise His Holy name.
But, while thus acknowledging the immense advantages
possessed by the sick in our advanced and enlightened age,
we are called upon the more loudly to honour the memory
of the faithful few, who, in olden times with the best
knowledge of medicine then to be obtained, devoted themselves night and day to God's poor in God's House. We
are invited to look upon the Infirmary and Church, the
sole remains of a very ancient and once very useful institution, as of inestimable worth—of which ecclesiastically
and archæologically Portsmouth, nay the whole county of
Hampshire, may well be proud. But there is another, and
a very strong reason, why the now Garrison Church of
Portsmouth should be dear to the hearts of Englishmen.
It contains and overshadows the dust of England's gallant
soldiers and sailors, the great Napier, the leader of a thousand battles, the conqueror of Scinde, lying close to its
western door. It is, in good truth, a national monument,
dedicated to the memory of the brave sons of a brave
land—of heroes, who under God have fought and conquered

in all quarters, and among all nations. Every patriot may well be proud to aid in its preservation. But there is yet a still higher, a more glorious reason, why this ancient House of God, this last earthly home of loving comrades, should be honoured and maintained; it is the gathering place, the rallying spot, where, apart from the strife and struggle of the world, England's army, regiment after regiment, falls down and worships the Lord of Hosts, lays its sins before the cross of Christ, and seeks the protecting influences of God's Holy Spirit.

My story has been told, and having told it, I most earnestly invite all who esteem and value the British soldier to cheerfully and liberally help us complete the restoration of the Royal Garrison Church of Portsmouth; and, in taking farewell of the reader, I can only ask him to join with me and say:—may England long continue a God-fearing country and her army never forget that it is the Lord God omnipotent who alone "treadeth down our enemies in the battle."

Bird's View

A.D. 1725

The PARADE

Main Guard

Governor's House

Wimbleton's

CALCOTT LITH: PORTSEA

Nº 13

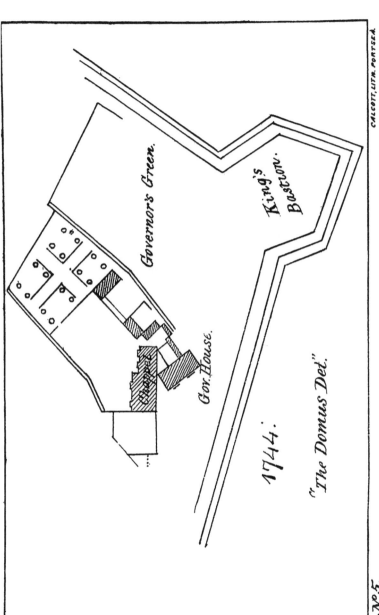

Governor's Green.

King's
Bastion.

Gor. House.

Chapel.

1744.

"The Domus Dei."

№ 5.

CALCOTT, LITH. PORTSEA.

NOTES.

Page 12. The Photograph is from a fancy picture. I give it as an illustration, because it represents very accurately the Borough Seal, and the Seal of the " Domus Dei" is seen hanging below it.

Page 24. It is stated that the " Domus Dei" was attached to the Southwick Priory; that is not true, the wording should have been :—" to which the Portsmouth 'Domus Dei' paid annually a chantry fee of 20s." The Bishops of Winchester always presented to the Wardenship of the Hospital. Margaret of Anjou, having landed at Portsmouth, went at once to the ' Domus Dei,' and having rested there, proceeded the same day to the Priory of Southwick, where she was married to Henry VI., on the 1st of April, 1445.

Mortimer's History of England, Vol II, p. 67.

Page 32. " That immortal hero, ever actuated by a sense of duty, awaited at the old ' Domus Dei' his royal Master's return from the Naval Review." It was little thought in those days that, before the close of the century, the church of the ' Domus Dei' would be restored, and a Stall therein be dedicated to the memory of the great Wellington. As there never was in any age a more distinguished, or a more patriotic soldier, the reader will, I doubt not, examine with pleasure the following list of honours gained by the " Iron Duke"—

1. The Garter.
2. The Bath.
3. The Supreme Order of the Annonciate of Sardinia.
4. The Golden Fleece of Spain.
6. The Tower & Sword of Portugal.
6. The St. Esprit of France.
7. The Elephant of Denmark.
8. The Sword of Sweden. (Military)
9. St. Andrew of Russia.
10. The Black Eagle of Prussia.
11. The Red Eagle of Brandenbergh (Prussia).
12. Fidelity of Baden
13. St. Alexander Newsky of Russia.
14. St. Januarius of the two Sicilies.
15. Maria Theresa of Austria (Military)
16. Military Merit of Wurtemburg.
17. St. George of Russia (Military)
18. The Lion d'Or of Hesse Cassel.
19. Max Joseph of Bavaria.
20. St. Ferdinand of Sicily (Military)
21. The Crown of Saxony.
22. St. Ferdinand of Spain (Military)
23. The Lion of Baden, sometimes called Lion of Zaringhen
24. St. Hermanagildo of Spain (Military)
25. The Guelph of Hanover.
26. Wilhelm of the Netherlands (Military)

The Duke of Wellington was Field Marshal of the Armies of eight different Nations, viz—

1. Great Britain. 2. Spain. 3. Portugal. 4. The Netherlands.
5. Austria. 6. Russia. 7. Prussia. 8. Hanover.

Page 141. I might have added to the list of murdered Bishops Thomas à Becket and Bishop Walcher of the See of Durham.

Thomas à Becket. All know that Henry II. solemnly swore, in the cathedral of Avranches, that he was innocent in word or deed of the murder of the Archbishop, and was as solemnly absolved of all censure. It is equally well known, that on the 11th of June, 1174, the king walked barefoot from Harbledown to Canterbury, and there knelt at the Tomb of Becket, and was scourged with a

knotted cord. But it is not so well known that, among the acts of unholy pre-
sumption committed by Henry VIII., we have to place that of formally un-
sainting the great Archbishop. The king ordered his Attorney-General to file
a " Quo Warranto" against him for usurping the office of a saint. Becket was
cited in court to answer to the charge. Judgement of " ouster " would have
passed against him by default, had not the king, *to show his impartiality and
regard for the administration of justice*, assigned him counsel at the public
expense. The case having been called on, and the Attorney General and Becket's counsel fully heard, sentence was pronounced to this effect :—" That Thomas,
sometime Archbishop of Canterbury, had been guilty of contumacy, treason, and
rebellion, and that his house should be publicly burnt, to admonish the living
of their duty by the punishment of the dead; and that the offerings made to
his shrine should be forfeited to the Crown, his images and pictures destroyed,
and his name erased from the list of Saints ."

There is a curious State Paper, dated August 18th, 1538, which gives a
letter from Cranmer to Cromwell. The Archbishop alludes thus to the Martyr :—" Farther, because I have in great suspecte that St. Thomas of Canterbury, his blodde in Christes' Church, in Canterburye, is but a fayned thing, and
made of some red okar or such like matier, I beseech your Lordship that Dr.
Lee and Dr. Barbour, my Chapleyn, may have the kinges' commisssion to trye
and examen that, and all other like things there.*

Bishop Walcher. The following passage by Sir Thomas Duffus Hardy
in his Preface to " Killoe's Register," gives an interesting account of the murder of Bishop Walcher, but I cannot hear of any paper or story of the excommunication which followed the cruel deed :—

Bishop Walcher, being of an unaspiring listless character, loving
quietude and detesting turbulence, permitted his officers, without check or
restraint to oppress his tenants and people. The general discontent which pre-
vailed, amounting almost to rebellion, having reached the Bishop's ears, he
appointed a day and place at Gateshed to hear their complaints and redress their
wrongs. The multitude however were too violent and impatient to wait for
deliberation or justice. Greatly outnumbering the Bishop's retainers, who were
quite unprepared for resistance, they fell upon them and massacred all without
mercy. The Bishop himself, who had taken refuge in the Church there, was
lanced to death with brutal ferocity on the 14th of May, 1080.

---

* Canterbury in the Olden Time by John Brent, F.S.A.

ERRATA.

Page 34	1862	read	1826
56	Space	,,	Span
56	No. 16	,,	No. 1 b.
57	Archœlogia	,,	Archæologia
120	Portissara	,,	Pontissara.
124	Conventional	,,	Conventual.
136	Fell Records	,,	Pell Records
139	Gedler	,,	Zedler.
184	£20	,,	£40
208	Foot note—instead of "raising fight" read "running fight."

There are, I dare say, a few other misprints. The above are the most
important. Some of the statements made in the "Story of the Domus Dei"
will be doubted, possibly declared inaccurate by antiquarians. I shall be very
thankful for any correction ; also for any information which may throw addi-
tional light upon a subject which I have studied with intense pleasure.

APPENDIX.

AMONG the valuable documents relating to ancient Hospitals we may place in the first rank the Inventory of St. Mary's Hospital, Dover, discovered by the eminent ecclesiologist and antiquarian, the Rev. Mackenzie E. C. Walcott, while making researches in the Record Office for his 'Cathedral Cities of England and Wales.' " Such lists (he justly observes) have been called, with more pithiness than injustice, the skeletons of monastic history; for it requires only a slight stretch of imagination, and a little thought, to reproduce the various chambers with their furniture complete, and present to the mind's eye a true and vivid portraiture of their inner and domestic arrangements. No description so complete has ever come under my notice. I regret that from the destruction of documents it is out of my power to contribute any information with regard to the internal working of a Maison Dieu."*

There is also another document, I may say, of equal if not greater interest, lately published by the Rev. C. A. Swainson, D.D.,† which exhibits the form of admission into a ' Domus Dei,' and then introduces us to that inner working of a Hospital, for a knowledge of which Mr. Mackenzie Walcott so earnestly yearned.

I publish them both as an Appendix to my " Story of the 'Domus Dei' of Portsmouth," because they are exactly what the reader requires to help him as he examines the old plans of that Hospital. The Inventory will enable him to furnish every building from the Warden's House to the Stable and Bakehouse, and will well suggest the style of life passed by the inmates; while the Oxford MS. tells him, with much detail, the way by which Brothers and Sisters were formally admitted, what their duties were, under what discipline they lived, and how they rendered themselves useful to " the poor and sick people," who in their sickness or distress sought help in the ' House of God.'

---

* Archæologia Cantiana, Vol. vii. p. 272.

† The Hospital of St. Mary of Chichester, by C. A. Swainson, D.D.

I.

The Inventory of all such goods and catalls as be in the house called the Meason de Dieu, of Douver, and of all catell, the which wer of the late Master and Brethren, ther taken by John Anthony,* servant to the most wurshipfull, Master Crumwell, Secretary to the Kyngs Hyghnes, the xxiii *daie of Jannuarye the* xxvjth *yere of the reigne of Kyng Henry the* viiith.

PLATE. first, iij gylt chalyses, with ij patens and ij gylt sponys, wherof one chalyce is coper and gylt, waying xlii uncs.

Item, ij olde fasshon pieces, with ij covers, parcell gylt, waying lx uncs.

Item, iij pownst† pecys of silver, waying xxj uncs.

Item, iij parcell gilt saltts, with a cover, waying xv uncs.

Item, ij standyng Cuppys, parcell gylt, with a cover, waying xv uncs.

Item, iij dosen of sylver sponys, waying xxvj uncs.

Item, a Cruett of sylver, parcell gylt, and a nut with a cover of sylver, parcell gylt, weying xv uncs.

Item, iiij Saltts, parcell gylt, with ij covers, waying xxxiii uncs.

Item, ij litell potts with covers of sylver, parcell gylt, and a flatt piece of sylver, parcell gylt, weying xxiiij uncs.

Item, iij dosen of sylver sponys, weying xxiij uncs.

Item, ij sponys of sylver gylt, waying

Item, v grete masers with small bonds of sylver and gylt, and a littell olde nut with a bonde of sylver and gylt, and a littell bonde of sylver and gylt, waying in all lx uncs.

Item, ij Nutts with ij covers of sylver and gylt, and the seid Nutts garnysshid with sylver and gylt, waying xxxiij uncs.

Item, iiij Masers, whereof iij of them be with gylt bonds, and the fourth with a sylver bonde, dailye occupied, waying xxiiij uncs.

Item, ij Masers with brode bands, sylver and gylt, and a litell maser with a fote and a small bande, sylver and gylt, waying xviii uncs.

---

* He was one of the visitors of monasteries (2 Cranmer, p. 271.)

† Pownced, punched, punctured, stippled, stamped, or pricked, by way of ornamentation. A pouncet-box was a perforated perfume-box, and a pouncer was used by gravers. This kind of work was called *pounsonnez* or *ponçonnee* in French, and in Latin *ponsatum*. (See 'Archæologia,' vol. xxix. p. 55.) Pownson is rendered 'puncto' in the 'Promptorium Parvulorum,' vol. ii. p. 411. The word occurs also in the MS. Inventory of Whalley.

Item, ij small masers with brode bands of sylver and gylt, waying lx uncs.

Item, a stone pot and a nut, garnysshid with sylver and gilte, with ij covers of sylver and gilt, waying xv uncs.

Item, a standyng Cuppe with a cover and a goblet with a cover all gilt weying xxii uncs.

IN THE VESTRYE.* First, iiij chalyces of sylver and gylt, and one other of coper and gylt, waying lxiii uncs.

Item, j chalice and a paxe† of sylver, parcell gylt, waying xv uncs.

Item, ij candlestycks of sylver, parcell gylt, waying xx uncs.

Item, ij cruetts, wherof one is of byrrall,‡ garnyshsshed with sylver and gilt, and the other sylver and gylt, waying vj uncs. d. i.

Item, ij Sensers, and a ship§ of sylver, parcell gylt, waying lxxv uncs.

Item, ij basens of sylver, parcell gylt, waying xxxix uncs.

Item, a Crosse of Coper and gylt, with certeyn sylver plate about the same.

Item, iiij Corporasses‖ with ther casys of clothe of golde and sylver.

Item, iiij Corporasses and ther casys, daylye occupied.

Item, iij Cortens of green sylke.

Item, ii Copes of black velvet, with a vestment for a preyst, decon, and sub-deakon, with that that apperteynith.

Item, v copys of cloth gold, with a vestment¶ for a priest, decon, and sub-deakon, with thappurtenances* the grownde of blewe velvett.

---

* Richard de la Wyche, the canonized bishop of Chichester, consecrated St. Edmund's Altar in the Maison Dieu on Mid-Lent Sunday, 1253, in the presence of King Henry III. The Chapel was dedicated to St. Mary in 1227.

† Pax, "asser ad pacem," or osculatory, "tabula ad osculandum"—a tablet of wood or round metal plate, which the priest kissed and gave to the people for the same purpose after the consecration, instead of the ancient kiss of charity.

‡ Beryl designated both the precious stone and fine glass, like crystal.

§ The incense-boat; furnished with a spoon.

‖ Corporas,—a consecrated white linen cloth, used in the service of the altar and placed over its ordinary coverings; upon it the chalice and host rested. (See Arch. Cant. V. p. 70, note 2.) The technical name of the embroidered case was "theca," "bursa," "repositorium," etc.

¶ Vestment was the technical name for a suit of mass-robes for priest, deacon, and sub-deacon—the chasuble, dalmatic, and tunicle. The cope (from cop, a covering,) which resembled an ample cloak, was used in processions. (Durandi Ration. lib. iii. c. 1; Canons, 960, c. 33.) The chasuble (casula, a little house,) like the ancient trabea, was of rich texture, with an aperture for the centre, and hanging down on every side almost to the ground; the dalmatic, so called from a robe of state worn in Dalmatia, was shorter, and open at the sides, which terminated in angles, and had wide sleeves and two stripes of embroidery; the tunicle was without embroidery, and the sleeves were narrower, and the whole dress of less dimensions. The dalmatic was not worn by the Cistercians. (Martine de Ant. Mon. Rit. iv. p. 78.)

* Appurtenances or appendages, viz. the albe, amice, stole, maniple, and girdle.

Item, ij copys of crymson velvet, olde, with a vestment for a preyst, decon, and sub-dekan, with thappurtenances.

Item, a cope with a vestment for a preyst, decon, and subdecon, with thappurtenances of grene clothe of bawdekyn.

Item, j cope of white sylke, embrodered with byrds of grene sylver, with a vestment for preist, decon, and subdecon, with thappurtenances.

Item, a vestment for a priest and decon of red sylke, embrowdered with byrds of golde, with thappurtenances.

Item, j red vestment with thappurtenances of bawkekyn* worke, olde.

Item, j vestment of red damaske, with the appurtenances.

Item, j vestment of purple velvet, with the appertenances.

Item, j vestment of white damaske with a grene Crosse, with the appurtenances.

Item, j vestment of red sylke, with the appurtenances.

Item, j olde vestment of black velvet for a priest and decon, with the appurtenances.

Item, xii copys of red satten of brugs.

Item, xj copys of whyte bustian, imbrodered with red rosys of saye† and cloth.

Item, iij copys of grene sylke, old bawdkyn worke.

Item, j vestment of red sylke, bawdkyn worke, with the appurtenances.

Item, j vestment of olde whyte fustyan, with a Crosse of red saye, with the appurtenances.

Item, ix olde vestments, with all thyng thereto belongyng, occupied dailye.

Item, iij olde carpetts, of tapestreye, to be laid before the aulter.

Item, ij carpetts of red wollen, and ij whyte wollen and iij other carpetts, to be laid before aulters.

Item, ii cusshons made of an olde cope, and ij other olde cushons.

IN THE GREAT CHAMBER CALLED THE HOOSTRYE.‡ First, in the same

---

* Bawdkyn (like the Italian *baldachino*, a canopy,) cloth of gold from Bagdad, Babylon, or Baldacca, whence the first rich stuffs of this kind were imported. (Vincent of Beauvais, 1. xxxii. c. 30.)

† Saye, a kind of woollen cloth, or serge, made in large quantities at Sudbury, near Colchester.

‡ The Guest House, or reception chamber, still remaining. The word in the Inventory of Hales Owen Abbey is spelt Ostre, and Ostripanes are mentioned at Rochester (Custum. Roff. p. 25). The Black Hostry at Ely adjoined the Infirmary. In the Hostry of Whalley I find mentioned the chief chamber, the parlour beneath, the lady chamber, the gallery chamber, the bishop's chambers, and the King's receiver's chambers. (MS. Invent. p. 310.)

chamber iiij tables, ij payer of trestylls, ij old Gentyshe* carpetts, j long setell, iiij formes, j litell olde cubbord, iij tornid cheyres, with iiij olde cusshyns, and j olde wyrred stole, a payr of andyrons with a fyre forke, and a lyttell olde chest, wherein is one olde Gentyshe coverlet.

Item, a grete bedsted, with a testure of wod, a fetherbed, and a coverlet of verdour.

Item, a litell bedsted with a fetherbed, and an olde coverlet.

In the Littell Chamber within the Hoostrye. First, j bedstede, a fetherbed, an olde blanket, a coverlet of verdour, olde, a littell olde quylt, a testour† of saye, with cortens of the same, and hangyngs of the chamber of olde saye, payntted, ij torned cheyres with one olde cusshon.

Item, j other littel chamber, wherein is j bedstede and an olde fetherbed.

In the Chamber over the Water. First, in the same chamber ij tables, ij formes, and j torned cheyer.

Item, in the chamber within that a bedstede, with j olde fetherbed and j olde coverlet of tapystry, with a testure and curteyns of other whyte clothe.

Item, an olde presse, wherein lieth an old quylt, an olde coverlet of tapystrye, and j coverlet of red wollen, very olde.

Item, another littell chamber within that, ij bedsteds, j olde matteras,‡ and j olde litell fetherbed.

In the Chamber called Sir Peer's§ Chamber. First, ij bedsteds, ij fetherbedds, j olde coverlet.

Naperye in the Custody of John Enyvers wife.‖ First, xxx payr of Canvass sheats, xij olde payr of olde sheets. Item, v payrs and j sheete for the Hoostrye. Item, v payr of olde sheets for the Firmerye.¶ Item

---

* In the custom accounts of Sandwich, temp. Henry VIII., six "Kentish" carpets occur, and in the Booke of New Rates, 2 James I., are Brunswick, China, Gentish, and Turkey carpets. There is an instance of the latter in the Prior's Chamber of the New-Work.

† Teester, rendered capitellum in the 'Promptorium,' vol. iii, p. 489. It was the upper hanging over a bed. The word also occurs for horse-equipage or housings, Wardrobe Issue, 6 Edw. III., 5 Ric. II., and a cover for a "mail," 1322.

‡ The matras occurs in the Inventory of Pulteney's effects, 25 Edw. III. Matras coopert. de carde Yndey, matras paley, matras de cirpis prec. 4 den.

§ The guest chambers were usually called after the name of some person, probably a former occupant of distinction.

‖ John Enyver was one of the brethren of the hospital.

¶ The Infirmary.

x pylowes, with vj pyllowberes. Item, vj table cloths of playne clothe, very olde, dailye occupied. Item, iiij towells of playne clothe, very olde. Item, iij olde dyaper clothes and ij diapre towells, with xij diaper napkins, very olde. Item, ij in woll, by estimacyon xxx quarters.

In the Kechyn. First, vj brasse potts, j grete ketell of coper and viij other ketells, iiij gredyrons, and x spytts, grete and small, ij trevetts, with another grete ketell with an iron bande, xl platters, x dishes, xx sawcers, xx podyngers.*

In a Chest in the Newe Kechyn. First, xv grete platters of the sylver fasshon, x large disshes of the sylver fashon, viij small disshes of the sylver fasshon. Item, vj other disshes, with the grete chargers.

In the Master's Chamber. First, platters of sylver fashion vj, disshes v, prodyngers xij, sawcers vi. Item of another sorte, xij platters, xij disshes.

In the Master's Stable. ij sorell† geldyngs, a white nag, a black nag.

In the Stable for the Best Cart Horses. ij grey horses, a black horse, a sorell horse, a sorell geldyng.

In the Second Stable. One sorell geldyng, ij grey geldyngs, j black geldyng, j white geldyng.

In the Fermery. For power preystes iij bedds, for power men ix bedds for power women ij beds.

In the Gardener.* x quarters of whete.

In the Bruehouse. l quarters of malt, and all thyng belongyng to a bruehouse

In the Bakehouse. All thyng and implements thereunto belongyng.

In the Barnes. Of whete, by estimacyon, xx quarters; of barleye, by estimacyon, xxx quarters; of tares, by estimacion, xx coppes; of heye, by estimacyon, v or vj lodes.

Catell pertaynyng to the house and being ther. Fyrst, iij mylke kyne, j bore, iij sowes, xvj lyeware, called yong hoggs.

Shepe remaynyng in ther owne hands. First, in ewys vᶜ di. xxiij. Item wethers iiiiᶜ viij. Item, teggs iiᶜ xlv.

Shepe put out to farme. First to William Haman, of Ewell, xx ewes. Item to Thomas Peper, of Charlton, lxiii wethers. Item to John Stelman, of St. Margarett's, xxx ewes. Item to ffag, of Dudmanston, iiᶜv wethers.

---

* Podyngers, porringers. The word is spelt Podegares in the Inv. of Langley Priory, 1485.
† A sorell denoted a kind of horse, 32 Edw. III.
A corruption of garner or granary

Catell remaynyng in Romney Marsshe. First, xx lene bullocks of North ern Ware. Item, viij contrey bullocks at the stacke. Item, iij fat oxen for the larder. Item, ij kyen. Item, iiij lene contrey bullocks. Item, viii maryes,* young and olde. Item, iij staggs of ii years age. Item, iij coltts of i yere of age. Item, j mare of ii yeres of age. Item, vj fat wethers. Item, v barens Item, xxiij lene ware. Item, teggs xxij.

Catell remaynyng at Whitfelde, beyng in their owne hands. First, xx yong oxen, xij bullocks of iij yeres of age, xiij bullocks of ii yere of age, xxxv kyen, xv calvys, vii yong hoggs, j colt, coloured baye.

Redy money left by the late master, xxiv *li.* vij*s.* vj*d.*

Sum. The weight of all sylver, one with thother, v^c xxvii unces and di.

The weight of the masers and nuts, clix uncs.

The some of all shepe, one with another, m^{li} vi^c.

The some of all bullocks and kyen, cxix.

The same of mares and coltts, xv.

The some of horse and geldyng, xiiij.

Per me dom. Henr. Wodd; per me dom Will. Coorte; per me dom. John Burnell; per me dom. William Nowle; per me John Evyner.†

II.

The form of admission of a Brother or Sister to a ' Domus Dei,' and the discipline exercised therein.

" If any one seeks the Hospital of St. Mary, at Chichester, let the Prior examine whether he is in sound or infirm health. If he is in sound health, whether male or female, let the Prior consider whether he is a person of good conversation, of honest life and character, likely to be useful to the house, whether in serving or labouring for the poor. If he should be found such, the Prior should first point out to him the poverty of the house, the poorness of the

---

* Mares.

+ The master and brethren of St. Mary's Hospital, or Maison Dieu, acknowledged the supremacy Dec. 1534; their names were John Clerke, master ; dom. Henry Wood, William Coorte, dom. John Burnell, dom. William Nowlde, and John Enyver. (Dep. Keeper's 8th Report, p. 285, App. ii.) It was surrendered Dec. 11, 36 Henry VIII., by Henry Wood, John Burnell, William Noole, and John Thompson. (*Ibid.* p. 19, App ii.) The latter name is that of the master, as appears from the title of the Inventory of St. Martin's; was his alias Enyver ? John Clerke, master of the Hospital, according to Holinshead built c. 1500, a round tower at the S.W part of the bay, to shelter it from winds, and enable ships to lie moored to it, and this " corner " was, in consequence called " Little Paradise." His successor, John Thomson, when Rector of St. John's in 1533, built a pier in the harbour.

food, the gravity of the obedience, and the heavy duties which may possibly deter him and induce him to recall his purpose. But if he persevere in knocking, then, with the counsel of the Lord Dean and the brethren of the House, he may be received in the name of the LORD, without the intervention of any money or any compact, unless he has any property of his own and is disposed to resign it into the hands of the Prior. But if the character of the man be insufficient he must be repelled entirely.

"He, however, who is to be admitted, must first swear that he will in all things be faithful to the house, and that he will observe to the utmost of his power the rules established in it. Then he must promise three things in this fashion. I, N., promise to God and to the Blessed Mary, that hereafter, with their assistance, I will observe towards myself chastity, towards my superiors obedience, and that I will hold no property of my own without the licence and consent of the Prior. This done, if he is a male, he will kiss the brethren; if a female, the sisters, in order. Then let the males be cropped below the ear; or the hair of the women be cut off back to the middle of the neck, and thenceforward they must be addressed by the name of brother and sister. If a brother under the instigation of the devil, fall into immorality, out of which scandal arises, or if he be disobedient to the superior, or if he strike or wound the brethren or clients, or commit any other grievous irregularity, then, if he prove incorrigible, he must be punished severely, and removed from the society like a diseased sheep, lest he contaminate the rest. But let this be done not with cruelty and a tempest of words, but with gentleness and compassion. Still should he promise amendment if he be allowed to return, and give security for it, let him be treated mercifully, as the judgment of the Prior, the Confessor, and the brethren of the House may decide, but so, that, without accepting of persons, the fair dealing of the House be maintained, and a worthy penance be enjoined. If the sin be concealed and without scandal, let the penance, though suited to the offence, be concealed too. But if the brother shall have a quarrel with a brother with noise and riot, then let him fast for seven days, on Wednesdays and Fridays on bread and water, and sit at the bottom of the table and without a napkin; and a sister likewise. If a brother or sister shall, against the wishes of the Prior, leave the House and stay either in the city or without it, then, if, changing his mind, he desire again to return, let him fast thirty days, on Wednesdays and Fridays, on bread and water, sitting as above. If a brother shall be found, whilst alive and in health, to have money or property which he had concealed from the Prior, let the money be hung round his neck, and let him be well flogged, and do penance for thirty days, as before. If he shall have acquired the money out of the goods of the Hospital, care must be taken thenceforward that he has no administration in its household matters. If a brother shall die in the House, and then it shall be discovered that he had property which he had concealed, he must be buried beyond the walls of the cemetery, unless on his death bed he shall have revealed it to the priest. Trivial and daily excess of the brethren and sisters must also be attended to, lest, whilst they are overlooked, small offences should become great.

"If however, any one in infirm health and destitute of friends should seek admission into the house for a term, until he shall recover, then let him be received gladly and assigned a bed. Let everything that he requires be administered to him as the means at the disposal of the House may permit; and if he has anything of his own let the Prior take charge both of it and of his clothes, until he is restored to health; then let them be given back to him without diminution, and let him depart, unless, of his own accord, he offer the whole or part to the house. If he die in the House, let his goods be distributed as he has disposed of them. If he die intestate, let his property be kept for a year in the House, so that if any friend of the deceased shall come and prove that he has a claim upon it, justice may not be denied to him. If no one claims within the year, let it be merged into the property of the Hospital..

"In regard to the poor people who are received late at night, and go forth early in the morning, let the Prior take care that their feet are washed, and, as far as possible, their necessities attended to. Care must be taken that they do not annoy the sick, that they do not pilfer, that they behave respectfully in word and deed. The sexes must be separated.

"The brothers and sisters must pray continually, or be engaged in work, that the devil may not find them with nothing to do. If they earn anything, let them not conceal or appropriate it, but let it be expended for the common good.

"When the seven canonical hours are being daily said in the Church of God, let the brothers and sisters who are ignorant of them say, every ordinary week day, at each hour, the Lord's Prayer seven times, with the Gloria Patri except at matins, when, instead, they must repeat fifty Paternosters. On feast days they must say fifteen Paternosters at each hour; at matins, a hundred. Let the brothers and sisters say every day a hundred and fifty Ave Marias. For a brother or sister who has died, let them say a hundred and fifty Paternosters. Let whoso knows it say the Psalter; and let one half keep watch before matins, and the other half after; but no one must, because of these prayers, omit the other things which may be enjoined him by way of penance.

"When the brethren meet for food, if a presbyter is present, let him publickly say the Benediction, and each brother say the Lord's Prayer in private. If no presbyter is present, let each make the sign of the cross over the bread, and say *In Nomine Patris*. After the meal let each lift up his hands and return thanks to God, and say Paternoster. Let them eat in silence, and without murmuring, whatever is placed before them, providing that what is prepared shall be sufficient for nature, and not addressed to the taste.

"Every evening, when the poor have been received and refreshed, let prayers be said for the Pope, for the Archbishop, and Bishop of the place, the Dean and Chapter of the Church of Chichester, and for all the Prelates of the Church; for the King and Queen, and for the peace of the realm; for Master Thomas, the Dean, Master ——— de Keynsham, Master G. of Gloucester, &c., and for all the Canons; for Dominus Martin, and for all the citizens of this city, for all the benefactors of the House, living and dead (their names being mentioned), who founded the House, who constructed it, or gave to it fixed rents. If a priest be in the Hospital, let him say the prayers with the Psalms accustomed to be said in the Church on the Lord's Day; but if no priest be there let one of the brethern say them; and at each prayer let each brother and sister say one Paternoster and one Ave Maria."*

Dr. Swainson remarks, that this "document of great moment" gives us the reason why endowments flowed so largely towards the House of St. Mary. "The Hospital was intended to be a temporary home for the sick and infirm; the brethren and sisters who dwelt within its walls were intended to act as nurses. It was also intended to act as a refuge for a night to the wandering poor—the *casuals* of the modern day." It was in fact a ditto of the "Domus Dei" of Portsmouth, only on a smaller scale.

That at Dover was, we may believe, about the same size as the Portsmouth Hospital, possibly somewhat more extensive.

If the reader will take the Plan of the Portsmouth Hospital, drawn in the days of Henry viiith, and make use of the Dover Inventory, he will be able "to reproduce the various chambers with their furniture complete, and present to his mind's eye a true and vivid portraiture of their inner and domestic arrangements." The University College MS. will help him still further, for by means of it, he may see the brothers and sisters at work, watch their discipline and rejoice over their active doings in behalf of God's poor.

*Dr. Swainson's valuable Papers from which this extract has been taken, will be found in Vol. xxiv. of the Sussex Archæological Society's Collections.

For EU product safety concerns, contact us at Calle de José Abascal, 56–1°,
28003 Madrid, Spain or eugpsr@cambridge.org.